Centaur Classics
GENERAL EDITOR: J. M. COHEN

POEMS AND SOME LETTERS OF
JAMES THOMSON

Engraving from a photograph of 1869, used as the frontispiece to the *Poetical Works*, Volume I, 1895

POEMS AND SOME LETTERS OF

James Thomson (1834-1882)

EDITED, WITH A BIOGRAPHICAL
AND CRITICAL INTRODUCTION
AND TEXTUAL NOTES, BY

ANNE RIDLER

Southern Illinois University Press
Carbondale
1963

WHITTEMORE LIBRARY
Framingham State College
Framingham, Massachusetts

© CENTAUR PRESS LTD., 1963

Library of Congress Catalog Card No. 62-14999

Published in Great Britain 1963 by Centaur Press Ltd.
Published in the United States of America 1963 by
Southern Illinois University Press
and printed in Great Britain by
The West Yorkshire Printing Co., Ltd., Wakefield, England

'There are moods when one is prone to believe that, in these last days, no longer by "clear spring or shady grove", no more upon any Pindus or Parnassus, or by the side of any Castaly, are the true and lawful haunts of the poetic powers; but, we could believe it, if anywhere, in the blank and desolate streets, and upon the solitary bridges of the midnight city, where Guilt is, and wild Temptation, and the dire Compulsion of what has once been done—there with these tragic sisters around him, and with Pity also, and pure Compassion, and pale Hope, that looks like Despair, and Faith in the garb of Doubt, there walks the discrowned Apollo, with unstrung lyre . . .'

> A. H. Clough, reviewing 'Poems by Alexander Smith and Matthew Arnold', 1853 (quoted by Katharine Chorley in *Arthur Hugh Clough*, O.U.P. 1962).

CONTENTS

Introduction ix

POEMS 1852-1860

    Four Points in a Life 1
    The Approach to St. Paul's 4
    Suggested by Matthew Arnold's *Grande Chartreuse* . . 5
    The Doom of a City 12
    A Chant 54
    Lines on his Twenty-third Birthday 54
    A Recusant 58
    The Lord of the Castle of Indolence 58
    A Real Vision of Sin 61
    Mater Tenebrarum 65

POEMS 1860-1874

    The 'Melencolia' of Albrecht Dürer 66
    Through Foulest Fogs 67
    To Our Ladies of Death 68
    Two Sonnets 73
    On George Herbert's Poems 74
    To Joseph and Alice Barnes 74
    The Three that shall be One 76
    Sunday at Hampstead 78
    Thomas Cooper's Argument 86
    The Fire that Filled 88
    From the Midst of the Fire 89
    Vane's Story 89
    Versicles 118
    Low Life 119
    Polycrates on Waterloo Bridge 121
    Once in a Saintly Passion 122
    On the Terrace at Richmond 122
    From Sunday up the River 125
    Art 126
    A Polish Insurgent 128
    Mr. MacCall at Cleveland Hall 129
    Life's Hebe 131
    Day 133
    Night 133
    Philosophy 134
    The Naked Goddess 135
    Two Lovers 142
    In the Room 146
    A Song of Sighing 151

CONTENTS

Weddah and Om-el-Bonain 151
L'Envoy 175
Lilah, Alice, Hypatia 176
In a Christian Churchyard 176
The City of Dreadful Night 177

POEMS 1878-1882

Lines, 1878 205
A Voice from the Nile 208
To H.A.B. 213
The Sleeper 214
At Belvoir 216
Modern Penelope 219
Proem: 'O Antique Fables' 221
The Poet and his Muse 222
Insomnia 225
Despotism Tempered by Dynamite 232

LETTERS

To Agnes Gray 239
To Mrs. Bradlaugh 239
To Hypatia Bradlaugh 240
To Mrs. Bradlaugh 242
To Mrs. John Thomson 243
To W. M. Rossetti 243
From Colorado to an unknown recipient . . . 248
To Hypatia and Alice Bradlaugh 249
To Hypatia Bradlaugh 250
To Alice and Hypatia Bradlaugh 251
To the Same 252
To Mrs. John Thomson 253
To Mrs. Bradlaugh 254
To Mrs. John Thomson 255

NOTES

Introductory Note 257
Abbreviations 258
Notes to Poems 259
Index of first lines 277

PLATES

James Thomson in 1869 . . . . . Frontispiece
From the MS. of 'The City of Dreadful Night' facing p. 178

INTRODUCTION

A GOOD deal of the ground covered in the first part of this Introduction has already been explored in biographical studies of Thomson, but as these are for the most part out of print, and as no study has taken account of all the manuscript material which is now available,[1] it seemed best to include a short biography here. The *Life* of Thomson by Henry S. Salt, and the Memoir which Bertram Dobell prefixed to his two-volume edition of the Poems, are the chief published sources of information.[2] These books are out of print, but Imogene Walker's valuable *Critical Study*, with a bibliography, is obtainable.[3]

I

MR. ROBERT GRAVES has told us that the nest of the Muse is 'littered with the jawbones and entrails of poets',[4] and certainly a glance at the lives of nineteenth-century poets discovers much evidence in his support. Yet

> I will not see myself the desolate bard,
> His natural friendships cast and his loves buried,
> Auguring doom like some black carrion bird

was Mr. Graves's own early protest against such a view,[5] and something of this ambivalence is to be found, I think, in James Thomson, the 'laureate of pessimism' as some admirers named him; a poet who often saw himself as dedicated to despair and as a son of the devil, who yet had in him a tough, practical capacity for humdrum work, and a longing for the delightful state that is disparaged as 'ordinary bourgeois happiness'. He had too keen a sense of the ridiculous to maintain a consistently Byronic pose, though he enjoyed referring to himself as an outcast and Ishmael, and as he grew older he came to think that no one would write poetry unless he were thwarted of the more satisfactory means of self-expression to be found in action.

> Who gives the fine report of the feast?
> He who got none and enjoyed it least.[6]

---

[1] In 1952 Bertram Dobell's son sold to the Bodleian Library his father's collection of MSS. relating to Thomson, containing holograph poems, notebooks and diaries, letters by him and addressed to him, and other writings and memoranda.
[2] Salt's *Life* was published in 1889 (Reeves & Turner and Bertram Dobell), reissued in 1898 (A. & H. B. Bonner) after a fire had destroyed most of the original edition, and revised in 1914 (Watts & Co.). My references are to the revised edition. Dobell's Memoir prefaces the *Poetical Works of James Thomson* (Reeves & Turner), 1895: he repeated the substance of it in other introductions, which are listed in Miss Walker's bibliography.
[3] Cornell University Press, 1950.
[4] *The White Goddess*, p. 22.
[5] 'The Poetic State', *Poems 1914-1926*.
[6] 'Art'. See p. 127.

INTRODUCTION

'Laureate of pessimism' is a romantic title, but there was nothing romantic about the ill-luck of Thomson's early life; nothing Byronic about his later endurance of lodging-house poverty, cold-mutton dinner and fireless grate. He was born of Scottish parents at Port-Glasgow on 23 November 1834—even the month of his birth contributing to gloomy reflections in later life, as he noted in his diary on his fortieth birthday:

'Third day of fog. Congenial natal weather. No marvel one is obscure, dismal, bewildered and melancholy.'

When he was five, his sister, two years younger, died of measles caught from him, and the following year his father, a merchant seaman and chief officer of his ship, had a paralytic stroke from which he never fully recovered, though he lived for another thirteen years. Thomson, in a letter written near the end of his life, recalled that after the stroke his father's temper was 'strange, disagreeable, not to be depended upon. I remember his taunting (Mother) with being his elder', and that later 'his mental perturbations settled down into a permanent weakness of mind'.[1] Thomson remembered his mother as loving towards her husband and children, but as having 'a cloud of melancholy overhanging her; first, perhaps, from the death of her favourite brother John Parker Kennedy, drowned on the Goodwin Sands; then probably deepened by the death of my little sister . . .'[2] She was an Irvingite in religion, and Thomson remembered Edward Irving's portrait at home, 'hung with yellow gauze', and 'some books of his on the interpretation of prophecy, which I used to read for the imagery'—this argues some precocity in the boy, since he left home for good when he was eight. He says also that his mother 'followed Irving from the Kirk when he was driven out.'

Now Irving had been appointed to the Caledonian Chapel in Cross Street, Hatton Garden, in 1822, and this was the time of his widest fame, when all the notables of the day flocked to hear him.[3] In 1827 a larger church in Regent Square was built for him,[4] and in 1828 and '29 he toured Scotland, preaching the second Advent. It may have been then that Sarah Kennedy, later Thomson's mother, became his follower, or she may have lived in London during some of the years of his ministry, for it was in London, in 1834, that she and Thomson's father were

---

[1] The letter is given on p. 255.
[2] Thomson was evidently drawing on these family memories in the narrative poem in terza rima which he began in 1858, where the one completed canto describes a seaman's wife made permanently melancholy by her brother's death at sea. This fragment is in the Bodleian MSS.
[3] See Hazlitt's *Spirit of the Age* for a description of his preaching, and Carlyle's *Reminiscences* for an account of their long friendship.
[4] The chapel then reverted to the Swedenborgians who had first built it. See A. L. Drummond, *Edward Irving & His Circle;* J. Hair, *History of the Regent Square Church.*

married. In 1830 began the 'glossolalia' in Irving's congregation which was to lead to his downfall: in 1832 he was deprived of the pulpit of the Regent Square church, and formed a new congregation; in March 1833 he was deprived of his ministry in the Church of Scotland, and in the following year, a couple of months after the date of Thomson's birth, he died. But Thomson's mother, presumably, continued a member of the new congregation (later to call itself the 'Catholic and Apostolic Church'), and the description Thomson gives of chapel meetings to which his father (after the onset of his illness) used to take him, with the 'groaning responses' of the congregation and their spiritual anecdote-swapping, sounds uncommonly like the same sect.

Such was Thomson's early religious training, continued in a Calvinist school. It was small wonder that the theme of the sheep and the goats was so recurrent in his early verse, and that in later years he was to prefer the Moslem version of heaven to the Christian one.[1]

It is not clear whether the father was able to do work of any kind after his stroke: Thomson records that he recovered the power of walking, though never the use of his right hand. However, another son, John, was born in February 1842, by which time we know that the family was living in London, for a note in Thomson's diary for 1867 records details of John's birth certificate (obtained for his wedding), from the 'District of St. Mary in the Parish of St. George in the East', the parents then living at 24 Mary Ann Street.

A fortnight after his own eighth birthday, when the baby was some nine months old, Thomson left home to become a boarder at the Royal Caledonian Asylum for the sons of poor Scottish soldiers and sailors, and soon after this his mother died. He seldom wrote of these early losses, but it was indeed a pitiable start in life for the little boy: it is not surprising that he kept the sense of loneliness to the end of his life, and that one of his failings as a poet is a certain monotony of self-pity.

However, Thomson was never a gloomy companion except to himself, and he was thoroughly popular at school. The Royal Caledonian Asylum was founded in 1815 at Cross Street, Hatton Garden, at first in close connexion with the Chapel where Irving found fame. But by 1828 the number of boys had risen from twelve to forty, and new buildings were erected at Copenhagen Fields, Islington. This, therefore, was the place of Thomson's schooling, and three years after he went there, the buildings were enlarged and girls were admitted as pupils.[2] The education he received would have been sound though limited, to judge from the

---

[1] See *The Secularist* for 19.8.76.
[2] I am indebted to the present Warden of the Royal Caledonian Schools, at Bushey since 1903, for this information.

Report on 'hospital schools' in general made by the Schools Inquiry Commission in 1861. He would have learnt no Latin or modern languages except possibly French, but he must have had natural talent as a linguist, since he acquired a good reading knowledge of German and Italian by his own efforts later on. He was good at mathematics; he played first clarinet in the school band,[1] and listening to music was always one of the chief pleasures of his life.

Thomson's holidays were spent with a family called Gray, where there were two daughters, and in the account which Salt gives of his relationship with them, is seen the invariable pattern of his feminine friendships—the relationship of a young tutor with his pupil, easy, bantering and affectionate. In one of his notebooks he makes a contemptuous equation of women with infants, but he was always able to get on to the best of terms with them, and he certainly venerated the great, such as George Eliot. One of his letters to the younger of the two Grays (the parents had forbidden correspondence with the elder) is given on p. 239.

When Thomson was nearly sixteen he was sent to the Royal Military Asylum, Chelsea, to train as an army schoolmaster, and a year later he went to serve as a probationary teacher in the regimental school at Ballincollig near Cork. He stayed there for eighteen months, under the supervision of Joseph Barnes, the garrison-master, in whose household he lived, and who with his wife became devoted to the clever young man, whom they nicknamed 'Co', short for Precocious. A pleasant reminiscence describes Thomson in a family emergency when Mr. Barnes was away and Mrs. Barnes was ill, writing on the blackboard in the classroom with the Barnes infant held on his other arm.[2]

This seems to have been a happy time for him, as the set of sonnets, written ten years later, records.[3] Moreover, two important things happened to him: he fell in love, and he met Charles Bradlaugh. Matilda Weller, daughter of an armourer-sergeant stationed at Ballincollig, was only fourteen, but it seems to have been understood that she and Thomson should marry later on, and her illness and death in the summer of 1853, some six months after he had returned to the Chelsea School to finish his training, was a disastrous blow to him. It is recorded that he would not touch food for three days, and 'lay about in the windows of the College' in hopeless grief. However much his later writings may idealize Matilda ('an Angel' and 'As lovely and beyond my love As now in your far world above'[4]) it is certain that her loss was deeply felt, and must have confirmed in the lad, who had begun to find happiness after his unlucky childhood, a sense of malevolence in the scheme of things. 'Se fosse amico il re del' Universo' . . . he might

---

[1] Dobell and Salt, op. cit.
[2] Salt p. 8.
[3] See p. 74.
[4] 'Vane's Story'.

have echoed the pathetic words of Francesca in the *Inferno*: 'If the King of the Universe were our friend . . .'

Thomson never forgot Matilda, and never, so far as we can tell, knew hopeful love again—unless fleetingly in the last year of his life. 'Affairs' he must have had, and his diaries contain some recurrent names, but he never married. Imogene Walker[1] thinks that he felt sexual desires to be shameful, and used Matilda's memory as a defence against any close relationship. Certainly his treatment of love in his poems is artificial and remote, and the early ones contrast the purity of spirit with the impurity of flesh, but that was very much in the idiom of his time, and I should say that a more likely explanation of his bachelorhood was his growing dipsomania (I refer to this later) and his hopeless material prospects.

The meeting with Charles Bradlaugh was to have much influence on the course of Thomson's life. Bradlaugh had enlisted in the army on running away from home shortly before, and his regiment was stationed at Ballincollig. They must have been in many ways an ill-assorted pair of friends: Bradlaugh tough, confident and pugnacious, where Thomson was sensitive, sceptical and irresolute. Their friendship, however, lasted for more than twenty years, and for much of that time Bradlaugh provided the means of material support and stability, of which his friend was increasingly in need. Bradlaugh was already an atheist when they met, which Thomson was not, and although Salt says that they made no attempt to convert each other, the fact that Bradlaugh was the only powerful thinker with whom Thomson came into contact at this impressionable age, cannot but have affected the development of his thought. If instead he had known someone who could have put before him the intellectual claims of Christianity, his development might have been different, and the religious instinct which was so strong in him might not have been left unsatisfied; but his polemics never show awareness of any but the most puerile definitions of the Christian faith.

On the evidence of his poems, Thomson in his early years seems to have been tormented by the conflict between doubt and the wish to believe, and he was strongly under the influence of Shelley's Idealism. *The Doom of a City*, written when he was twenty-three, shows a belief in God and a rejection of the formulae of the churches. His later belief, formulated here and there both in poetry and prose, seems to have been that only the material part of man is immortal ('One part of me shall feed a little worm . .' etc.[2]), and that the laws of the Universe are entirely indifferent to man and his needs. There is no space here to document this development: Miss Walker's *Study* discusses it fully, though I think that Thomson's final position was less tolerant and more positively atheist than she allows.

---

[1] op cit. p. 16.   [2] 'To Our Ladies of Death', l.215.

Thomson completed his probation and took up his first appointment as a fully-trained Army schoolmaster, some three months before his twentieth birthday. He was first at Plymouth, then at Aldershot, then again in Ireland from the summer of 1856 until 1860; another year at Aldershot followed, and then a year in Jersey. In some ways the life, with its recurrent changes of scene, suited him well—at any rate in retrospect it seemed to him to have contained his happiest days—but although he made two lasting friendships with fellow schoolmasters,[1] and he seems to have been a popular teacher, an army mess cannot have been the best of nurseries for a literary talent, and the teaching (of children in the morning and soldiers in the afternoon) had much of drudgery in it. The verse which Salt quotes from a letter of this time[2] has a characteristic modesty, and tells us more of Thomson than his utterances in the grand style, such as the poem written on his 23rd birthday (p. 54).

> And if now and then a curse (too intense for this light verse)
> Should be gathering in one's spirit when he thinks of how he lives,
> With a constant tug and strain—knowing well it's all in vain—
> Pumping muddy information into unretentive sieves:
> Let him stifle back the curse, which but makes the matter worse,
> And by tugging on in silence earn his wages if he can;
> For the blessed eve and night are his own yet, and he might
> Fix sound bottoms in these sieves too, were he not so weak a man.

In October 1862 Thomson was discharged from the army for an offence so trifling (refusal to give names after a bathe in a prohibited pond) that it is obvious his periodic bouts of drinking must already have imperilled his position.[3] This may therefore be the place to discuss his malady of dipsomania, which was to ruin his life and cause his death in middle age. He and his friends believed that it was inherited, and he once said that all the members of his family who had any brains were so afflicted. Although opinion nowadays might not be able to solve the problem as simply as that,[4] it seems certain that Thomson's drinking was the direct result of constitutional melancholia of a cyclic kind,

---

[1] James Potterton, whose death he notes in his diary for 1869, and John Grant, who outlived him. Many of the MSS. poems in the Bodleian collection were copies made for Grant. A memorandum by Dobell in the collection says that Grant made a drunken scene because he had not been invited to his friend's funeral.

[2] op. cit. p. 21.

[3] Salt, op. cit. p. 35, does not record whether the other schoolmasters involved were discharged too. Dobell repeated Salt's account in his 1895 Memoir, but added, in his later version of the Memoir, 'His great infirmity had, I believe, already begun to show itself . . .'—see *The Laureate of Pessimism* p. 18. Salt, op. cit. p. 20, dates its onset from 1855.

[4] I am told by a psychiatrist that someone can inherit not only the 'special personality-structure' which causes him to crave for drugs and stimulants, but also the physical ability to absorb alcohol unusually quickly, or to 'metabolise abnormally'. Such people feel none of the unpleasant physical sensations, and rapidly lose the power of judgement, which might act as a deterrent.

which afflicted him with periodic insomnia. G. W. Foote, a free-thinker who saw much of him towards the end of his life, has the clearest account of it.[1]

> He was not a toper; on the contrary, he was a remarkably temperate man, both in eating and drinking. His intemperate fits came on periodically, like other forms of madness; and naturally as he grew older and weaker they lasted longer, and the lucid intervals became shorter. The fits were invariably preceded by several days of melancholy, which deepened and deepened until intolerable. Then he flew to the alcohol, so naturally and unconsciously that when he returned to sanity he could seldom remember the circumstances of his collapse.

Salt also quotes a statement made to him by another friend, J. W. Barrs:[2]

> After the fit had spent itself would come a dreary week of feebleness and self-abhorrence, then returning health would bring back the normal Thomson, and a few months of work would be the prelude to another attack. No mortal ever strove against an overpowering disease more grimly than Thomson, and when friends were to be pained by his succumbing to the mania it was always combated and repulsed to the last moment. His absolute abandonment during these attacks was sufficient to attest their nature, and no more pregnant illustration of the metamorphosis he underwent could well be found than the remark made by his landlord's children on one such occasion. Thomson was naturally very loving with children, and children invariably returned his affection. Once, when he came back to his rooms in Huntley Street in the fulness of the change wrought by his excesses, the children went to the door to admit him, but closed it again and went to their father, telling him that 'Mr. Thomson's wicked brother was at the door'; and for some time they could not recognise 'our Mr. Thomson' in the figure of the dipsomaniac claiming his name.

'There is some evidence that he had now and then taken opium', Salt remarks,[3] but clearly this never became a habit. Brandy and whiskey are the spirits mentioned by his friends (though there is no mention of them in his own meticulously-kept accounts), and he must have had strong recuperative powers to have survived as long as he did. It is only in the later eighteen-seventies that the deterioration in his beautifully clear handwriting is visible, and even then he was capable of steady writing in good intervals.

On his discharge from the army, Thomson found a home in the household of Charles Bradlaugh, who had purchased his own discharge in October 1853 and was now an active leader of the party of Free-thought, supporting himself by lecturing and by work as a solicitor's clerk.[4] He was married, with two daughters, and Thomson shared their family life for the next four years, first in Bishopsgate and then at Park, near Tottenham. He became devoted to the two Bradlaugh girls and their mother, and the younger of the two has left a delightful account of him as he appeared to them—how he would tell them stories of his own

---

[1] *Progress*, April 1884: quoted by Salt.
[2] op. cit. p. 107. [3] op. cit. p. 79.
[4] See *Life of Charles Bradlaugh*, by Hypatia Bradlaugh-Bonner, T. Fisher Unwin, 1895.

invention, one instalment each Sunday, and would take them to the Opera, keeping the English text of the words open for them to glance at; or how he came with their father to fetch them from a Christmas party, and carried them pick-a-back through the snow.[1] In a ball-room, she writes, 'his light feet and merry tongue made him one of the most desired partners', and her memory of his gaiety made her angry with those who after his death portrayed him as devoured by melancholy. She records, however, that after his 'fits of intemperance', 'comparatively rare at first', he had to be searched out, brought home, and nursed until he was well, for 'it often happened that he was bruised and wounded, and unfit to go out for some days'.

All observers comment on the expressiveness of Thomson's eyes—'full of shifting light, soft grey in some moods and deep blue in others' was Foote's unscientific but positive impression.[2] His hair and beard were black; his height, W. M. Rossetti estimated, only about five foot six.[3] 'There was', Rossetti adds, 'a rather peculiar expression in his mouth; something of a permanently pained expression, along with a settled half-smile, caustic but not cynical, not "put on", but adopted as part of his attitude towards the world . . . He talked extremely well, and without, I think, any symptom of defective education, except that his *h*'s were sometimes less aspirated than they should be. Not that he *dropped* his *h*'s, and he certainly never inserted them when they ought not to come.[4] . . . He was quite as ready to listen as to talk, and his conversation was in no degree pragmatic[5] or controversial.' Another account of his conversation as heard in the last year of his life, when he was dependent on the stimulus of alcohol to rouse him, is given by Frank Harris,[6] somewhat flowery, but worth quoting.

> As the spirit took effect Thomson talked better than I had ever heard anyone talk up to that time; his shrunken features seemed to fill out . . . the eyes now grey pools of soft light; now dark blue, deep beyond deep, held one enchanted with their play of expression; the face took on a certain nobility of power . . . Whenever he spoke of a poet he would quote a line of verse and these were often new and always intensely characteristic; a verse of Shelley about music and violets; a line of Keats: 'There is a budding morrow in midnight.' . . .

Thomson 'modified nearly all the accepted judgements', 'flashed agreement' when Harris refused Byron the title of poet, and said that Browning had produced twenty times as much high poetry as Tennyson and far more even than Wordsworth.

---

[1] Hypatia Bradlaugh-Bonner, op. cit. and two articles in *Our Corner*, August and September, 1886. Some of Thomson's letters to the family are given in my selection.
[2] op. cit.   [3] quoted by Salt, p. 53.
[4] In support of this point—T.'s MS. for the poem 'Our Ladies of Death' reads *Thine hair*, which he corrected in the 1880 volume.
[5] So Salt's quotation, but presumably *dogmatic*.
[6] *Contemporary Portraits*, 2nd series, published by the author, New York, 1919.

Bradlaugh found work for Thomson in the solicitor's office which he managed, and, in the spring of 1863, as secretary to the 'Polish Committee' which had been formed to help the cause of the Polish rebellion against Russia. A letter of May 1863 from one of the sponsors, quoted by Hypatia, complains that Thomson has disappeared, and has 'not been at [the office] this week', but he was evidently not sacked at once, for a note in his diary says '25.8.63. Cease connection with Polish Committee. Commenced 23.4.63. Four months and two days. £1.1. since end of July.'

Meanwhile, Thomson was contributing to Bradlaugh's weekly paper, *The National Reformer*, which, as it provided his chief literary outlet until 1875 and published his major poem, must be described here. The prospectus of 1859 announces it as 'Atheistic in theology, Republican in politics, and Malthusian in social economy'. It cost 2d., and its public must have been drawn chiefly from the working classes, but Thomson's 'City of Dreadful Night' attracted notices in the *Academy* and *Spectator* when it appeared, and there must have been a number of readers of the type of Bertram Dobell, who first saw Thomson's work there. Writing to W. M. Rossetti in 1874 Thomson said:[1]

> The *National Reformer* has now a circulation of between 7000 and 8000 copies, I believe; which is very large for a paper of its extreme views. It is, probably, the only periodical of the kind which has succeeded in paying its way. Of course the great bulk of its readers are poorly educated, and care little or nothing for poetry or any other art; care, in fact, nothing for literature as literature, but only as a club to hit parsons and lords on the head with . . . For me its supreme merit consists in the fact that I can say in it what I like how I like; and I know not another periodical in Britain which would grant me the same liberty or license.

The paper combines the tone of habitual opposition which is familiar to us in journalism of the extreme left, with the parochialism of a parish magazine and the naïveté of a crank health-magazine. Capably-written attacks by Bradlaugh on the Establishment, ecclesiastical and secular, jostle advertisements for cocoa free from adulteration, and the Works of Tom Paine. There are accounts of the happily *non*-pious deaths of free-thinkers, and reports of Secularist Sunday-School meetings :—the Superintendent of the Huddersfield Secular and Eclectic Sunday School is presented with the complete Works of J. S. Mill and Smiles's *Self Help*, and is 'sensibly affected': '"You have gone too far", he said: "I am not deserving of such a treat as this."'

Thomson provides the chief literary merit of the paper, and some of his work is extremely good. He wrote a discerning review of Blake's poems at a time when recognition of Blake's genius was rare, and his criticism of his contemporaries is almost always just and perspicacious. His admiration, admittedly, was extended to

[1] Bodleian MSS.

a practitioner of automatic writing called Garth Wilkinson,[1] whom he considered the equal of Blake in some respects—but did not Coleridge extol the sonnets of Bowles? He was among the earliest admirers of Meredith and Browning, and although he was prejudiced against Tennyson, there is some truth in his criticism. Where he was sympathetic, he could turn a stricture neatly—witness this comment on 'Aurora Leigh', who 'sets out determined to walk the world with the great Shakespearian stride, whence desperate entanglement of feminine draperies and blinding swirls of dust.'

There is certainly an insensitiveness and cheapness about much of Thomson's satirical writing which jars—perhaps the result of too much association with Secularists, eager to score debating points. In a serious article on Jesus of Nazareth he describes the 'My God, My God, why hast Thou forsaken me?' as a 'womanish cry of desperation', a curious comment from the author of the 'City'. But he knew slovenly work when he saw it, and his reviews of Stigand's translation of Heine, or the egregious 'Secularist Hymn Book' of Mrs. Besant,[2] are devastating and well-documented. As to his lighter work, it is always readable and sometimes delightful, as when he pokes fun at his fellow free-thinkers (especially Bradlaugh) in the piece called 'A National Reformer in the Dog Days':[3]

> The glass registers between 90 and 100 in the shade, and a trifle under boiling point in the sun ... Body and soul I am limp and fuming as a boiled rag, fit for nothing but to take off my flesh and loll in my bones and sip iced-claret cup; and the barbarous Editor is urgent for copy ... Lo, our Editor strideth stalwart in the van of the Army of Progress, brandishing his pen as a keen lance ... waving on high as the banner of the hopes of Humanity the last broadsheet of this noble periodical ...

And Thomson, with not an idea in his head 'except iced claret-cup', takes his seat on a green bluff overlooking a bay, and watches the Army of Progress march out of sight, sure that if he waits long enough they will come round to the same place again.

Thomson's contributions to the *National Reformer* continue from 1860 to 1875, and before this he had contributed a good deal of verse to a Scottish publication called *Tait's Edinburgh Magazine*, and earlier still (1858-9) both verse and prose to a paper of Bradlaugh's called *The London Investigator*, where he used for the first time the pen-name under which he always wrote thereafter—Bysshe Vanolis (later abbreviated to B.V.), from Shelley's middle name and *Novalis*, the pen-name of the German poet von Hardenburg, who like Thomson had lost his early love.

From time to time Bradlaugh withdrew from the editorship of the *Reformer*, and Thomson performed a good deal of the editorial and sub-editorial work, with the editor-in-charge, Charles Watts.

---

[1] In 'A Strange Book' (reprinted in *Biographical and Critical Studies*, Reeves & Turner and Bertram Dobell, 1896) T. gives long extracts from his poems, which are very insipid.

[2] *The Secularist*, 8.4.76.

[3] Reprinted in *Essays and Phantasies*, Reeves and Turner, 1880.

He was not paid anything for his verse contributions,[1] and whatever he received for his other work was not sufficient to support him, on the evidence of a letter to his sister-in-law, quoted on p. 243. In the autumn of 1866 he ceased to live with the Bradlaughs, perhaps because Bradlaugh feared his influence on his wife, who herself became a drunkard,[2] or possibly because the expeditions to retrieve him after his disappearances had become an intolerable burden on the family. In a notebook of that year Thomson records the addresses at which he searched for lodgings:

> Thurs. 11.10.66. Hunted the W.C. district north of Holborn and Oxford Street. Dusty, musty, fusty, rusty, and *dear* . . . Saty 13.10.66. Hunted the Pimlico district with Potterton. Took Bed and sitting room 11 Denbigh Street Belgrave Road S.W. 14/- a week with Breakfast and Tea. Rooms on first floor. Seem decent people.

Then follows the pathetic note: 'Shall probably settle down.'

Thus began Thomson's London lodging-house existence, which was to last with few breaks until his attempt to burn the house down over his landlord's head, shortly before his death:—that solitary existence in anonymous London rooms which pervades his nightmare poems—literary forerunners of the drab poverty of Gissing's novels, and the 'dingy shades In a thousand furnished rooms' of Mr. Eliot's London. Thomson's diaries and notebooks, with their careful entries and accounts, supplement his poems, for he was an inveterate note-maker, dating all his manuscripts, putting particulars about the weather at the top of his daily entries and remarking on current events such as the result of the Boat Race. I quote some typical notes.[3]

> 8 Nov. 1874 First fire.
> 28 Nov. 1874 No regular dinner since Saturday.
> 6 Nov. 1878 Got out Watch and Clothes (i.e. from pawn).

In contrast to this is a laundry list of 20.10.66, quite lavish to modern ways of thinking, which includes '11 shirts plus four (sent on 15.12.66), 2 white waistcoats, 20 collars, 2 merino undershirts'. At about this date, too, there is an interesting entry of the service-times at various churches, including the Catholic and Apostolic in Gordon Square, and the Swedenborgian in Hatton Garden, though there is no reason to suppose that this argues anything more than curiosity, or perhaps some projected article on different creeds.

On 4 March 1879 he notes that the British Museum tried electric light for the first time, and in the same year, on a cold Ash Wednesday, he is infuriated to find it shut. This year also he notes 'Little Harry's fourth birthday' (I think the landlord's son),

---

[1] Letter to Dobell, 9.7.75.
[2] Four years later her malady brought about a partial separation, and she took the girls to live with her father at Midhurst, where Bradlaugh visited them at intervals. She died in 1877 of heart-failure induced by alcoholism. See Hypatia Bradlaugh-Bonner, op. cit.
[3] The diaries before 1872 are fragmentary. The diary for 1875, the year of Thomson's rupture with Bradlaugh, is missing.

and in 1881: 'Mrs. Israel next room, died last night about 10.20, after I heard her crying and moaning.'

On 4 Nov. 1869 is an entry describing how he has burnt all his old papers 'save the book MSS': it took him five hours to get them burnt without setting the chimney on fire. ' . . . after this terrible year, I could do no less than consume the past'. Salt and Dobell both quote this in full, but can give no hint as to why this year in particular should have been a terrible one for Thomson. What is certain is that two months later he began to write the 'City of Dreadful Night'.

This dreary picture is a little brightened when one remembers that Thomson never lacked friends with homes in which he was a welcome visitor. He continued to spend his Christmases or part of the Christmas season with the Bradlaughs until 1874, and after that he was generally with hospitable friends in Gower Street,[1] where he had a refuge until the end of his life.

Thomson made many efforts to get his poems accepted by other than free-thinking journals: in the 1866 notebook there are memoranda of poems and translations offered to the *Cornhill*, *Argosy*, *Belgravia* and *Daily Telegraph*, all rejected. His one success was in 1869, when Froude printed 'Sunday up the River' in *Fraser's Magazine*, but although he invited Thomson to breakfast and lent him Spinoza, nothing further came of their meeting, and Froude refused the next poem which Thomson sent him. Early in 1872, Thomson sent a copy of the numbers of the *National Reformer* containing his 'Weddah and Om El Bonain' to William Rossetti, whose cheap edition of Shelley he had reviewed in the previous year, and this led to some half-dozen meetings and a literary correspondence over a number of years. Rossetti showed the poem to Swinburne, who at first gave it enthusiastic praise, but afterwards partially withdrew the praise, with expressions of moral condemnation in which the voice of Watts Dunton seems to speak.

'The City of Dreadful Night', half written by the end of 1870, was then laid aside for $2\frac{1}{2}$ years, and meanwhile Thomson wrote no more poetry except a handful of epigrams and part of a draft for the 'Proem' which he rewrote in 1882. In April 1872 he was sent out to Colorado, in his capacity as Secretary to the 'Champion Gold and Silver Mines Company', to report on conditions at their mines there, and remained in America until the end of the year. It was an experience that he enjoyed, in spite of the unsatisfactory condition in which he found his company's affairs, and the fact that they defaulted on part of his salary. 'When travelling about', he wrote in a letter of the time,[2] I always find myself immensely better than when confined to one place. With money, I believe I should never have a home, but be always going to and fro on the

---

[1] T. R. Wright and his family: see below.
[2] See p. 249.

earth, and walking up and down in it, like him of whom I am one of the children.' (The ending is characteristic.) The Colorado landscape made a strong impression on him, as can be seen from the long letter he wrote to William Rossetti,[1] and the diary he kept at the time is full of minute descriptions of scenery, besides notes of gravestone-inscriptions and of local words. His descriptions of scenery are always full of colour:

> 19.8.72. Lovely walk up Cañon between 8.30 and 9.45 or 10 . . . At first the southern hill-mass, solid sombre green, like bronze; then the light green crater; then the Squaw and Chief to the right; then on the divide the whole line under horizontal white clouds, and northwards the well known hills (high mottled green to right, sharp spinal ridge centre, noble ridge to left with precipices now like three black eyes white-ringed). Between the Gulch and the lefthand hill, seamed with trails and watercourses, stripped, gashed, pitted, lacerated, and the idle mills down Russell Gulch like ships in ordinary at Spithead or Plymouth. The pines on the sombre southern hills fine, thick and sleek as the soft warm fur of some monstrous animal. The hills sharply defined against the azure daylight as usually against a clear moonlit or gleaming sky.[2]

During the spring after his return, Thomson again started work on his major poem, but broke off when he was sent out as correspondent to the *New York World*, to report on the civil war in Spain. This assignment, obtained through Bradlaugh's influence, was also much to Thomson's liking, but his employers were not satisfied with his reports[3] and recalled him after two months—according to Thomson because the participants would not fight enough to furnish him with material. He was prostrate with sunstroke[4] for more than ten days, as his fragmentary diary records, and during this time[5] mentally composed some more of the *City*. Soon after his return on September 23 he set to work again on the poem, in spite of ill-health resulting from his visit to Spain, and had finished drafting it by the end of October, as the MS. dating makes clear. Early the next year he was polishing it[6] and on Easter Eve, 4 April, his diary records that he went through the last two parts of the poem, and adds: 'Walked self after tea. Imagination deeply stirred.'

From Thomson's diary for this year it is plain that he was existing from hand to mouth on his work for the *National Reformer* and a short-lived Company venture in the City. Austin Holyoake, the editor in charge at this time, from whose house the *Reformer* was published,[7] was mortally ill, and Thomson was helping to carry on the paper. Several diary entries say 'Austin's all week', and after Holyoake's death in April is the note 'Saw Austin—still

---

[1] See p. 243.   [2] Bodleian MSS.
[3] He only sent back three during his first month: Salt, p. 71-2.
[4] Perhaps also with the effects of alcohol, but there is no proof of this except a statement by Hypatia in the *Life* of her father quoted above.
[5] Salt, p. 71, reports that T. 'told a friend' this.
[6] Letter to W. M. Rossetti, 24.6.74.
[7] The Holyoakes were among the apostles of Secularism: Austin a publisher of free-thought literature, and his elder brother George Jacob imprisoned for six months in mid-century for atheism.

looking better than I have lately seen him sometimes in life—jaw fallen, right eye a little open, leg a skeleton from the large kneebone.'

Meanwhile the 'City' had begun to appear in instalments in the *National Reformer* (March-May 1874), and although it did not please some of the regular readers of the paper, it did attract the notice of fellow-writers, of which Thomson had hitherto received so little. Bradlaugh received letters of protest after the first instalment, and delayed the second for three weeks, which caused Bertram Dobell to write to ask when the rest was to appear. Thomson replied under his own name, and thus began their friendship, and Dobell's selfless devotion to the cause of publishing and preserving Thomson's work. A laudatory notice of the poem in the *Academy* (known to have been by Edith Simcox[1]) gave it some publicity, and the numbers of the *Reformer* in which it appeared were soon sold out. Thomson sent them to George Eliot, who replied graciously, though expressing the wish that he would soon utter 'more heroic strains with a wider embrace of human fellowship in them'—to which Thomson replied comparing her to 'that grand and awful Melancholy of Albert Dürer which dominates the City of my poem'. 'I am aware', he added later, 'that the truth of midnight does not exclude the truth of noonday, though one's nature may lead him to dwell in the former rather than the latter.'[2] Meredith too read and admired the poem, though he and Thomson did not correspond until some years later.

The copy sent to William Rossetti arrived,[3] perhaps somewhat inopportunely, to greet him on his return from his honeymoon, but this does not seem to have biased his judgement, and he responded with an invitation to dinner, which Thomson accepted, thanking 'for the freedom as to dress .. [as] .. I am a barbarian who has not evening dress.'[4] But alas, Thomson must have been seized by one of his drinking fits, and, as subsequent allusions in the correspondence make clear, not only failed to turn up at the dinner, but never wrote to apologize. Rossetti did succeed in getting him to a New Year's dinner of 1877, when he was 'about the best talker in the company', but he again defaulted on a later invitation, and 'the matter was never alluded to' on the two or three further occasions when they met.[5]

---

[1] T.'s letter to W. M. Rossetti, 22.11.74.
[2] Quoted Salt, p. 82.
[3] Letter to W. M. Rossetti, 14.5.74, enclosing the numbers: 'I fear that you will find it altogether too pious and cheerful.' Letter of 24.6.74: '(I am sorry that) I happened to salute you on your return from your wedding tour with such a dismal raven's croak.' It is clear from the correspondence, which Imogene Walker had not seen, that she is quite unfair in saying that Rossetti extended no invitations to Thomson until after Miss Blind had taken him up: op. cit. 132-4.
[4] 27.7.74.
[5] Letter from W. M. Rossetti to Salt, copy in Bodleian made by Dobell in July 1898.

Those who would befriend Thomson had to put up with such uncertainties, and Ford Madox Ford describes a similar experience at a dinner given by his parents in B.V.'s honour, when he himself was sent out to look for the missing guest, and found him hopelessly drunk at a whelk stall in the Euston Road.[1]

Although Thomson, in replying to Dobell's enquiry about the instalments of the *City*, had referred to Bradlaugh as 'my very dear friend . . . always anxious to stretch a point in my favour', their friendship must in fact have been cooling for some time, and the final break between them came in the summer of 1875. Perhaps it would have come earlier, but for the mutual affection between Thomson and the girls and their mother. On Bradlaugh's part there was evidently a growing exasperation and disillusionment, for which Thomson certainly gave him good cause. It cannot have been easy to swallow the annoyance of recommending him for jobs on which he defaulted, but even worse was what Bradlaugh considered his betrayal of the Secularist cause by bringing it into disrepute.[2] On Thomson's side, I imagine that there must always have been a certain envy of Bradlaugh's extravert confidence and physical strength,[3] and he did not share Bradlaugh's belief in human progress; but apart from this, Thomson was only one of many who were becoming alienated by Bradlaugh's overbearing ways, which must have grown upon him with the years.[4] When Mrs. Besant joined forces with him on the *National Reformer* in August 1874 Thomson found himself gradually crowded out of the paper, and the friendship seems to have ended with Bradlaugh's discharging him from his service 'for drunkenness',[5] and with a later meeting in the presence of solicitors when Thomson refused Bradlaugh's proffered hand. The break with the family was complete, for the girls' first loyalty was to their

---

[1] *Ancient Lights*, Chapman & Hall, p. 36. Thomson is not named here, but it is clear from the context that he is referred to. Dobell notes the story, though only at third hand, in his memoranda deposited in the Bodleian.
[2] See Bradlaugh's letter in Bodleian, dated 12 Nov. [1882], subscribing £1 to the Thomson Memorial Fund, to be given anonymously 'In memory of Bysshe Vanolis and Ballincollig'. 'I once very dearly loved him and rescued him at least twenty times from delirium tremens and misery—I housed him fed him and clothed him for more than twelve years . . . and only broke with him with deep pain in 1875-6 because drink had utterly accursed him.—If you are honoring a fine poet and mighty prose writer you do well—If you are honoring a freethinker for his devotion to the cause you are utterly wrong.'
[3] See letter to Mrs. Bradlaugh, p. 242. 'He appeared as though he could have supped off a creature the size of me, and not have been troubled with indigestion . . .'
[4] Hypatia's *Life*, I, 96 quotes an early letter which shows a more attractive side of him.
[5] Letter of 'Oliver H. S. Leigh' (i.e. G. G. Flaws) to T. B. Mosher (American publisher of T.'s poems) of early 1893, describing how T. had confided to him the slip of paper with the discharge, and 'I was to avenge his memory on that'. Bodleian MSS.

father, and though they met again in public, they did not speak to each other.¹

On 1 January 1876 the first number of a rival weekly appeared, to which Thomson was a frequent contributor. This was *The Secularist*, edited by a young free-thinker named G. W. Foote (already quoted on Thomson), and the veteran G. J. Holyoake, who had quarrelled with Bradlaugh some years earlier, but was soon to quarrel with his fellow-editor and lend his name to the support of the Bradlaugh-Besant faction, setting up an independent paper called *The Secular Review*. The changes in editorship of these papers resembles the crossings of a country dance: first Foote and Holyoake, Watts and Bradlaugh, are partners; Holyoake is then alone, to be joined shortly by Watts after his dismissal by Bradlaugh; then Foote joins Watts on *The Secular Review* and Holyoake steps down; finally Foote disappears from that paper and Holyoake joins it again, while Foote starts a fourth paper, a monthly called *The Liberal*. In each change there must have been some awkward memories of printed insults to swallow, and B.V. joined heartily in the polemics, especially in his references to Bradlaugh, 'the little great man' as he termed him, borrowing a phrase of Bradlaugh's own. When in 1880 the 'City' came out in book form, he made no acknowledgement to the *National Reformer*, and in August 1881, when Bradlaugh tried to take his seat in the House of Commons without swearing the statutory oath and was ejected, Thomson was among the watchers and seems to have enjoyed himself, to judge from his diary entry.²

Thomson contributed some poetry to Foote's monthly *The Liberal*, for which he says that he only charged for the time taken in correcting proofs,³ but Foote got in arrears with his payments, and this friendship too turned to a vindictive bitterness on Thomson's side.⁴ Considering the debts owed by Thomson himself to people without resources,⁵ the rancour with which he pursued his former friends seems particularly unpleasant, and one cannot but think it a sign of deterioration in a character which was naturally generous. Yet in these years he was still capable of the acute

¹ See Thomson's diary entry for 27.1.76.
² 'Grand field day for J. W. B(arrs) Percy (Holyoake) and I.' See I. Walker, p. 129 for a discussion of Salt's very different version of the incident; but one must add that J. W. Barrs seems to have given him the basis for his account: see letter from Salt to Dobell in Bodleian.
³ Letter from T. to Dobell, 19.10.79, Bodleian MSS.
⁴ Bitter references to Foote, 'that skunk', abound in letters and diary entries. Percy Holyoake, writing to J. W. Barrs, 11.5.82, speaks of serving a writ on Foote at a public meeting: there is no proof that this was on Thomson's behalf, but it seems likely, and the Bodleian MSS. include a memorandum 'given to H. Hood Barrs' of money due to T. from Foote.
⁵ Dobell records in his memoranda that he visited T.'s former lodging at 60 Tachbrook Street, where the landlady told him that he owed her £4 or £5 when he left, and had owed about £30 to his previous landlady in Vauxhall Bridge Road.

self-knowledge shown in this passage from his journalism of the time:[1]

> It is so much easier to set about reforming the world than oneself, it is so pleasant to be comprehensive in our plans and vast in our aspirations . . . it is so cheerless to fight vice after vice in the silent and solitary arena of one's own heart, that ninety-nine out of a hundred will ever persist to understand in somewhat of a parliamentary sense the 'making our calling and election sure.'

Thomson's main livelihood from September 1875 until 1881 came from a monthly trade paper called *Cope's Tobacco Plant*, which paid him well and regularly for literary articles on any subject which could conceivably be of interest to smokers—and this could include quite serious studies, such as that which he wrote on Ben Jonson, provided that they contained some references to tobacco. Salt spoke in his *Life* of the work for this paper as having been 'congenial' to him, and a later editor commented on the adjective as follows:

> It would perhaps be too much to assume that the analysing of blue books, the tabulating of statistics, the cataloguing of laws relating to tobacco and the preparing of trade memorials is precisely the kind of work that Thomson would have deliberately chosen. But it was Thomson's distinguishing merit that whatever he undertook to do he did with thoroughness. Tasks which an inferior man would have despised because they were 'hack-work', and done grudgingly if at all, he accepted and made as perfect in their own way as the finest of his poems. It was 'congenial' to him to be thorough.[2]

I have quoted this at length, since it shows how conscientious Thomson could be in his profession, when the demon did not hold him by the throat.

Early in 1876, Thomson moved his lodgings to 7 Huntley Street, in Bloomsbury, where he remained till just before his death. This was conveniently near the British Museum,[3] and the landlord, named Gibson, and housekeeper, Miss Scott, seem to have treated him with much kindness. Moreover, it was near a hospitable home in Gower Street where Thomson spent most of his leisure hours. Austin Holyoake's widow had married another Secularist writer, T. R. Wright, and G. W. Foote lodged at this time in their house. Thomson gave Italian lessons to Adeline, the Holyoake daughter, and made regular Sunday morning walks with Percy, the son, as his diaries record. There is frequent mention of games of billiards; and (for instance) on 29 December 1880 he returns there to dine after attending George Eliot's funeral in dismal weather, and notes that they are on their third turkey.

Ever since their first acquaintance, Bertram Dobell had been active in trying to procure publication of a volume of Thomson's poems. Various attempts on the larger publishing houses having

---

[1] *The Secularist*, 19.8.76.
[2] Preface by Walter Lewin to a volume of Selections from Thomson's contributions to the *Tobacco Plant*, Liverpool 1889.
[3] Miss Walker considers the move a symbol of defeated hopes, but most Londoners would think it a change for the better from Vauxhall Bridge Road.

failed, Dobell at last succeeded in finding a firm to share the risk with himself—a third of any profits to be given to Thomson—and in April 1880 appeared *The City of Dreadful Night and Other Poems* under the imprint of Reeves and Turner. It sold unexpectedly well, and Thomson notes in his diary on 17 August that he had got £10 'unasked' from Reeves, and that the volume has already paid its expenses—of which he is justifiably proud, as 'Other publishers all firm that *no* vol. of verse, however good, can now pay its expenses, unless bearing one of three or four famous or popular names.' There were some hostile reviews, but the *Fortnightly* gave it a sympathetic article headed *A New Poet*, and Saintsbury in the *Academy* praised the book, though he expressed a dread lest it should herald a fashion of 'Leopardism'. George Meredith wrote an enthusiastic letter, which led to a visit by Thomson to Box Hill in June, recorded in his diary as 'A Day to be marked with a white stone'—after which he notes down the topics they had discussed. He had long admired Meredith's work (he published four pieces of criticism of the novels), and though he only paid one other visit to Box Hill, they continued to correspond, and Meredith wrote very warmly about him after his death.[1]

After this modest success, the publishers were ready to risk another volume, and in October of the same year they brought out *Vane's Story and Other Poems* (with the date of 1881 on the title page). This was not quite so well received as the *City*, but had a reasonable success—more than the collection of his prose, *Essays and Phantasies*, which was brought out in the spring of 1881, with such swiftness did books then roll from the press. Early in that year, *Cope's Tobacco Plant* was discontinued, thus cutting off Thomson's only regular source of income, and the introduction which Meredith had given him to John Morley, though it led to the publication of a long poem in the *Fortnightly Review* later in the year, was not likely to make up the difference. But Thomson, who had never lacked good friends, now made new ones who were to give him some weeks of happiness and fresh hope, during the last year of his life.

Thomson first met J. W. Barrs and his sister during a visit to Leicester in March 1881, on the occasion of the opening of the new Secular Hall, for which he had composed an Address in verse, to be declaimed by Mrs. T. R. Wright. His diary entry says: 'Mr. Barrs drove us to his place, round by Braunstone Wood . . . His sister. Nice place and grounds . . . All of us plus Adeline and Percy *must* go in summer.' This they did, and letters and diary entries of the time show with what cheerful results.

We are here four miles from Leicester,[2] with railway station a few

---

[1] Salt p. 136.
[2] The house, Forest Edge, Kirby Muxloe, still stands with its pleasant grounds unspoilt, though now on a busy main road, so I am told by Mr. L. Adey who visited it recently.

minutes off, in a pleasant villa surrounded by shrubbery, lawn, meadow, kitchen garden. Host and hostess (sister) are kindness itself, as are all other Leicester friends. We lead the most healthy of lives, save for strong temptations to over-feeding on excellent fare and host's evil and powerfully contagious habit of sitting up till about 2 a.m. smoking and reading or chatting. I now leave him to his own wicked devices at midnight or as soon after as possible. Despite the showery weather we have had good drives and walks (country all green and well-wooded), jolly little picnics, and lawn-tennis *ad infinitum* (N.B. Lawn-tennis even more than lady's fine pen responsible for the uncouthness of this scrawl).[1]

His host wrote of Thomson as being 'chief jester' on these summer outings, for 'Whatever has been said or written of his charm of manner and conversation . . . cannot give a just representation of them. Few men have known so delightful a friend, and his hilarity could equal his sombreness when in congenial company.'[2]

The diary entry 'his sister', quoted above, is eloquent enough to anyone who reads Thomson's poems and letters of this year. Beyond question he fell in love with her, though it is impossible for us to say how far she returned his feeling. The poem 'At Belvoir' (p. 216) written in the following winter and recalling their summer visit to Belvoir Castle, would seem to imply some shared feeling. I should guess at least that Miss Barrs ('the divine Dick' as Thomson called her) would have been enchanted by his talk, and flattered by the admiration of a poet who was distinguished even if not widely famous, and was valued by the free-thinking circles in which she lived; then also she would have been moved by pity, and by the thought that she alone might have the power to cure him of his malady. Her relations must have thought that there might be some stronger feeling, as a letter from another brother, a lawyer called Henry Hood Barrs, written to J. W. Barrs in January 1882, attests: 'It was however all a mare's nest. There is nothing between Dick and B.V. but friendship, of which I am glad.'[3]

To anyone who knows Thomson's history, the poems of what Salt calls his 'Indian summer' are sadder even than the avowedly pessimistic poems, for they show a flowering of the affections which had no hope of any lasting fulfilment—as he must have realized in dispassionate moments. Miss Barrs and her brother hoped that the peace and security which their home provided, would enable him to cure himself of his disease, but the knowledge that he could not permanently depend on them for support, and

---

[1] Letter to Dobell, 21.6.81, Bodleian MSS.
[2] Salt p. 122.
[3] Bodleian MSS. Salt and Dobell were naturally reticent about Miss Barrs, writing as they did in her lifetime, but I have been able to trace her marriage certificate at Somerset House. Nineteen months after T.'s death (1.1.1884) Harriette Annie Barrs, daughter of John Barrs (deceased), Tea Merchant, was married in the Register Office at Leicester, in the presence of her two brothers, to Auguste Paul Pelluet, Professor of Languages, son of Jacques Ambroise Pelluet, farmer; her age being then 26 and his 27.

that the future held only the unending alternations of anxiety and delirium, must have sapped his will to recover. Perhaps the contrast between Forest Edge and the drab loneliness of Huntley Street drove him to drink more quickly than ever—at any rate, directly he returned from the seven weeks of summer holiday he took to the bottle, and Percy Holyoake writes to J. W. Barrs on 25 July: 'Thomson is again on his Mazeppa-like journey ... for the *first time* he dismissed me this morning, would do nothing, say nothing.'[1]

The Barrs pressed Thomson to return to them, and he did so in November, staying on till after Christmas. During this time he wrote a number of poems, and thanks to his careful dating of MSS. they can be read in more or less the order in which they were written. The despondent poem he addressed to Miss Barrs ('H.A.B.') on his 47th birthday—always a time of melancholy recollection for him—and the interesting if derivative *Voice from the Nile*, are succeeded by some rhapsodic love poetry which seems to imply a few weeks at least of hopeful love. But no sooner did he return to London in January than he began to drink again, and Percy Holyoake's letters to J. W. Barrs trace the fluctuations of his friends' hopes.

21.1.82 After all our united efforts, we are done in the end ... Dick is very cut up about it as well she may be, after all the trouble she had taken, and the promises he had given her to be good, however genius is its own reward.

30.1.82 [B.V. is] again on the upward path ... has sworn an oath not to touch spirits again ... packed up all his 'comforts' (corks and all) and made that resolve, notwithstanding that on the following day there was to be a wedding in the house.

4.2.82 I saw him last evening and relieved him of about half a pint of firewater from various pockets ... On Thursday I took him to be measured for some things to go away with, he was so well, and penitent ... Dick has not seen him yet, nor will she, I think.

However, the hospitable Forest Edge received him again in early February, and during this visit was written the terrible poem 'Insomnia', so poignant a contrast to the lines written when he watched Dick Barrs asleep:[2]

       Sweet sleep; no hope, no fear, no strife;
        The solemn sanctity of death,
       With all the loveliest bloom of life;
       Eternal peace in mortal breath:
       Pure sleep from which she will awaken
       Refreshed as one who hath partaken
       New strength, new hope, new love, new faith.

Here as before the Barrs tried to make it impossible for Thomson to find the means of buying drink, but at last he outwitted them and had to be retrieved in a hopeless state from the local inn. Miss Barrs at this point refused to have him in the house, and he

[1] Holyoake's letters and J. W. Barrs's account of his and his sister's efforts on T.'s behalf are in the Bodleian collection.
[2] The Sleeper, p. 214, referred to by H. Hood Barrs as 'B.V.'s poem on Dick'.

spent the rest of the night in the coach-house, returning to London next day. He wrote his host a pathetic but dignified letter of regret and farewell (the handwriting is surprisingly steady): 'In one fit of frenzy I have not only lost more than I yet know and half murdered myself (were it not for my debts I sincerely wish it had been wholly), but justly alienated my best and firmest friends old and new both in London and Leicester.'¹

Thomson had not alienated his friends (indeed, J. W. Barrs sought him out in Huntley Street and begged him to return once more to Forest Edge), but this time there was to be no recovery for him. He was several times taken up by the police and bailed out by Percy Holyoake and others—Holyoake wrote wryly to Barrs that 'Bow Street will probably in the far distant free-thought future be the Mecca of the party'—and in his need of money he would pester the proprietress of a bookshop, where he had formerly dealt, for loans, even running off with books to sell when she refused him. His long-suffering landlord finally shut the door of 7 Huntley Street on him, but Thomson sometimes forced an entry, would threaten suicide, or hide upstairs. At last in his desperation he tried to set fire to the kitchen there—after which a magistrate sent him to prison for a fortnight, advising his friends not to stand bail for him, but to let him be treated in the prison hospital.²

He has now become 'the great Pitiable' in Holyoake's references, and pitiable indeed is the description of his meeting with two Secularist friends at the bar of the Holborn Restaurant, his clothes 'worn, soiled, and deeply-creased' as though he had lain in the street, his feet 'protected from the slushy streets only by a pair of thin old carpet-slippers, so worn and defective that, in one part, they displayed his bare skin.'³

Holyoake was making enquiries at a home for inebriates, in the hope that they might still persuade him to go to such a place, but it was too late. Emerging from the prison hospital, Thomson began the same 'Mazeppa-like journey'.⁴ At last on Thursday 1 June 1882, he collapsed with intestinal haemorrhage in the rooms of

¹ 22.4.82, Bodleian MSS.
² The Barrs seem to have been afraid of possible publicity, presumably on Miss Barrs's account, for Holyoake writes on 12 May in his account of Thomson's trial: 'Nothing concerning Forest Edge was on him, nor has there been for some days past.' The landlord, Gibson, had taken him coffee and toast at the police station, and next day in court said that he did not want punishment for Thomson, only protection for himself and his property.
³ 'Saladin' (W. Stewart Ross) in the *Agnostic Journal*, 6.4.89. The other friend was Gordon Flaws ('Gegeëf'): see Notes, p. 270.
⁴ Percy Holyoake's letter of 28 May describes how B.V., having guineas in his pocket after a visit to Morley, 'convivialised at the Bedford Head', and then went to Miss Scott at Huntley Street and 'as often before announced his intention of jumping off the viaduct.' After this he 'turned in with the youngster George' and slept till one, when he woke everyone up with shouts of 'Brandy', which he kept up until 4 a.m., when he dressed and went out saying that he would *do it*.

Philip Bourke Marston, the blind poet, whom he knew from Pre-Raphaelite gatherings.[1] He was taken to University College Hospital near by, but recovered consciousness enough to see Marston and another friend next day, and to declare that he would leave the hospital on the Monday, even if he left it in his coffin. He died on the Saturday evening, June 3rd, and his prophecy came true.

He is buried in the Highgate Cemetery for non-Christians, in the grave of Austin Holyoake. Miss Scott, the housekeeper at 7 Huntley Street, produced a purse (perhaps one woven for him by the elder of the two Gray sisters) and a locket containing some of Matilda Weller's hair, which were buried with him. Gibson, the landlord, stood with the Barrs and Wrights and other friends by the grave,[2] and T. R. Wright read the Secularist Burial Service which had been written by Austin Holyoake. Thomson's poems paid the expenses of the funeral.[3]

II

'As for this "City of Dreadful Night", it is so alien from common thought and feeling that I knew well ... that scarcely any readers would care for it'—so wrote Thomson to Dobell about his poem, and in writing to his sister-in-law he describes it as 'sombre and atheistical and generally incomprehensible', advising her to skip the first 77 pages of his book, as they will only distress her. Yet to us, as we look back on the poetry of the last half of the nineteenth century, it seems that Thomson is much more typical of his time than the Victorian of solid and bewhiskered optimism who has often been presented to us. Certainly, the nostalgia and despair of the poets alternated with bursts of exaggerated manliness, and even Thomson might be judged a cheerful poet of the great outdoors by anyone who looked only at the quite untypical selection of his work printed by Quiller-Couch in the Oxford Book of English Verse. It is only too easy to derive a false picture from anthologies, or from taking the statements of dramatic characters as though they represented their authors' opinions: the song of Pippa has been taken as typical of Browning's optimism, when one might as well judge him from his words after his wife's death— that he and she had been walking on a straw over a torrent—and call him a pessimist.

---

[1] Meantime Percy Holyoake had lost track of him and was vainly searching for him. Eyewitness accounts of this final collapse are given in Dobell's Memoir (account by William Sharp, which Salt used for the first edition of his *Life*), and in Salt, 1898 and 1914 (account by Herbert Clarke).
[2] Account of the funeral in *Secular Review*, 17.6.82.
[3] A memorandum by Dobell of 19.6.82 says that Reeves has paid the funeral expenses. There seems to have been a certain amount of haggling over the price which should be put on the copyright of Thomson's unpublished poems, which Dobell eventually purchased from Percy Holyoake. Bodleian MSS.

No one who reads Signor Mario Praz's analysis of nineteenth-century romanticism[1] is likely to think too much of Victorian optimism, and at first sight it seems that Thomson's themes qualify him for a place in the gallery, though it happens that Signor Praz does not quote him. These are the themes recurrent throughout his work, from early to late: the futility of mortal hopes of happiness, the blessedness of oblivion, the inevitable loss of the beloved and the hopeless division between her purity and his own unworthiness, the callousness of Nature. The passage which Signor Praz quotes from Baudelaire's *Journaux Intimes* on Beauty—

> C'est quelque chose d'ardent et de triste . . . qui fait rêver à la fois . . . de volupté et de tristesse; qui comporte une idée de mélancolie, de lassitude, même de satiété . . . une ardeur, un désir de vivre, associés avec une amertume refluante, comme venant de privation et de desesperance . . .

would serve as a description of Thomson's approach to love; and equally striking is the likeness between his 'Melencolia', the stoical Queen-Mother-figure whom he describes in the 'City' and in an earlier poem (comparing her also, as we have seen, to George Eliot), and the poem to the Medusa by Shelley which Signor Praz takes as being 'almost a manifesto of the conception of Beauty peculiar to the Romantics'.

> It lieth, gazing on the midnight sky,
>   Upon the cloudy mountain-peak supine;
> Below, far lands are seen tremblingly;
>   Its horror and its beauty are divine . . .
>
> Whilst in the air a ghastly bat, bereft
>   Of sense, has flitted with a mad surprise . . .

so Shelley, describing the picture ascribed to Leonardo: and Thomson in the same stanza-form, with Dürer for his model—[2]

> She sits, a Woman like a Titaness . . .
>
> But, O, the stern, strong, swarthy countenance!
>   O, the intensely fixt sole-thoughted eyes
> Gazing athwart the sullen sea's expanse,
>   Wherein the sun is drowning from the skies!
> A Sphynx thus gazes in eternal trance
>   Athwart the desert's gloomy mysteries,
> Thus images a soul beyond the scope
> Of all fond frailties of fear and hope.
>
> A bat is floating in the waste of air . . .

a creature which becomes in the later poem an imp 'dog-headed, from the Pit' with 'batlike' pinions.

Yet in important respects Thomson differs from the Romantic as thus documented. Although his love-poetry may be languorous and enervating, it has none of the sado-masochism of Swinburne, the necrophily of Wilde, or (to compare him with a far greater poet) the delight in cruelty of Baudelaire. Thomson may sometimes luxuriate in his apocalyptic effects—the sun like a 'bleeding

---

[1] *The Romantic Agony*, 1933.
[2] Undated poem, hitherto unpublished.

eyeless socket, red and dim', the flames writhing like a 'Sabbath of the Serpents', but there is nothing voluptuous about the suicide's death of *In the Room*; its 'dingy urban images' (to use Mr. Eliot's description of his own youthful subject-matter[1]) are starkly presented.

In this poem Thomson perhaps comes nearest to a pure pessimism, because the death is presented as completely without significance, importance or consolation. 'Insomnia' impresses one as the fruit of terrible experience, certainly, but the piling up of superlatives, the overplus of adjectives—

> Death's ghastly aureole,
> Pregnant with overpowering fascinations,
> Commanding by repulsive instigation
> Despair's envenomed anodyne to tempt the Soul . . .

inevitably dull the impact. In the early poems, death is yearned for like the 'easeful death' of Keats—

> [I] yearn for Thee, divinely tranquil Death,
> To come and soothe away my bitter pain.[2]

As to the 'City' itself, though Herman Melville called it 'the modern book of Job',[3] there is in it a consolation of stoicism akin to Housman's

> O never fear man, nought's to dread,
> Look not left or right,
> In all the endless road you tread
> There's nothing but the night.

As Paul Elmer More says in an interesting essay on Thomson:[4] 'So necessary for the soul is some place of stability outside of nature's vortex that, if no other peace is allowed, it will make its account with death.'

> Her subjects often gaze up to her there:
> The strong to drink new strength of iron endurance,
> The weak new terrors; all, renewed assurance
> And confirmation of the old despair.[5]

There is something in common between the pessimism of Thomson, Arnold, Clough and Hardy—indeed, two of Clough's lines were quoted by Kipling as coming from the 'City'.[6] But a comparison shows that the element of self-pity, present in some degree in Arnold if not in the others, is considerably more dominant in Thomson. The mood, as a literary habit, was no doubt derived to some extent from Thomson's sources: from Novalis, and perhaps from Leopardi, with his 'stanco mio cor', though an enervating, inward-gazing, self-pity is rarer in him than in Thomson. Leopardi

---

[1] In his Preface to the *Selected Poems* of John Davidson, 1961.
[2] 'To our Ladies of Death'.
[3] In writing to H. S. Salt: Bodleian MSS.
[4] Shelburne Essays series V, 1908.   [5] *C.D.N.*, last lines.
[6] See *Longman's Magazine*, January 1892, an imaginary Dialogue by Andrew Lang. The lines:
> We are most hopeless who had once most hope
> And most beliefless, that had most believed
are from *Easter Day*, though they are not consecutive in the poem.

cannot have influenced Thomson's early poetry, since he did not begin to learn Italian until 1866,[1] but the pessimism of his later poems is undoubtedly coloured by Leopardi's expression of his own, and especially in the conviction that Nature is indifferent to man, an idea which Thomson often repeats in prose and in verse, but most strikingly in the 'City':

> The world rolls round for ever like a mill;
> It grinds out death and life and good and ill;
> It has no purpose, heart or mind or will....
>
> Nay, does it treat him harshly as he saith?
> It grinds him some slow years of bitter breath,
> Then grinds him back into eternal death.

compare Leopardi:

> So che natura è sorda
> Che miserar non sa.
>
> Che non del ben sollecita
> Fu, ma dell'esser solo...[2]

'Pessimism comes when self-consciousness is developed at the expense of irrational instinct',[3] and Thomson sometimes quoted Coleridge in reference to himself:

> And haply by abstruse research to steal
> From my own nature all the natural man.[4]

It is, as William James saw, essentially a religious disease, and in its extreme form which leads to despair, Thomson himself regarded it as a disease. 'Despair', he wrote in 1876, 'is constitutional as Hypochondria ... as animal spirits, as the hopefulness of sanguine people. It undoubtedly is a symptom of weakness, but the weakness is constitutional not volitional.'[5]

Despair becomes a fruitful ground for poetry in proportion as the poet has power to express the common lot through his own: a power which depends partly on sheer technical ability, partly on sincerity of artistic purpose, and partly on the breadth of his sympathies. The sense of isolation from one's fellows, known to every human being as a mood, and very pervasive in Matthew Arnold for instance, is damaging to poetry if it becomes absolute, and the experience of life as 'one dark maze of dreams'[6] ends in sterility. Thomson maintained easy surface relationships with his fellows (as we have seen), but his inner life became more and more divorced from these, and from any sense of reality.

> Of old I was conscious of an impenetrable veil between myself and nature: of late I have been conscious also of an impenetrable veil between my inner and outer self; I have to live, think and work with

---

[1] Diary notes: '9.10.65 Began the Italian'; '23.8.66 Began the Italian for the second time—having forgotten the little I learnt last year'. No English translation of Leopardi's poems had then appeared, though an article in *Blackwood's Magazine* (Oct. 1855) had given verse translations of portions of several Canti—see Bibliography to G. L. Bickersteth's *Leopardi*.

[2] 'Il Risorgimento', 119. *I know that nature is deaf and does not know how to pity. That she was never solicitous for (our) good, but only for (our) existence.*

[3] Paul Elmer More, op. cit. [4] 'Dejection, an Ode'.

[5] *The Secularist*, 26.8.76. [6] 'Insomnia'. See p. 232.

the latter, and cannot get at the former, cold and vague and dim aloof. This is a painful puzzle, to be shut out and cut off from one's very self, and conscious of the disabling separation.[1]

So it happened that Thomson's power of apprehending reality and transmuting his experience into poetry did not develop after the 'City', finished when he was forty. Of his later poems, the only really valuable part expresses hallucination in one form or another: his attempts to write of the natural world or the emotion of love become more and more derivative from other literature. To write good love-poetry, one must have a vivid sense of another person's existence, but in Thomson the sense of separation is the only reality. This had always been true of his serious love poems:

> You were an Angel then; as clean
> From earthly dust-speck, as serene
> And lovely and beyond my love
> As now in your far world above . . .[2]

but in the playful vein there had once been something more alive.

> Oh, what are you waiting for here, young man?
> What are you looking for over the bridge?
> A little straw hat with the streaming blue ribbons
> Is soon to come dancing over the bridge.[3]

In the late love-poems nothing gets through but the second-hand image, the stock response: the pure neck burns, the little white arms cling, maidens murmur like doves, and the nightingale is in attendance as inevitably as Koplik's spots attend upon measles.[4]

As to technical ability, Thomson undoubtedly had a remarkable imitative facility from his earliest days, and one wonders what his poetry might have been if, like Hardy, he had learnt his technique from William Barnes rather than from Shelley and Swinburne. J. M. Robertson remarks on his 'defect in artistic austerity and patient devotion' in the craft of poetry, which made him fail fully to appreciate those qualities in Tennyson—a defect which Robertson thought was not present in his prose, 'which he writes with perfect ease'.[5] And J. M. Cohen[6] cites 'The Poet, High Art, Genius', to support this view—an essay[7] in which Thomson develops his theory that art is only a second-best substitute for life. Yet Thomson did toil at his poems, as the verbal alterations in his manuscripts show, and I feel that the stale diction he employed and his insensitive use of words were due more to the bad influence of Shelley (a great poet but a bad model) and the prevailing acceptance of a worn-out coinage, than to a failure of care. The lack of perception which made him adopt some of Shelley's

---

[1] Notebook, 21.9.78.
[2] 'Vane's Story', l.715.
[3] 'Sunday up the River', part II.
[4] I refer to 'Richard Forest's Midsummer Night' and 'He heard her Sing', neither of which is included in this selection.
[5] Preface to Thomson's *Poems Essays and Fragments*, 1892.
[6] 'Mr. Thomson and his wicked brother', *Penguin New Writing* 36.
[7] *Essays and Phantasies*, 1881.

worst faults of style—the inflated sentiment and the profusion of generalised adjectives—may also have been partly due to his inadequate training: after all, he achieved everything for himself. And however much Shelley may teach a disciple about the imagination, he does not teach him to use his eyes. Thomson's Colorado notebook shows that he *could* use his eyes, but in his poetry the colours are always 'literary' colours—azure, vermeil, crimson—the landscapes are dream scenes.

I do not think, therefore, that Thomson should be accused of a want of devotion, but rather of a want of taste, and of auditory imagination (to which I shall return later). 'It was congenial to him to be thorough', as the passage quoted above said of his journalistic work: he was accustomed to mark with underscorings and a tick in the margin the lines in his poems which he wanted to improve, and there are many such marks in his manuscripts, with attempts at improvement. In the 'Proem' to the *C.D.N.* he changes 'To blot the sunshine of *exulting* years' to 'exultant', as the first version would have conveyed 'exulting ears'; he notes fortuitous internal rhymes and the ambiguity caused by the *s* in 'torrent swirled';[1] he writes to Rossetti that if the animal in Dürer's engraving is indeed a wolf-hound and not a sheep, he will have to alter his line to

With the keen wolf-hound sleeping undistraught

'a villainous makeshift'. Yes indeed, and the worse because 'undistraught' has been brought in for makeshift duty in other places in his verse. But those shifts for the purpose of rhyme did not really seem as villainous to Thomson as they did to a purer tradition, or to poets writing after the revolution of the early twentieth century: they seemed regrettable perhaps, but not unforgivable.

Where ideas were concerned, Thomson was not in the least tied to the fashions of his day. I have said that he admired Blake when his poetry was little known; he was among the first to admire Walt Whitman; he knew Leopardi before translations had appeared in England. It is curious that he does not seem to have read Baudelaire,[2] since he knew French quite as well as he knew Italian —Balzac meant much to him, and he drew on Stendhal for some of his subjects. Dante also Thomson knew well—the *Inferno* at any rate, as we could deduce from the 'City', especially section II, and the 'rooted congregation' swaying 'as black fir-groves in a large wind bow' of section XIV.[3] Some of his contemporaries thought him 'terse', an adjective which certainly does not spring to the mind of one who peruses, say 'The Doom of a City', or even its greater successor: he does in fact need space for his effects, which

[1] 'Insomnia'.
[2] The *Fleurs du Mal* appeared in 1857, and Swinburne's enthusiastic praise of the book was published in the *Spectator* in 1863.
[3] Thomson wrote 'A Supplement to the Inferno', a satire on Lord Lytton in terza rima (not included here), in May 1870, when he was writing the 'City'.

are cumulative and not epigrammatic. He has an ear for a grand-sounding line, a sonorous word—
> Most cold, imperial, unlamenting Bride.[1]

One is never quite sure that such a line may not come from some other poet, however, as with
> Islanded in the boundless sea of air[2]

which turns out to be a borrowing from Shelley's 'A Boat on the Serchio', though an improvement on its original:
> Islanded in the immeasurable air.

The refrain, too, Thomson used with splendid effect in his major poem
> As I came through the Desert, thus it was

and
> I wake from daydreams to this real night ...

the more so because an effect of monotony is one of the legitimate aims of the poetry here. Elsewhere the monotony cannot be so defended, and there are few of his poems which would not be the better for cutting.

Thomson has little or no auditory imagination—the power that enables a poet to recreate a word by his use of it in certain contexts, and to make coined or technical or archaic words serve his purpose. He is fatally fond of the word *riant*, which occurs in his work from first to last, and *fulgent* is another unresisted temptation. In a letter to Bertram Dobell[3] which refers to some criticisms of 'Our Ladies of Death', he quotes the dictionary in support of his use of sombrous, tenebriously, ruth, but adds: 'I looked into the Dictionaries, not knowing whether their authority would sustain or condemn me, as I am used to trust in careful writing to my own sense of what is right; this, naturally, having been modified and formed by reading of good authors'—a defence effective enough if the 'sense of what is right' had in fact been alert to the associations of words, their evocative power. I cannot recall any observations in his notebooks about words, except of some dialect words in Colorado—*hornswoggle* and *lickity-brindle*. The stock rhyme-words ruth-truth, June-moon-boon, Death-breath, are repeated again and again without self-consciousness, though it is fair to say that the pervasive influence of Shelley, seen in such lines as
> A splendour lamping all eternity[4]

and in the recurrence of words like pard-beautiful, halcyon, hyaline, is most noticeable in the early poems, such as this:
> Then the shining silver Lily of the Night
> Opens broad her leaves divine,
> Afloat on the azure hyaline
> Of the heavenly sea; and her purest light
> Kisses the Earth that dreaming lies

---

[1] 'Doom of a City'. [2] 'A Voice from Nile'.
[3] Quoted by Salt, p. 98. [4] 'Ronald and Helen', not included here.

> In a still enchanted sleeping;
> While the heavens with their countless starry eyes
> Still watch are keeping.[1]

It is difficult to say whether or not Thomson was aware of his own plagiarisms: he underlined the 'moving moon' in the last stanza of the 'City', as though he thought to avoid the echo of Coleridge, but went no further than that. There are echoes of *Sohrab and Rustum* in 'A Voice from the Nile', and of Keats's 'Autumn' in the 'Lord of the Castle of Indolence'—

> Whom all the laws of Life conspire to love and bless.

The echoes are sometimes of poetry which Thomson did not admire. For instance, he writes contemptuously of Tennyson's 'maudlin Maud', yet there is a strong reminiscence of that poem in his 'Richard Forest':

> My Lotus, my Lily, my Dove . . .
> I shall find her all alone
> At the wicket of garden and lane,
> Or out of the porch by the rose o'ergrown
> She will glide all flushed and fain . . .

Swinburne he defended, so that it is less surprising to find some very Swinburnian lines in the same poem

> Like a sudden bountiful beautiful birth

and, in 'He heard her sing', echoes of the 'Hymn to Proserpine':

> Slain by the agitation, by the stress and the strain of the strife
> And the pang of the vain emulation . . .[2]

Because neither of these poems, written in the last year of Thomson's life, has anything to offer that is not derivative, I have not included them in this selection. But 'Vane's Story' and 'Sunday at Hampstead', where the rhythms of Heine (of whose poems Thomson made many translations in the early eighteen-sixties) have been successfully transposed to suit his own purpose, I have included. 'Vane's Story', admittedly, has some passages as bad as anything in Thomson, showing his tastelessness when he is trying to be *épatant*, and his lack of self-criticism. As he is neither neat, witty nor epigrammatic, the octosyllabic couplet was not a happy form for him. But I have included it in this selection because of its biographical interest, and for one or two good passages: a complaint—

> The same old stolid hills and leas,
> The same old stupid patient trees . . .
> The same old way of getting born
> Into it naked and forlorn,

---

[1] 'Ronald and Helen'.
[2] Kipling seems to have learnt from Thomson's earlier use of the long line, without the internal rhyme: from such lines as these from the 'Doom of a City' (IV, 149):
> When thy thousands of harlots abroad with the other thousand are met
> Of those who made them first and who keep them harlots yet . . .

And other evidence proves that Kipling admired Thomson—see *The Light that Failed*, and p. xxxii note.

xxxviii INTRODUCTION

> The same old way of creeping out
> Through death's low door for lean and stout...

and a passage with obviously sexual imagery about a fountain with 'lance of silver', sealed off by the stone of loss. As so much of the poem is consciously autobiographical, his deliberate choice of the name *Vane* as signifying something 'vain or unreal'[1] is another proof of his sense of inner unreality, his lack of belief in his own significance.

Edmund Blunden dismisses both the 'Sunday' poems alike as 'banjo music'[2] but the Cockney narrative part of the 'Hampstead' seems to me delightful and quite individual. The young Cockney is entertaining his girl and their friends by picturing themselves, and the spot where they are sitting on Hampstead Heath, in prehistoric times:

> Ten thousand years ago, ('*No more than that?*')
> Ten thousand years, ('*The age of Robert's hat!*')...
> This place where we are sitting was a wood,
> Savage and desert save for one rude home
> Of wattles plastered with stiff clay and loam;
> And here, in front, upon the grassy mire
> Four naked squaws were squatted round a fire:
> Then four tall naked wild men crushing through
> The tangled underwood came into view.....

Ten thousand years earlier they are four 'grave meek' women with horsemen lords; earlier, four Atlantis goddesses; earlier still, four mermaids. Something of the gaiety and liveliness of fancy that Thomson's friends found in his company is transmitted to the verse, without the exaggerated tone of *bonhomie* that he thought it fitting to adopt in some of his other proletarian poems. One should beware of deducing direct biography from poetry, certainly: Thomson was scornful of someone who objected to the rower's dress in 'Sunday up the River'—

> My shirt is of the soft red wool
> My cap is azure braided...
> My tie mauve purple-shaded—

saying 'Does she think *I* ever went boating in that style? I write what I have seen.'[3] But we know that Thomson did go boating of a Sunday, and walked upon the Heath, and it is only when he attempts a more serious vein in the short love poems of the two pieces, that he falls into mawkishness and unreality. I have therefore included only the 'Hampstead' in its entirety, with the first two parts of the 'River'. I do not think it vandalism to truncate the poem, as the manuscripts show that it was not conceived as a whole, but put together out of scattered pieces.

As a satirist Thomson is generally heavy-handed, in verse as well as in prose; in narrative he shows some skill—the story in 'Weddah and Om El Bonain', after a rather slow opening, moves

[1] Letter to W. M. Rossetti 15.12.80, and a note by Dobell in his Memoir.
[2] Preface to his 'Selection', 1932.
[3] Quoted by Foote in *Progress*, April 1884.

at just the right pace towards an effective climax. Thomson is more successful with the stanza than with blank verse, in spite of the temptation to use stock rhymes. Among his early poems, 'The Lord of the Castle of Indolence' is an attractive piece of pastiche— as its original, by Thomson's namesake, was itself a pastiche of Spenser, but Thomson's is more reminiscent of Keats than of Spenser.

> He there reclined as lilies on a river,
>   All cool in sunfire, float in buoyant rest;
> He stirred as flowers that in the sweet south quiver;
>   He moved as swans move on a lake's calm breast,
>   Or clouds slow gliding in the golden west;
> He thought as birds may think when 'mid the trees
>   Their joy showers music o'er the brood-filled nest;
> He swayed us all with ever placid ease
> As sways the throned moon her world-wide wandering seas.

It is now time to consider Thomson's major poem in more detail, and with it the early poem ('The Doom of a City', 1857) which foreshadows it both in form and content. Passages in the prose 'A Lady of Sorrow' (1864) are also relevant, but I want here to show how the form of the 'City of Dreadful Night' developed from the much more diffuse shape of the 'Doom', written some thirteen years earlier. This is a remarkable work for a young man of twenty-three, and has value in its own right: it shows the influence of Shelley's 'Triumph of Life' (a favourite poem of Thomson's), but not overwhelmingly, and the main theme is derived from the *Arabian Nights*, while the 'Judgements' are reminiscent of those books of Edward Irving which Thomson recalled reading as a little boy.[1]

The narrator leaves his native city (where, as in the later poem, the lamps burning in streets deserted save for himself are a symbol of gloom and loneliness)

> To dare the desert sea . . .
> The unknown awful realm where broods Eternity.

The reiteration which follows his arrival at another City across the ocean, foreshadows the terrible reiterations of the *C.D.N.*

> What saw I in the City, which could make
>   All thought a frenzy and all feeling madness?
> What found I in the City . . .

The horror is that its inhabitants are all turned to stone,[2] and he hears a Judgement pronounced upon them, and sees destruction overtake all but the few 'spirits who had conquered Life' (compare the 'Triumph of Life'), who are beckoned to join a company of the blessed on their mountain—[3]

---

[1] See p. 260, col. i.
[2] In the *Arabian Nights* story (of the Three Ladies of Baghdad) they are petrified because they have turned from worship of the One God and his Prophet to worship Fire.
[3] The blessed, one may note in passing, are playing harps, an activity for which Thomson in his later days expressed an extreme distaste—see *The Secularist*, 19.8.76, already quoted.

> And still the glory-stream flowed back to God;
> And they with it were floated up the sky;
> Whose gates shut blank against my straining eye,
> And left the earth a dark and soulless clod . . .

The Avenging Justice withdraws from 'Penal smitings dire' (Miltonic phrase), and the Narrator sees the statues begin to be brought back to life, whereon he returns to his boat and to his own city, with a message of warning and of hope.

The noticeable thing about the Argument of the poem, as compared with Thomson's later philosophy expressed in the 'Dreadful Night', is that doom falls as a retribution for wrong-doing, and the Narrator himself, after first renewing his self-dedication to Misery and Death, comes to realize that it is a madness which has made him cut himself off from his fellows and from life. It is a sad commentary on the poet's own later sense of isolation.

> Dire Vanity! to think to break the union
> That interweaveth strictly soul with soul
> In constant, sane, life-nourishing communion:
> The rivers ever to the ocean roll,
> The ocean-waters feed the clouds on high
> Whose rains descending feed the flowing rivers:
> All the world's children must how quickly die
> Were they not all receivers and all givers!

The form is very diffuse: a series of long irregularly-rhymed stanzas, varied in the later parts of the poem by sections of couplets, octosyllables, and long dactylic or trochaic lines. Thomson kept something of this variety in the *C.D.N.*, but he must have realized that a long poem needed a backbone, so that he there employed two main stanza-forms, one of six lines for most of the narrative, and the other, of seven, for meditation and commentary. As Edmund Blunden describes it:[1] 'This recurrent, slow-uncoiling, backward-coiling stanza, with the overhanging rhymes toward the close only suggesting a freedom of movement in order that the close may be more ironically definite, is the pulse of the City.' Thomson had used something like it nine years before in the poem called 'To our Ladies of Death', and wrote of it at the time that it was 'moulded under the influence of "The Guardian Angel" in Browning's "Men and Women"'. In fact, however, the earlier poem lacks the feminine endings of the two penultimate lines which are the distinctive feature of Browning's stanza, and which Thomson adopted for the *C.D.N.* Here it is as Browning used it, addressing the Angel:

> Then I shall feel thee step one step, no more,
> From where thou standest now, to where I gaze,
> And suddenly my head is covered o'er
> With those wings, white above the child who prays
> Now on that tomb—and I shall feel thee guarding
> Me, out of all the world; for me, discarding
> Yon Heaven thy home, that waits and opes its door!

---

[1] op. cit.

The irony was perhaps unconscious, but any reader of the two poems cannot but be aware of it, when he compares the childlike trust displayed towards the Guardian Angel, with the powerlessness of the angel in the 'City', his wings, his sword, and finally his body shattered by the mere influence of the Sphinx (who represents perhaps things-as-they-are; the Truth).

In the later poem there is no definite journey to reach the City—
> How he arrives there none can clearly know ...
> To reach it is as dying fever-stricken—

in fact, 'Hell is a City much like London' the reader feels—but once having visited it, Thomson says, no one can escape it for long. The Narrator passes through the City and its suburbs, and the visions which he sees, the circles of its Inferno, are all aspects of Thomson's own mental misery, the forms of his obsession—so much is clear to anyone who has studied his other writings. First, is a man tracing out an endless round, revisiting the places where died Faith, and Love, and Hope—and Thomson has a mathematical footnote:

'Life divided by that persistent three $= \dfrac{LXX}{333} .2\dot{1}\dot{0}.$'

The poetry of this, the first part of the poem that Thomson wrote, seems to me to look back to Dante and forward to Mr. Eliot.

Next is an orator (his 'stalwart shape, the gestures full of might, The glances burning with unnatural light' perhaps reminiscent of Bradlaugh, as is the second orator in section XIV with the 'organ-like vibrations of his voice'), declaiming to no one his schizophrenic vision on a shore, where a woman carrying her own burning heart bears off his corpse, leaving behind the 'vile me', the part of him that watches, alone on the shore.

Next comes a strange episode of two spirits who could not enter Hell because they could find no hope to abandon at the portal. This is, to me, the least satisfactory of the episodes, because of the intellectual contradiction contained in such a situation, where two people wishing to enter the place of the hopeless, are forbidden because they *are* hopeless. Next follows a dialogue (already quoted) between the defiant and the fatalistic—as it might be Thomson in his earlier blasphemous mood, and the calmer voice of Leopardi: the one indicts the Maker of the Universe, and the other responds that there is no such Being—
> Man might know one thing were his sight less dim;
> That it whirls not to suit his petty whim,
> That it is quite indifferent to him.

Next appears a 'mansion' which, unlike the other houses of the City, is lighted up—but only to reveal a young man kneeling by the dead body of his love, whose picture is in all the rooms of the house, 'the mansion of (his) heart'. Then the Narrator enters a cathedral, where all who enter 'wake from daydreams to this real night', and hears the preacher (speaking the doctrines which

Thomson must often have heard Bradlaugh enunciate) give comfort to the assembly by telling them that all illusions have vanished—

> There is no God, no Fiend with names divine
> Made us and tortures us ...

such a sad comfort as Thomson perhaps himself found in abandoning a faith which held too many contradictions for him. A man in the assembly laments his lost chance—again with Thomson's own bitter backward-looking glance—the one chance of happiness 'frustrate from my birth'.

Next, the Narrator, meeting a man who is trying to retrace the thread of his life in order to begin it again,[1] sees the folly of it, for 'His life would grow, the germ uncrushed', whereas death lies close at hand for the taking. A meditation on suicides follows, with the arguments that Thomson must often have had with himself, as to why he did not put that 'End it when you will' into practice. Then comes the episode of the angel defeated by the sphinx. And last, in the seven-line stanza, the vision of 'Melencolia' which had been in the poet's mind for so long, with its consolation of stoicism.

The poem is wonderfully comprehensive: at the close, the reader feels that he has travelled the whole range of despair, and although the light is the lurid one of nightmare, the City is so consistently and passionately seen that it becomes for ever a part of experience for those who have read the poem, even if they are not among those who 'Travel the same wild paths though out of sight'. It has been blamed for monotony, and even though hell be monotonous, it will always be a question how far its reproduction in art is permissible. Certainly, one or two of the intervening meditations could be cut without damage to the matter of the poem, but this would damage the musical structure, and we can see from the manuscript that this was carefully planned.

Thomson's compulsion to put the date of composition on all his poetry, portion by portion, when he copied it out, enables us to trace the development of the 'City'. The manuscript[2] evidence shows that he began in January 1870 with three 'episodes' in an ababcc stanza,[3] and that the description of the City in Part I, in the 7-line stanza, was not written till July of that year. We cannot tell, of course, how much of the plan was formed in his mind when he began, but it is clear that he composed much of

---

[1] G. M. Harper, relating this conception to Blake's 'golden thread'
> 'I give you the end of a golden string
> Only wind it into a ball,
> It will lead you in at Heaven's gate ...'

seeks to trace a connection between the crawling figure and Blake's drawing of Nebuchadnezzar, which Thomson might have seen. (*Studies in Philology*, Jan. 1953.)

[2] see the Notes for a full account of this.

[3] The 'perpetual circle' of lost hope; the crawling figure seeking his lost innocence; the Angel and the Sphinx.

the now-divided commentary verse in one piece, and broke it up later by the alternating episodes, sometimes changing his mind about the exact sequence. The risk he ran was that the two modes would not be sufficiently related, and one reviewer[1] thought that there were really two different poems combined under one title, but I think that when one has read the poem two or three times and grasped its structure, the unity is felt. The Narrator is, to put it crudely, alternately looking and thinking, and the final Melencolia piece, in the 'meditative' stanza, combines the two modes.

'In the Room', written some three years earlier, is perhaps Thomson's best poem after the 'City'. The way in which the inanimate objects surrounding a lonely man in lodgings come to appear to him to have an actual, and hostile, life of their own; the dramatic delay of the clue—that the tenant of the room is lying there dead while the furniture is talking; the ironic contrast between his deadness and the comparative liveliness of objects that can still be used; and the sudden harsh introduction of the 'hero'—

> It lay, the lowest thing there, lulled
>   Sweet-sleep-like in corruption's truce;
> The form whose purpose was annulled,
>   While all the other shapes meant use.
> It lay, the *he* become now *it*,
>   Unconscious of the deep disgrace,
> Unanxious how its parts might flit
>   Through what new forms in time and space—

all these are masterly. The flat, dull rhythm of the stanza is exactly right, and the reminiscence of *Lear* (whether conscious or unconscious) only enriches the irony:

> I know when men are good or bad,
>   When well or ill, he [the bed] slowly said;
> When sad or glad, when sane or mad,
>   And when they sleep alive or dead ...

which is followed by the mirror's reminiscence of how a relation of hers was brought to prove whether a man was still alive to 'blur her with his breath' or not.

What has Thomson to say to a mid-twentieth-century reader? Before I read Mr. T. S. Eliot's preface to a recent selection of John Davidson's poems,[2] it had struck me that the 'unreal City' of the 'Waste Land' owed something to Thomson as well as to Baudelaire, and that Thomson might even have some part in the 'familiar compound ghost' of 'Little Gidding', Part IV:

> Because he seemed to walk with an intent
> I followed him; who, shadowlike and frail,
> Unswervingly though slowly onward went ...
> Thus step for step with lonely sounding feet
> We travelled many a long dim silent street.[3]

The preface confirmed me at least in that Mr. Eliot there acknowledges an early debt to the 'City'.

---

[1] G. A. Simcox in the *Fortnightly*. See also W. D. Schaefer in P.M.L.A. Dec. 1962, published after this edition was in proof.
[2] Edited by Maurice Carpenter, 1961.   [3] 'City' part II.

I have no such proof that Edwin Muir ever read Thomson, but
certainly the crawling figure in the 'City' who is seeking for
> the long-lost broken thread
> Which reunites my present with my past . . .
derived perhaps from Blake, foreshadows one of Muir's main
themes. Of course, the idea that the development of a man's life
tarnishes his early purity is common enough, especially since
Wordsworth, but Thomson's expression seems very close to our
own time:
> And I become a nursling soft and pure,
>   An infant cradled on its mother's knee,
> Without a past, love-cherished and secure;
>   Which if it saw this loathsome present Me,
> Would plunge its face into the pillowing breast,
> And scream abhorrence hard to lull to rest.

Compare Yeats—
> What youthful mother, a shape upon her lap
> Honey of generation had betrayed,
> And that must sleep, shriek, struggle to escape
> As recollection or the drug decide,
> Would think her son, did she but see that shape
> With sixty or more winters on its head,
> A compensation for the pang of his birth,
> Or the uncertainty of his setting forth?[1]

Thomson's line in his 1878 poem[2] anticipates even Yeats's phrasing—
> What compensation for the throes of birth—

as the line close before it:
> Why were we ever brought to life at all?

anticipates Wilfred Owen's 'Futility'.

> Je sais que la douleur est la noblesse unique
> Où ne mordront jamais la terre et les enfers—[3]

Sorrow in Thomson has no such nobility: he saw its effect on the
soul as being, ultimately, an ignominious enslavement,[4] and there
have been many in the twentieth century to hold such a view:
'Pain never improved anyone: pain makes man a devil' said an
experienced surgeon recently, in an interview for a Sunday newspaper. The uncompromising courage with which Thomson rejected
all facile consolations is sympathetic to an age in which disillusion
has seemed the only honest starting-place. Moreover, in his 'cold
rage' to 'show the bitter old and wrinkled truth' he seems very
close to our time. His own contemporaries, though recognizing
the power of the 'City', turned with relief to his love poems and
his lyrics, which seem to us—as I have said—largely derivative
and written in a worn-out mode. It is no use looking to him for
freshness of diction, for subtleties of metrical variation, or for the

---

[1] 'Among School Children'.   [2] p. 208
[3] Baudelaire, 'Bénédiction'.
[4] see 'A Lady of Sorrow' (*Essays and Phantasies*) written in 1862-4, which foreshadows in prose much of the matter of the 'City'.

natural observation which illumines the flattest page of Barnes or the most ornate page of Hopkins; the colloquial rhythms which give life to the poems of Browning and Clough are rarely found in him. But the unromantic pessimism of his maturity, his midnight view of an unhomely city, his 'dingy urban images', these speak directly to us.

I have tried to choose favourable specimens of Thomson's verse at every stage from early to late, opening the door a little wider than my judgement would approve, in order to admit some examples of his late love poetry. I have printed the poems in chronological order (though this was not his own method of arrangement) so that the development of his powers can be seen. There is too much dross in the Collected Edition of 1895 for a reprint of this to be acceptable, but something a good deal more substantial is needed than the selections which have been printed since then. There are a few poems hitherto unpublished which are of interest for one reason or another, though of no great artistic value, and the manuscripts show a certain number of interesting variants—in particular, that of the 'City of Dreadful Night' itself, which has not hitherto been compared with the printed version. The principles which I have followed in printing these variants will be found set forth in the Notes, which are placed at the end of the book: footnotes in the text of the poems are Thomson's own.

My grateful thanks are due to the Curators of the Pierpont Morgan Library, New York for permission to collate the printed versions of the 'City of Dreadful Night' with the manuscript in their care, and to reproduce two pages from it; also to the Curators of the Bodleian Library, Oxford and to the Trustees of the British Museum for the use of their collections of Thomson manuscripts. I am also indebted to the Directors of Messrs. C. A. Watts & Co. for permission to quote from Henry Salt's *The Life of James Thomson*.

OXFORD 1963   A.R.

POEMS

FOUR POINTS IN A LIFE

I
LOVE'S DAWN

STILL thine eyes haunt me; in the darkness now,
The dreamtime, the hushed stillness of the night,
I see them shining pure and earnest light;
And here, all lonely, may I not avow
The thrill with which I ever meet their glance? 5
At first they gazed a calm abstracted gaze,
The while thy soul was floating through some maze
Of beautiful divinely-peopled trance;
But now I shrink from them in shame and fear,
For they are gathering all their beams of light 10
Into an arrow, keen, intense and bright,
Swerveless and starlike from its deep blue sphere,
Piercing the cavernous darkness of my soul,
Burning its foul recesses into view,
Transfixing with sharp agony through and through 15
Whatever is not brave and clean and whole.
And yet I will not shrink, although thou piercest
Into the inmost depths of all my being,
I will not shrink, although thou now art seeing
My heart's caged lusts the wildest and the fiercest, 20
The cynic thoughts that fret my homeless mind,
My unbelief, my selfishness, my weakness,
My dismal lack of charity and meekness;
For, amidst all the evil, thou must find
Pervading, cleansing, and transmuting me, 25
A fervent and most holy love for thee.

II
MARRIAGE

COME to me, oh come to me!
Time is long since we were parted;
I am sad and weary-hearted,
Foiled and almost overthrown,
Fighting with the world alone: 5
What am I when thou art gone?
Come darling, soon!

Come to me, oh come to me!
Let my failing head find rest, Love,
On thy pure and tender breast, Love;
  Calm my overwearied brain,
  Soothe away my heart's chill pain,
  Bring me hope and strength again:
    Come darling, soon!

Come to me, oh come to me!
Evermore the memory lingers,
How your gentle flower-soft fingers,
  With a touch when I lay ill
  Through my fevered frame could thrill
  Cool rich life divinely still:
    Come darling, soon!

Come to me, oh come to me!
Dearest heart of love and meekness,
Is not this unmanly weakness?
  Ah, with thee such pure sweet calm
  Heals my wounds with heavenly balm,
  I fighting feel my spear a palm:
    Come darling, soon!

Come to me, oh come to me!
Though its perils gloomed more fearful
I could fight undaunted, cheerful,
  This stern Agony called Life,
  Were the pauses of the strife
  Blest by thee, my noble Wife:
    Come darling, soon!

Come to me, oh come to me!
Strength and hope and faith are waning
With this fierce and pauseless straining;
  Ere my soul be conquered quite,
  Ere I fail from Truth and Right,
  Come, my Life, my Joy, my Light,
    Come Darling, soon!

III

PARTING

WEEP not Dearest, weep not so;
Soon again we two shall meet
Who now part in bitter woe:
After pain shall bliss be sweet.

PARTING

Few more years of numb despair
Must we wander far apart
Through the desert dead and bare:
Love is courage in the heart.

Few more years of bitter moan
O'er the rugged mountain height,
Must we toil on each alone:
Love can make all burthens light.

Few more years of stricken woe
Erring on an alien shore
Lone and friendless each must go:
We will love then more and more.

Few short hours of doubt and dread
Trembling on the brink of Night
Spectre-haunted, each must tread:
Love can burn all darkness bright.

All the long lone years must die;
Then shall we together come
Where beneath a calm bright sky
Bright waves bear us to our home.

Weep not Dearest, weep not so;
Soon again we two *must* meet
Where the calm deep waters flow,
Soothing surely care and woe,
With their mystic murmur sweet.

IV
AT DEATH'S DOOR

Is this the second childhood's feeble sadness?
My eyes are dim now and my hair is white;
Yet never did the sunshine give more gladness,
Never young Spring burst forth in green delight
More freshly; never was the earth more fair,
Never more rapture in the common air.

Still as I near great Death, it seems his portal
Glides gently backward, that I may gaze through
And glimpse far glories of the realm immortal;
The world becomes transparent to my view,
Diviner Heavens expand beyond the skies,
The stars grow thoughtful with eternal eyes.

How the green grass and every flower swell yearning
To hint more clearly some high loveliness
Whose mystic soul within their forms is burning; 15
How strives the sea for ever to express,
With infinite heavings, murmurings manifold,
Some secret grandeur that will not be told!

The life of day is lulled to dreamful musing,
And true life waketh in the world of dream; 20
While with the Present strangely interfusing
The Future and the Past together stream,
As if the long-drawn waves of Time should be
Settling and mingling in Eternity.

With every golden dawn awakened lightly, 25
I think I must have slept through Death's calm night;
For lo, how purely, silently and brightly,
The Heavens unfold their gates before my sight;
The trancèd sea of crystal spreadeth slowly,
The burning Throne lives out with splendours holy. 30

Whereon I look to see thee come swift-greeting
From where thou waitest for my laggard feet,
Assured beyond impatience for the meeting,
Crowned with triumphant love and faith complete:
I look in vain as yet; but every hour 35
So summer-rich may make the bud a flower.

How well, my Love, the thoughtful Heavens endeavour
To make this world and life and time all bear
Dream-lightly on the soul, ere it for ever
Be parted from them! Did I once despair 40
Through years of lonely anguish unassuaged?
This calm can scarce believe that storms have raged.

Here is the blessing: I now muse enchanted
In this sweet dawnlike sunset; night comes then
Of restful sleep by gracious visions haunted; 45
So with new morning I shall rise again
Full of young life, and find my Love for aye,
My Love whom I have missed this long sad day.

THE APPROACH TO ST. PAUL'S

EASTWARDS through busy streets I lingered on;
   Jostled by anxious crowds, who, heart and brain,
   Were so absorbed in dreams of Mammon-gain,
That they could spare no time to look upon
The sunset's gold and crimson fires, which shone 5
   Blessing keen eyes and wrinkled brows in vain.

THE APPROACH TO ST. PAUL'S

   Right in my path stood out that solemn Fane
Whose soaring cupola of stern grey stone
Lifteth for awful beacon to the sky
   The burning Cross: silent and sole amid
   That ceaseless uproar, as a pyramid
Isled in its desert. The great throngs pressed by
Heedless and urgent: thus Religion towers
Above this sordid, restless life of ours.

SUGGESTED BY MATTHEW ARNOLD'S
STANZAS FROM THE GRANDE CHARTREUSE

THAT one long dirge-moan sad and deep,
   Low, muffled by the solemn stress
Of such emotion as doth steep
   The soul in brooding quietness,
Befits our anguished time too well,
Whose Life-march is a funeral knell.

Dirge for a mighty Creed outworn—
   Its spirit fading from the earth,
Its mouldering body left forlorn:
   Weak idol! feeding scornful mirth
In shallow hearts; divine no more
Save to some ignorant pagan poor;

And some who know how by Its light
   The past world well did walk and live,
And feel It even now more bright
   Than any lamp mere men can give;
So cling to It with yearning faith,
Yet own It almost quenched in death:

While many who win wealth and power
   And honours serving at Its shrine,
Rather than lose their worldly dower
   Proclaim their dead thing 'Life divine';
And sacrifice to coward lust
Their own souls' truth, a people's trust.

And will none mourn the mighty Dead,—
   Pillar of heavenly fire and cloud,
Which through this life's wild desert led
   For whole millenniums each grand crowd
Of sages, bards, saints, heroes, all
Whose names we glory to recall?

None mourn Him, dead, with deep-moved soul,
   Whom, living, all our sires adored?
None feel the heavy darkness roll
   Stifling about us, when the Lord
Leaves us to walk by our own light,   35
That one pale speck in boundless Night?—

That earthly lamp when sun and star,
   When all the heavenly lights are lost:
Does it shed radiance round afar?
   Our pathway is by deep gulfs cross'd: 40
It fathoms none. We lift it high:
It casts not one beam on the sky.

If He thus died as no more fit
   To lead the modern march of thought,
Supreme,—commanding, guiding it,   45
   With noblest love and wisdom fraught;
He was at least Divine; and none
Of human souls can lead it on.

We pine in our dark living tomb,
   Waiting the God-illumined One   50
Who, only, can disperse the gloom;
   Completing what the Dead begun,
Or farther leading us some space
Toward our eternal resting-place.

But Israel wanders shepherdless,   55
   Or gloom-involved unmoving lies,
And in despair's stark sinfulness
   Reviles the promised Paradise
It cannot reach—Father divine!
Let us not long thus hopeless pine.   60

Still the deep dirge-notes long and low
   Breathe forth strange anguish to recall—
Could we forget—our direst woe:
   A proud strong Age fast losing all
Earth has of heaven; bereft of faith;   65
And living in Eternal Death.

And loudly boastful of such life:
   Blinded by our material might,
Absorbed in frantic worldly strife,
   Unconscious of the utter Night   70
Whose palpable and monstrous gloom
Is gathering for our spirits' tomb.

SUGGESTED BY ARNOLD'S STANZAS

We feel as gods in our own hearts;
  Seeming to conquer Time and Space;
Wealth gorging our imperial marts; 75
  Earth pregnant, from the fierce embrace
Our matter-lusting spirits press,
With unexampled fruitfulness.

God, answering well our worldly prayer,
  Our hearts' chief prayer through all the hours 80
Of selfish joy and sordid care,
  Comes down to us in golden showers:
God turns to Mammon at our cry;
Our souls wealth-crushed, dross-stifled lie.

Those few, how rich! while this great mass, 85
  Myriads with equal greed for gold,
Sink in such want and woe, alas!
  As never can on earth be told:
These starve, and those yet wealthier rise;
Meanwhile in both the spirit dies. 90

Hear now the thrilling dirge-notes peal
  The anguished cry in thunder rolls:—
The few yet left who think and feel,
  Who yearn with strenuous soaring souls
For more than earth or time can grant; 95
Where, where shall they appease their want?

Black disbelief, substantial doubt
  Wreathe—blent into one louring cloud
Through which Heaven's light can scarce shine out—
  Round all the Faiths: all in such shroud 100
Fade ghostlike to th' entombing Past:
Our Heaven is wildly overcast.

Yet each Creed, senile, sick, half-dead,
  With bitter spite and doting rage
Reviles all others. Whoso, led 105
  By thirst of love to pilgrimage,
Seeks now old God-given Wells of Life,
Finds drought-dry centres of vain strife;

And turns away in blank despair,
  To scoff or weep as fits his mood. 110
O God in Heaven, hear our prayer!
  We know Thou art, Allwise, Allgood,
Yet sink in godless misery:
Oh, teach us how to worship Thee!

Part II

The great Form lies there nerveless still:
   But as we fix our longing gaze
It grows in grandest beauty, till
   We worship in entranced amaze;
Such holy love and wisdom seem
To be there rapt in heavenly dream.

Oh, if He may once more awake!
   Oh, if it be not death, but sleep!—
And He from that dread slumber break
   Refreshed and strong, full-powered to sweep
The darkness from our path again;
Once more the Guiding Star of men!

Yet—though it be death—view It well.
   The brow, how nobly high and broad!
What love on those shut lips might well!
   This Form sublimely templed God:
And, if not perfect, is a shrine
Approaching well the most divine.

Do not turn hastily away
   From mighty death to petty life;
Gaze in deep reverence on the clay
   With such a soul's expression rife:
Read here, read long, the features worn
By One incarnate Heavenly-born.

So may we hope to recognise
   That Greater One who shall succeed
This death-bound Monarch, who now lies
   In mute appealing for our need:
God cannot long desert His earth;
In the Old's death the New has birth.

What say we?—we know well this truth,
   There is no death for the Divine,
Which lives in ever-perfect youth:
   The Form alone—its earthly shrine—
Is subject to earth's mortal sway;
Sickens, and dies, and rots away.

Thus each Form in its turn expires,
   No more with all revealed Truth rife,—
Which even at that time inspires
   Some new and nobler form with life,
Grander and vaster to express
More of Its infinite heavenliness.

Thus has it been since Time's first birth,
　　Thus must it be for evermore:
Still lie, moth-eaten, on the earth
　　Old garments which this Spirit wore;
Till, soiled and rent, they were off-thrown,
And wider-flowing robes put on.

They could not grow with His great growth,
　　Pauseless though slow throughout the years;
And vainly worshippers—so loath
　　To leave what lengthened use endears—
May still the empty robes adore;
Their virtue was from Him who wore.

Let none say the Divine is dead,
　　Although this Form be soul-less quite:
The Heavenly Sun doth ever shed
　　His lifeful heat, His saving light;
Never our earth doth lose His ray,
Save when she turns herself away.

Let none say the Divine is dumb,
　　Although His voice no more we hear:
It is that we are deaf become.
　　For measured to each eye and ear
His glory shines, His voice outspeaks;
To each He gives the most it seeks.

Our spirits may for ever grow;
　　And He will fill them as before,
And still their measure overflow
　　With His unlessened infinite More:
He gives us all we can receive;
He teaches all we can believe.

The pure can see Him perfect-pure;
　　The strong feel Him, Omnipotence;
The wise, All-wise; He is obscure
　　But to the gross and earth-bound sense:
Alas for us with blinded sight
Who dare to cry, There is no light!

Part III

Nay, ask us not to rise and leave
　　Him from whom power and life seem gone;
Say not that it is weak to grieve;
　　Duty does *not, now,* urge us on:
In vain *ye* urge; too well we know
We cannot by our own strength go.

Vainly ye choose you Saviours now
    Of men,—however good and wise
Be those your mean faith would endow
    With power to which no man can rise:
No best men living lure our faith
From the Divine though veiled in death.

Vainly ye wander every way
    Throughout the earth in search of Heaven,
Changing your useless path each day
    With each new transient impulse given
By human guides, who still agree
In naught but fallibility.

We should know better from the lore
    Of worldly wisdom—keen mistrust—
On which our minds so love to pore;
    Nor leave for any child of dust
This One Divine: to Him adhere
Till the diviner One appear.

My brothers, let us own the truth,
    Bitter and mournful though it be,—
That we, who spent our dreary youth
    In foul and sensual slavery,
Are all too slavish, too unmanned,
For Conquerors of the Promised Land.

In unprogressive wanderings
    We plod the desert to and fro;
And fiery serpents' mortal stings,
    Earthquake and sword and weary woe
And pestilence deal fearful death
Amongst us for our want of faith.

Far-scattered o'er the Waste forlorn
    Our bones shall whiten through the years,
And startle pilgrims yet unborn;
    Our noblest captains, priests and seers,
Dark death shall one by one remove,
For lack of wisdom, faith, or love.

Yet be we patient, meek and pure,
    Unselfishly resigned to God's
Mysterious judgements; and endure
    Our sore scarce-intermitted loads
Of grief and weary pain, imbued
With sternly passive fortitude:

And pray that those who shall succeed
　　Prove worthy of a happier life
Than we dare ask for as our meed;
　　That they a constant noble strife
Victorious against Ill may wage,
And gain the glorious heritage.

Cease now to cry and storm, and move,
　　By such tumultuous toil opprest
As, without guidance, vain must prove.
　　When God keeps still can *ye* not rest?
When He sends night so dark and deep,
Why shrink from renovating sleep?

Sleep, to His care resigned, a space;
　　That when He rises in His might
To lead our hosts from this dire place,
　　We may have strength and heart to fight
All evils that would bar our way,
And march unfaltering all the day.

Yes, let us stay in loving grief,
　　Which patient hope and trust yet cheer,
Silent beside our silent Chief,
　　Till His Successor shall appear;
Till death's veil fall from off His face,
Or One anointed take His place.

Nay,—our adoring love should have
　　More faith than to believe that He,
Before Another comes to save,
　　Can leave us in blind misery
Without a Guide: God never can
So utterly depart from man.

We will move onward!—let us trust
　　That there is life and saving power
In this dear Form which seems but dust.
　　Arise, arise! though darkness lower,
Earnest, bold-hearted, cease to mourn;
It shall before our hosts be borne.

Triumphantly He ever led
　　Our faithful armies while alive;
What though His form be cold and dead,
　　His Spirit doth that death survive:
We conquer by that Soul this Form
Enshrined, not ill, while free and warm.

Thus men have honoured fellow men,
  Who dying left a lofty fame;
And won most glorious victories then
  By inspiration of a Name:
If in men's names such life abode,   95
Shall there not in *His*,—Son of God?

A dawn-light creeps throughout the gloom,
  Sullenly sinks the storm of wrath;
Life blossoms in our desert tomb;
  Mysteriously we find a path   100
Which leadeth on to Paradise.
Thus to our love's faith He replies!

But, while the dirge still rolls away
  In passionate thunders wildly blent
With mournful moanings, let us pray—   105
  Still on our Holy War intent—
'O God, revive the seeming Dead;
Or send Another in His stead!

'The wintry midnight drear is past,
  But still the dawn gleams grey and cold;   110
Dread phantoms haunt each restless blast,
  Our stumblings still are manifold:
Oh, let Thy cloudless Sun rise soon,
And flood us with His summer noon!'

THE DOOM OF A CITY
A FANTASIA
PART I
THE VOYAGE

I

From out the house I crept,
The house which long had caged my homeless life:
The mighty City in vast silence slept,
Dreaming away its tumult, toil, and strife:
But sleep and sleep's rich dreams were not for me,   5
For me, accurst, whom terror and the pain
Of baffled longings, and starved misery,
And such remorse as sears the breast,
And hopeless doubt which gnaws the brain
Till wildest action blind and vain   10
Would be more welcome than supine unrest,
    Drove forth as one possest

To leave my kind and dare the desert sea;
    To drift alone and far,
Dubious of any port or isle to gain,
    Ignorant of chart and star,
Upon that infinite and mysterious main
Which wastes in foam against our shore;
Whose moans and murmurs evermore,
    Insupportably sublime,
Haunting the crowded tumult of our Time,
    Suspend its hurrying breath—
Like whispers of sad ghosts and spirits free
    From worlds beyond our life and death,
The unknown awful realm where broods Eternity.

II

I paced through desert streets, beneath the gleam
Of lamps that lit my trembling life alone;
Like lamps sepulchral which had slowly burned
Through sunless ages, deep and undiscerned,
Within a buried City's maze of stone;
Whose peopling corpses, while they ever dream
Of birth and death—of complicated life
    Whose days and months and years
Are wild with laughters, groans, and tears,
    As with themselves and Doom
They wage, with loss or gain, incessant strife,
Indeed, lie motionless within their tomb,
Lie motionless and never laugh or weep,
    All still, and buried deep
    For ever in death's sleep,
While burn the quiet lamps amidst the breathless gloom.

III

    My boat lay waiting there,
    Upon the moonless river
    Whose pulse had ceased to quiver
In that unnatural hush of brooding night.
I thought, Free breezes course the billowy deep!
And rowed on panting through the feverous air,
Leaving the great main waters on my right
For that canal which creeps into the sea
Across the livid marshes wild and bare.
    So slowly faded back from sight,
    As doth a dream insensibly
Fade backward on the ebbing tide of sleep,
That city which had home nor hope for me,
That stifling tomb from which I now was free.

IV

Like some weak life whose sluggish moments creep
Diffused on worthless objects, yet whose tide
With dull reluctance hard to understand
Refrains its death-in-life from death's full sleep,
The river's shallow waters oozed out wide,
Inclosing dreary flats of barren sand;
So merged at last into the lethal waste
That bounds of sea and stream could not be traced.

V

    Long languidly I rowed,
      With sick and weary pain,
Between the deepest channel's bitter weeds
    Whose rankness salt slime feeds;
And so out blindly through the dismal main,
Now shaken with a long hoarse-growling swell.
And soon the Tempest—as a King who had slept
The sleep of worn-out frenzy, while his slaves
Cowered still in stupor till he woke again
Refreshed for carnage—from his torpor leapt
Breathed swarthy pallor through the dense low sky,
    And hurrying swift and fell
Outspeeded his own thunder-bearing glooms;
Then prone and instantaneous from on high
    Plunged down in one tremendous blast,
Which crashed into white dust the heaving waves
And left the ocean level when it past. . . .
There was a moment's respite; silence reigned;
Such shuddering silence as may once appal
    The universe of tombs,
Ere the last trumpet's clangour rend them all:
And I sank down, one frail and helpless man
Alone with desolation on the sea,
To pray while any sense of prayer remained
Amidst the horrors overwhelming me.

VI

How shall I tell that tempest's thunder-story?—
The soldier plunged into the Battle-stress,
Struggling and gasping in the mighty flood,
Stunned with the roar of cannon, blind with smoke,
'Midst yells and tramplings drunk and mad with blood,
What knows he of the Battle's spheric glory?
Of heavenly laws that all its evil bless—
Of sacred rights of justice which invoke
Its sternest pleading—of the tranquil eye
Triumphant o'er its chaos—of the Mind

Commanding all, serene and unsubdued,
Which having first with wisest care designed 100
Works to the end with vigilant fortitude;
And from that field so drenched with angry blood
Shall reap the golden harvest, VICTORY?

VII

There was a stupor stung with pain and fear,
Amidst the strangling surf flung on and on; 105
There was bewilderment above all dread,
Delirious calm and desperate joy austere
Of revelling through the tempest lorn and lone.
My boat and I with dizzy swiftness sped,
In strange salvation from the certain doom, 110
Along the urgent ridges over-reeling
And gathering up their ruins as they fled;
And down into the depths of scooped-out gloom
Whose crystal walls glowed black in the revealing
Of lightning-kindled foam; and up again, 115
Perched on the giddy balance of two waves
Which fiercely countering mingle with the shock,
And rush aloft confused, and tower and rock
Foaming with wild convulsion, till amain
The mass heaves down from struggling, self-destroyed, 120
And leaves us shuddering in a gulfy void.
Confused and intermingled, fire, sea, air,
Wrought out their ravage; for the thunders there
Were echoing in the dreadly stormless caves
And shook the deep foundations of the seas; 125
The air was like an ocean, drenched with spray
Whose meteor-flakes outflashed tumultuously
Against the sinking heaven's black incline,
When sudden lightnings seemed to burst their way
Up through the deep to flood and fire its brine, 130
Ingulfing for each moment all the Night,
The blackness and the howling rage, in light
More lurid and appalling, a World-pyre. . . .
But heart and brain were overwrought; and soon,
All vision reeling from my powerless eyes, 135
I lay in quiet mercy-granted swoon
As senseless as the boat in which I lay:
And we two things through all the agonies
      Of night, tornado, sea, and fire,
Were drifted passive on our fearful way. 140

VIII

I know not for what time I lay in trance,
Nor in what course the tempest hurled us on.

At length to scarce-believed deliverance
I woke; and saw a sweet slow silent dawn
Upgrowing from the far dim grey abyss,— 145
So slow, it seemed like some celestial flower
Unfolding perfect petals to its prime,
And feeling in its secret soul of bliss
Each leaf a loveliness for many an hour,
With amaranthine queenship over time. 150
It grew: its purple splendours, flecked and starred
With golden fire, spread floating up the steep
Until they sole possessed the mighty sweep
Of crystal lucent æther: its regard,
The blessing of a light of peace and love, 155
Charmed with a gradual spell the sullen mood
Of the sea-giant, until all-subdued
No more his huge bulk livid shook and hove
The meteor-threatenings of his tawny mane,
No more growled lingering wrath and turbulent pain; 160
But calm and glad th' unmonstered monster lay
Beneath the royal sun's perfected sway.

IX

And there was Land. Where seemed a bank of clouds
Piled in the South, now nobly, one by one,
The pinnacles of lofty mountain-peaks 165
Flamed keen as stars, enkindled by the sun;
Emerging as with life from out their shrouds
Of silvern haze far-cleft with roseate streaks:
And far beneath them, down along the shore,
A wave of low round hills gleamed pure and pale. 170
  But soon—like any human life,
The golden promise of whose dawn doth fail
Into the same drear noon of barren strife
Of which our hearts were weary-sick of yore—
  The day grew chill and dark; 175
And through its sullen hours the wintry gale
  Beat restlessly my bark,
Beside that coast-line drifting to and fro
Upon the ocean's vapour-shrouded flow.

X

I saw grey phantoms, fading as they fled, 180
  Glide hurrying in loose rank
O'er livid backgrounds of the upper sky,
Whose vast and thunderous threat'ning overfrowned
  Abysses strangely dread—
Cold, glassy gulfs, each like an evil eye 185
Of serpent-malice which is dead and blank

To every sight but woe and agony.
The fascination of their wan green glance
Was fixed upon the hills which (at the foot
Of that stern wall of mountain lifted proud   190
Above the firmament of level cloud)
        Lay stretched out cold and mute,
In leaden bulk, beneath the long expanse
Of dark and desert sky, whose brooding gloom
Was blanched with cruel pallor here and there—   195
Pallor of wrath or dread, instinct with doom.
There stretched they far, a dark and silent host,
Like monsters stranded from their deep-sea lair
        Benumbed with terror cowering;
Still unrecovered from the storm whose ire   200
Had drowned them in wild floods of pitiless fire,
Or prescient of some deadlier tempest lowering.

XI

At intervals, opposing the sun's track,
        Circling about the North
        Shone strangely blazoned forth   205
Wild rainbow-fragments on the sweeping rack,
The gale's rent symbol on rent banners borne.
For ever and anon the sun gazed down
From dizzy summits of the cloud-crags black;
        Or where the wind had torn   210
Vast jaggèd rifts athwart their mass
        (Behind whose heavy frown
Faint smiles of soothing like a robe of grass
Had fallen from him on the frozen hills),
He gazed out powerless o'er the rain-grey sea: 215
        No eye which sorrow fills
        With constant bitter tears,
Drowning all life and lustre, joy and pride,
Can gaze more faint and wan and hopelessly
Into the homeless world and waste of years   220
Spread out between it and the grave's sweet sleeping;
Can let the dark lid sink upon its weeping
        More often, fain to hide
The chilling desolation blurred with strife
Which, seen or unseen, maps its future life.   225

XII

        Ere sunset came a storm of rain
        Ploughing up the barren main
        With fierce and vital energy,
While brief bright lightnings flashed incessantly.
And then the South stood up, one solid wall   230

Of battlemented cloud, in which the mountains
And hills were fused together out of sight:
The sinking sun from his intense fire-fountains
Poured out against its heaven-absorbing might
   Seas of lurid purple light   235
And fulvous meteors, surging and devouring
   The shattered crests, the crumbling slopes,
   The massive walls, the riven copes,
In fortitude of glowing bronze far-towering.

XIII

From all the secret caverns of the air   240
Night's gloomy phantoms issuing, gathered dense
To blot and stifle out the pageant there;
The murmur of their motions breathing wide
Through that new silence thrilled upon the sense;
When gazing southward I became aware   245
Of some slow movement by the dim sea-side,
As of a wind arousing from its lair
To rend the settled vapours. I descried,
After an interval of rapt suspense,
By what faint gloaming yet was left of day,   250
Two startling lamps uplifted slowly glide
From out the thick and dun immensity,
Fronting a long dark line like some array
Of men that came in silent mystery,
Across the undulations of the shore   255
Long-winding coil on coil unbrokenly,
To celebrate weird rites and sorceries hoar,
Shrouded in gloom beside the moaning sea.

XIV

   I knew, but would not know,
I knew too well, but knowledge was despair.   260
   It came on vast and slow,
And dipt those baleful meteors in the brine;
Whence soon it lifted them with hideous cries
That flung strange horror through the shuddering air.
Haling its length in many a monstrous twine,   265
It bore on steadfastly those loathsome eyes,
Set in the midst of intertangled hair
Like sea-weed in whose jungle have their lair
   All foul and half-lived things:
With such a gleam as haunts the rotting graves   270
They fixed upon me their malignant stare;
Shallow and slimy, fiendish, eyes of death.
It neared me soon with ponderous wallowings
Athwart the heaving and repugnant waves;

Then paused a moment, and with one harsh roar
Heaved up its whole obscene and ghastly bulk,
To rankle in my memory evermore.
With hissing shrieks and bursts of strangled breath,
Torn by some agonising pang, it fell,
And lay upon the sea a vast dead hulk;
But raised yet once the huge and formless head
Whence blood-dark foam was showering; and those eyes
Glared blinking on me with the hate of Hell,
Before it turned reluctantly and fled.
Down, down, convicted by the holy skies,
Away, away, O God! it hurtled forth;
To cower in frozen caverns of the deep;
To haunt—a nightmare in that ghastly sleep—
The death and desolation of the North.

XV

A man forlorn has wandered, cursed from rest,
Through Time's dead wastes and savage howling seas,
Bearing a fateful Horror in his breast,
Formless and dim, but mighty to disease;
Devouring, poisoning, stifling his pure life.
And suddenly, when Hope can hope no more,
He feels its coils unwinding from his heart,
And rich vitality with glorious strife
Surging through veins all shrunk and numb before:
But also sees the Incubus depart,
Coil after coil reluctant dragged away
As were a serpent's from its strangled prey;
And thus in his first health is clearly shown
What still was hidden from his lunacy,
The full obscene and deadly ghastliness
Of that which held and ruled him to this day:
Abhorrence almost chills him into stone,
And that great blow which struck the prisoner free
Hath nearly slain him by its mighty stress.
Such was my agony of joy that hour,
When saved for ever from the monster's power.

XVI

The sky was spacious warm and bright,
The clouds were pure as morning snow;
In myriad points of living light
The sea lay laughing to and fro.
Above the hills a depth of sky,
Dim-pale with heat and light intense,
Was overhung by clouds piled high
In mountain-ranges huge and dense;

Whose rifts and ridges ran aloft
Far to their crests of dazzling snow,　　　　　　320
Whence spread a vaporous lustre soft
Veiling the noontide's azure glow.
Through mists of purple glory seen
Those dim and panting hill-waves lay,
Absorbed into the heavens serene,　　　　　　325
Dissolving in the perfect day.

But when the sun burned high and bare
In his own realm of solemn blue,
The clouds hung isolated there,
Dark purple grandeurs vast and few;　　　　　　330
Like massive sculptures wrought at large
Upon that dome's immensity,
Like constant isles whose foamlit marge
Rose high from out that sapphire sea.

And all the day my boat sped on　　　　　　335
With rapid gliding smooth as rest,
As if by mystic dreamings drawn
To some fair haven in the West;
Flew onward swift without a gale
As if it were a living thing,　　　　　　340
And spread with joy its snow-white sail
As spreads a bird its snow-white wing;
Flashed on along the lucid deep
Dividing that most perfect sphere,
A vault above it glowing steep,　　　　　　345
A vault beneath it no less clear;
Within whose burning sapphire-round
The clouds, the air, the land, the sea,
Lay thrilled with quivering glory, drowned
In calm as of Eternity.　　　　　　350

Part II
THE CITY

I

Anear the dying of that royal day
Those amber-vested hills began to swerve;
And soon a lofty Pharos, gleaming white
Upon its isle set darkly in the light,
Beckoned us onward to the spacious bay　　　　　　5
Encompassed broadly by their noble curve.
And so at length we entered it; and faced
The thin dark lines of countless masts, all traced
Upon the saddest sunset ever seen—

THE CITY

Spread out like an interminable waste
Of red and saffron sand, devoured by slow
Persistent fire; beneath whose desolate glow
A City lay, thick-zoned with solemn green
Of foliage massed upon the steeps around.
Between those mast-lines flamed the crystal fires
Of multitudinous windows; and on high
Grand marble palaces and temples, crowned
With golden domes and radiant towers and spires,
Stood all entranced beneath that desert sky,
Based on an awful stillness. Dead or dumb,
That mighty City through the breathless air
Thrilled forth no pulse of sound, no faintest hum
Of congregated life in street and square:
Becalmed beyond all calm those galleons lay,
As still and lifeless as their shadows there,
Fixed in the magic mirror of the bay
As in a rose-flushed crystal weirdly fair.
A strange, sad dream: and like a fiery pall,
Blazoned with death, that sky hung over all.

II

Where, eastward from the town, the shore was low,
I drew at length my shallop up the sand,—
The quiet and gloomless twilight gathering slow;
And took my way across the lonely strand,
And onward to the City, lost in thought.
Who shall his own wild life-course understand?
From terror through great terrors I am brought
To front my fate in this mysterious land.
In my old common world, well fenced about
With myriad lives that fellowed well my own,
Terror and deadly anguish found me out
And drove me forth to seek the dread Unknown;
Through all whose terrors I have yet been brought,
Though hopeless, helpless, utterly alone.
May yet my long wild night be blessed with morn?
Some revelation from the awful Throne
Awaits me surely: if my life, torn free
From dire Egyptian bondage, has been led
In safety through the all-devouring sea;
If, lost in foodless deserts, it was fed
Though murmuring ever; hath it truly trod
Such paths for nothing? Shall it not be brought
To stand awe-stricken 'neath some Mount of God
Wrapt in thick clouds of thunder, fire and gloom,
And hear the Law of Heaven by which its doom
To good or evil must be henceforth wrought?

III

The moon hung golden, large and round,
Soothing its beauty up the quiet sky
In swanlike slow pulsations, while I wound
Through dewy meads and gardens of rich flowers,
Whose fragrance like a subtle harmony 60
Was fascination to the languid hours.
A tender mist of light was interfused
Upon the hills and waters, woods and leas,
Throughout the gloomless gloaming: and I mused
Dim thoughts deep-floating in delicious dream, 65
Until the long stern lines of cypress trees,
Amidst whose plumes funereal there did seem
To creep with quivering sobs a moaning breath,
Awed back my heart to life—to life and death.
Far in the mystic moonlight lay outspread, 70
In trance of solemn beauty still and weird,
That Camp and City of the ancient dead;
And far around stood up in dense array
Those monumental marbles ever reared
By men still battling with the powers of Life 75
To those released before them from its sway:
Victors or vanquished in the fearful strife,
What matters?—ah, within our Mother's breast,
From toil and tumult, sin and sorrow free,
Sphered beyond hope and dread, divinely calm, 80
They lie, all gathered into perfect rest;
And o'er the trance of their Eternity
The cypress waves more holy than the palm.

IV

A funeral train was gathered round a bier:
The reverend priest with lifted hands and face, 85
Appealing silently to Heaven's grace
For this young soul called early from our sphere;
And white-robed maidens pale, whose hands scarce held
What further symbol-flowers they had to shed
Upon their sweet lost sister,—awe and dread 90
Numbing their noisier grief, they stood compelled
To meet Death's eyes which wither youth from Life;
And leaning sole against a tree apart,
As one might lean just stricken to the heart,
A youth, wrought calm by woe's self-slaying strife— 95
His head was sunken nerveless on his breast,
He stood a dumb blind statue of Despair.
While all yet moved not, I approached them there,
Murmuring: They bring this maiden to her rest
Beneath the pure sad moon, in thoughtful night, 100

Rather than in the garish day whose King
Rides through the heavens for ever triumphing
Throned above ruth in never-darkened light;
That ere the blank dawn chills them they may gaze,
And see her soul as some white cloud on high 105
Floating serenely up the star-strewn sky. . . .
My steps were now close near them, when amaze
Convulsed me with a swooning suddenness—
What people dwell within this Silent Land,
Who thus have placed, through day and night to stand, 110
This Scene complete in all its images
Of Life in solemn conference with Death,
Amidst the wide and populous solitude
Of Death's own realm?—a people of strange mood.
For all,—the maidens meek with bated breath 115
And eyes weighed down by awe and fear and sorrow,
The priest appealing to the heavens above,
The youth whose mortal night could hope no morrow,
The sweet young girl new-riven from his love,—
All save the flowers, the withered flowers alone, 120
Were carven weirdly in unconscious stone.

V

Beneath my gaze was spread the princely mart.
From out the folded hills came broad the stream
Whose pulse flowed lifeful through the City's heart—
The City dead in ever-voiceless dream. 125
From all her stately mansions, reared apart
'Midst lawns and gardens, came no lamplight gleam,
No cheerful glow and smoke of household fire;
No festal music dying through the night,
Sad in its death as joyous in its birth; 130
No serenades intoning soft desire,
To which young hearts in secret throb delight;
No noise of banded revellers issuing forth
  With shouts and songs and jars,
Who find the pale moon reeling jollily 135
And twinkling laughters in the high cold stars.
  Between the hills and sea
  Only a dark dead dearth
Of soulless silence yawned in dreadful mystery.

VI

My limbs were shuddering while my veins ran fire, 140
  And hounded on by dread
  No less than by desire,
I plunged into the City of the Dead,

And pierced its Mausolean loneliness—
Between the self-sufficing palaces,   145
Broad fronts of azure, fire and gold, which shone
Spectrally pallid in the moonlight wan;
Adown great streets; through spacious sylvan squares,
    Whose fountains plashing lone
Fretted the silence with perpetual moan;   150
Past range on range of marts which spread their wares
Weirdly unlighted to the eyes of heaven,
Jewels and silks and golden ornaments,
Rich perfumes, soul-in-soul of all rare scents,
Viols and timbrels: O wild mockery!   155
Where are the living shrines for these adornings?
Shall love-tormented phantoms hither hie,
Resolvèd that the tomb be no more mute,
And thrill their heart-sick plaints from lyre and lute
To plead against fair phantoms' cruel scornings;   160
Wakening thin ghosts of buried melodies
To shiver out beneath the scornful skies,
And wander homeless till they fail of breath
About this desert realm of timeless death?

VII

What saw I in the City, which could make   165
All thought a frenzy and all feeling madness?
What found I in the City, for whose sake
Blank death were welcome as a restful gladness?
I hold it truth, that what the stars and moon
Can gaze upon with clear and steadfast eyes, 170
Still soaring as of old to reach their noon,
Serenely regnant in unwithered skies;
That scene should never fill a human being
With hopelessness of horror in the seeing.
Can souls be blighted where the mere trees grow?   175
Can lives be frozen where the dead streams flow?
Can Man be prostrate where the fleeting mountains
Stand up and fling abroad their joyous fountains?
Could oceans, hills, stars, heavens, those imageries
And shadows of our sole realities,   180
Endure but for a moment undestroyed
Were we extinct—Eternity left void?
O truth beyond our sin and death's concealing!—
The ghastliest den, worst Hell of pain and fear,
In which a spirit can have will, thought, feeling,   185
Is to that spirit no unnatural sphere;
Nor justifies that spirit for the death
Of firm self-trust, of love and hope and faith.

VIII

What found I in the City, then, which turned
My deep and solemn hope to wild despair? 190
What mystery of horror lay inurned
Within the royal City great and fair?
What found I? Dead stone sentries stony-eyed,
Erect, steel-sworded, brass-defended all,
Guarding the sombrous gateway deep and wide 195
Hewn like a cavern through the mighty wall;
Stone statues all throughout the streets and squares,
Grouped as in social converse or alone;
Dim stony merchants holding forth rich wares
To catch the choice of purchasers of stone; 200
Fair statues leaning over balconies,
Whose bosoms made the bronze and marble chill;
Statues about the lawns, beneath the trees;
Firm sculptured horsemen on stone horses still;
Statues fixed gazing on the flowing river 205
Over the bridge's sculptured parapet;
Statues in boats, amidst its sway and quiver
Immovable as if in ice-waves set:—
The whole vast sea of life about me lay,
The passionate, heaving, restless, sounding life, 210
With all its tides and billows, foam and spray,
Arrested in full tumult of its strife
Frozen into a nightmare's ghastly death,
Struck silent from its laughter and its moan;
The vigorous heart and brain and blood and breath 215
Stark, strangled, coffined in eternal stone.

IX

Look away there to the right—How the bay lies broad and bright,
    All athrob with murmurous rapture in the glory of the moon!
See in front the palace stand, halls and columns nobly planned;
    Marble home for marble dwellers is it not full fair and boon? 220
See the myriads gathered there in that green and wooded square,
    In mysterious congregation,—they are statues every one:
All are clothed in rich array; it is some high festal day;
    The solemnity is perfect with that pallid moon for sun.
See the theatre ranged high to its dome of deep blue sky; 225
    Tier on tier of serried statues glare impassioned on its stage,
On its background of deep night, on its sculptured Chorus white,
    On its lofty sculptured actors locked in deadly tragic rage:
Perhaps the drama was *too* great—Titans, Furies, eyeless Fate,

Brooded in such sulphurous darkness thunder-swollen o'er 230
    its doom,
That the multitude abide overwrought and petrified,
    Waiting till satyric sun-bursts rend away the crushing gloom.
Turn, and o'er the river mark that huge structure scowling
        dark:
    It is black stone seamed with crimson, hopeless death with
        cruel gore:
In it stony jailers guard stony prisoners evil-starred; 235
    Dungeoned thus within their dungeon, they are calm and
        groan no more.
Note the temples every one—How the great gods are undone!
    Not a steer or goat or doveling for their holy hunger dies:
Cold, long quenched their sacred fires; dull, long dumb their
        flattering quires;
    All the very priesthood staring at rich gifts with stolid eyes! 240
Not a maid whose yielding charms can enrich a god's bold
        arms;
    Yet perchance they dwell contented though thus shorn of
        joy and state:
Nectar-and-ambrosia-blest, they may bask in perfect rest,
    Since (with marble joints and larynx) Man rests unim-
        portunate!
Ha! search eagerly around—every vault beneath the ground, 245
    Every mansion, every chariot, every galley, everywhere;
And for ever, ever find all this blissful human kind
    Lifted up from clay's corruption into marble firm and fair:
Fear and shame and anguish stilled, every evil passion killed,
    Crooked forms and ugly faces grown transcendent works of 250
        art;
While the grand or lovely mood of the fair and young and good
    Is beatified in beauty that can nevermore depart. . . .
And the full moon gazeth down on the smokeless lampless town,
    In a solemn trance of triumph, with her choir of radiant
        stars;
For their peace is vext no more by a curse-and-shriek-swelled 255
        roar,
    By ferocities, obscenities, inebriate brawls and jars:
Nay, the very grass and trees, and the disencumbered breeze,
    And the stainless river-waters, and the broad bright
        glittering bay,—
Do they all joy that the strife of our sordid restless life
    Is now locked in adamantine bonds of perfect peace for aye? 260
Ever-loved and gracious Earth, Mystic Mother of our birth,
    This is cruel, bitter, terrible, this joy in our dead rest!
Canst thou still leap forth and run, glory-speeded round the
        Sun,

O thou Niobe of World-stars, with thy fairest and thy best—
With thy vigorous youthful darling lying stone-cold on thy   265
    breast!

X

The Palace gates stand open wide and free.
The King and Queen and all their company,
Transfigured in full splendour of their pride,
Came flowing forth in one refulgent tide,
While trumpets rang their silver-throated blare   270
Of jubilation through the sunny air;
Swept onward slowly 'neath the azure skies
Between the myriads of adoring eyes,
And poured into the Theatre's dense sea
Of many-billowed life triumphantly;   275
As some grand river in the sunset shine
May pour its boon of gold and crimson wine,
Brimming the fulness of the purpled ocean
Which heaves and sparkles, murmuring proud emotion.
Gathered together, all awaited there   280
Such scenic storms as purify life's air;
Whose scathless lightnings shimmer wildly grand,
Whose lofty thunders soothe sure peace more bland;
And now, without a throb, without a breath,
They wait, all frozen into icy death.   285

XI

O marble Monarch, far more awful now
Than when thy crown begirt a throbbing brow!
No tyrant ever lived so dire and dread
As He who sways the sceptre in thy stead;
Never before on earth did any state   290
Beneath Oppression cower thus desolate,
Thus utterly resigned to crushing Fate!
SILENCE broods ghastly on the dead realm's throne:
Whatever life in prayer or sigh or moan
Would shake the Nightmare of his tyranny,   295
Shudders with anguish, horror, lunacy,
To feel its scorned and strangled pleadings creep
Like homeless spectres through the vacant deep,
And wither into nothingness at last—
Devoid of refuge, unrelieved, aghast.   300

XII

The Palace gates indeed stand open wide:
Perchance the stately sepulchre may hide
Some single life amidst the desolation,

Preserved alone in mystical salvation,
Entranced apart in holy contemplation? 305
Pace up the steps, tread through the hall,—and see
In scattered groups all lounging listlessly
Those armoured gallants of the Royal Guard—
Poor fellows! they have found it sadly hard
To make their stately moments speed along, 310
Though spurred with wine and gaming, jest and song,
Cruelly mulcted of their sumptuous share
In the great festival proceeding there.

XIII

Haste on, haste on; awaken from their tomb
The ghostly echoes, swarming through the gloom, 315
Haunting your footsteps, gathering rank on rank,
Rustling demoniac through the deadly blank:
Better, far better that the air be rife
With weird deliriums of demoniac life,
Than void with utter idiotic death. 320
Haste on, with burning blood and breathless breath;—
How clear are all things round the rapid flight!
Shrouded in gloom or washed with pale moonlight,
The chemistry of terror thus intense
Burns them all lurid on the shrinking sense.— 325
See the mild maiden letting loose her soul
In tears and blushes o'er the tender scroll
Which plains his anguish since they two were parted,
And raves that she, poor thing, is stony-hearted.
Hurry from room to room, from hall to hall; 330
And mark the effigies on every wall—
Warriors and minstrels, nobles, kings, and priests,
Adoring, conquering, feasting regal feasts;
Olympian forms, ladies divinely fair
With lily-sceptred hands and flower-crowned hair; 335
See each and all, ev'n as you hurry past
Burst into sudden life, and swarming fast
Join in the tingling chase through death and night,
While clamorous echoes voice their mad delight.

XIV

Most sweet young Mother! thou hadst ample pleasure 340
Left quiet alone here with thine infant treasure;
Which, poised unsurely on its feeble limbs,
Across the sea-strange marble toward thee swims,—
One foot half-lifted, while the arms outplead
For thine extended arms to help its need: 345
It stands, thou kneelest; never on thy breast
Shall it fall forward in triumphant rest.

XV

Far in his lofty turret whence the bay
And half of heaven's vault were seen alway;
The bay, the distant ocean, and with these 350
Broad scope of temples, streets, and palaces,
The theatre, the square; the moving throngs,
Whose converse-murmurs flashing into songs
And laughters winged with joy were wont to rise
And wander bird-like through the sun-tranced skies, 355
Rippling deliciously the languid air;
Alone, yet not alone, the Sage dwelt there.
Doubtless his individual life required
In seeming solitude to be inspired
By constant intercourse with general Life, 360
And with the universal Spirit rife
In Man and Nature,—One in all their forms,
Alike contented with its worlds and worms,
Through all its countless masks alike resplendent,
The Breath of Life, eternal and transcendent. 365

XVI

He sits, the full-length statue of a Sage,
Amid the busts of those of every age
Who handed on the torch of Wisdom, bright
With growing splendour, 'thwart the billowy night
Of shoreless Ignorance. Before him lies 370
The roll which telleth on what mysteries
He shed its lustre till they shone out clear:
I trace its periods by the moonlight here.
It is with swelling reverence dedicate,
'Unto the King magnifical and great; 375
The bounteous Sun by whom we live and move
And flourish ever: Who commands our love
Even more throughly than our perfect awe;
Swaying His burning Throne by heavenly law,
While lifted far—by nature as by birth— 380
Above the petty statutes of our earth:
Who, while His warmth createth and sustaineth
Rich life in all, lights all; and no less deigneth
To feed abundantly with life and light
What humble spheres may strive to temper night 385
In realms left dark while His imperial sway
Vouchsafeth happier realms their boon of day:
To Him, by Whom our heritage is grown
The flower o' the world; to Him, whose godlike throne
Shall ever stand beside its subject sea, 390
Fulgent with valour, arts and equity,

Based on a princely people's love and bliss:
CHRYSANDROS, TYRANT OF COSMOPOLIS!'

XVII
Follow the problems which he hath resolved
Though heretofore in clouds of doubt involved:
'Shall this fair World consume in course of Time?
Our Earth is young, or old, or in her prime?'
Whereto the Theses proud, less said than sung
In liberal phrases of his golden tongue:
'This glorious Universe shall live for ever;
By all decay and death diminished never,
Nor added to by constant birth and growth;
But in the balanced interchange of both,
Ascending slowly by successive stages
Of nobler Good and Beauty through the Ages;
Until its infinite Æther and the Whole
Of stars and spheres that through it flashing roll
Shall be informed with conscious Life and Soul:
The All, one perfect Sphere, breathing one breath
Of cosmic Life too pure for birth or death. . . .
Our Earth has scarcely ceased to be a child,
Sweet in its grace, but ignorant and wild:
She putteth on about these very years
The bloom of maidenhood, whose smiles and tears
Are all of Love: She openeth out her heart
In throbs of passionate rapture, to impart
The dearest secrets of her treasured beauty
To Man, her Lord; constrained by yearning duty
Which he shall recompense with wiser love:
How blest are we all previous men above,
Born in this Spring of her millennial Youth!—
O gracious Truth, divine and tranquil Truth,
As I long years have worshipped only Thee,
Thou hast at length unveiled Thy face to me,
That I may ever of Thy priesthood be!'

XVIII
I trace not further in the tingling scroll
The steps by which he reached this glorious goal.
It is too horrible—alone, alone,
I make mad dalliance with the empty flesh,
Whose form is whole, whose ghastly bloom is fresh;
And by my side, that hater of the soul—
The grinning, the accursèd Skeleton!
It is too horrible—O dreadful God,
    Thou knowest—only Thou,

What dismal paths my shuddering feet have trod;   435
Yet never knew I agony until now;
Never,—O Thou who heardst me when I said
Coldly and quietly, with confirming heart,
'I take thee, Misery, for my faithful Bride:
Despair hath smoothed the secret marriage-bed   440
Wherein we two, embracing close, may hide,
      And wreak our stern unwitnessed vow—
Never in life, nor after death, to part.
I love thee for the love which only Thou
      Dost bear me: Thy caresses   445
Sting my faint heart, Thy kisses on my brow
Are fire and numbing frost, Thy tingling tresses
Like serpents creep about me even now.
O my enamoured Darling, deadly sweet!
      Sorcery-smitten Sorceress!   450
      Queen of lurid loveliness!
Most tender-hearted Ministrant of Ill!
My life, my soul, is lying at your feet;
Possess me, use me, at your own wild will!'

            XIX

O fool, fool, fool! cherishing fatal madness!   455
Mad with self-consciousness of guilt and woe,
Mad with the folly of the world's much gladness
While it was no less sunk in guilt and woe;
I shut myself up from the lives around me,
Eating my own foul heart—envenomed food;   460
And while dark shadows more and more enwound me,
Nourished a dreary pride of solitude;
The cords of sympathy which should have bound me
In sweet communion with earth's brotherhood,
I drew in tight and tighter still around me,   465
Strangling my best existence for a mood.
What—Solitude in midst of a great City,
In midst of crowded myriads brimmed with Life!—
When every tear of anguish or of pity,
When every shout of joy and scream of strife,   470
When every deed and word and glance and gesture,
Every emotion, impulse, secret thought
Pent in the soul from all material vesture,
Through all those myriads spread and interwrought;
Inspiring each the air with its own spirit,   475
Rayed forth as light is from a fount intense;
The universal Æther forced to bear it,
A certain though mysterious influence
Affecting duly every other creature
That breathed its breath of life; for good or ill,   480

For pain or pleasure, acting on each nature,
Beyond the consciousness, despite the will.
Dire Vanity! to think to break the union
That interweaveth strictly soul with soul
In constant, sane, life-nourishing communion: 485
The rivers ever to the ocean roll,
The ocean-waters feed the clouds on high
Whose rains descending feed the flowing rivers:
All the world's children must how quickly die
Were they not all receivers and all givers!   490

XX

But this is Solitude, O dreadful Lord!
My spirit starves in this abysmal air—
     Of every human word,
Of sigh and moan, of music and of prayer,
Of passionate heart-beats felt though never heard,   495
     So utterly stript bare:
The awful heavens are tranquil and divine,
Serene and saintly in their purple deep
     The moon and young stars shine;
No living souls beneath their influence leap,   500
No other eyes are fixed on them with mine.
     Men said that Death and Sleep
Are brothers: yes, as lurid lightnings may
Be kindred to the glory of calm day,
Or darkness of the restful night-tide boon   505
To darkness of the sun eclipsed at noon.
The Soul is murdered; and her world bereft
     By some dire doom still left—
A fadeless corpse whose perfect form is rife
'With ghastly affectations of true life.'   510

XXI

How long, how long, I cowered beside the Sage;
Whose head was lifted, fronting full the skies
In tranquil triumph from his victory lone.
Beneath that broad brow rough with thought and age,
The pitiless light-beams glittered on his eyes,   515
Like fatal swords flashed keen against a stone
To sharpen them for piercing to the heart:
How was his triumph smitten, pierct, and slain!
     But cowering there apart,
Upon those swelling eyeballs, that stern head,   520
I ever gazed; while in my burning brain
     A cold thought soothing spread:
As one who drains a poison-chalice slowly,

THE CITY

In fixed and infinite longing to be dead;
So let my yearning vision cleave amain 525
To this grand marble image melancholy,
Till I have drunken in to the last drain
That poisonous Spirit of Death which fills it wholly. . . .
The flesh that crept like worms is growing numb;
The raging fire of blood is dying cold; 530
The rout of fiendish thoughts are almost dumb:
The heavens fade like a Vision cycles-old,
Where from dead eyes gaze thoughts uncomprehended:
Thank God, I soon shall cease to be alone;
My mad discordant life is nearly blended 535
With all this realm's unsuffering death of stone.

Part III
THE JUDGEMENTS

I

A multitudinous roaring of the ocean!
Voices of sudden and earth-quaking thunder
    From the invisible mountains!
The heavens are broken up and rent asunder
    By curbless lightning-fountains, 5
Streaming and darting through that black commotion,
In which the moon and stars are swallowed with the sky.
Throughout the Mausolean City spread
Drear palpitations, long-drawn moan and sigh;
And then—an overwhelming whirlwind blast? 10
Or else, indeed, the irrepressible cry
Of all its statues waking up aghast!
Doth God in final Judgement come thus heralded?

II

I saw Titanic forms, dark, solemn, slow,
Like thunderclouds imperious o'er the wind, 15
Sweep far with haughty tramplings to and fro;
I heard great voices peal and trumpets blow:
Strange fragments of their chanting shook my mind.
'If the owl haunts doleful ruins and lives in the sombre night,
Could it joy in the cheerful homes of men, could it love the 20
    noonday light?
If the serpent couches in jungles and deserts of burning sand,
Would it rather cast its slough in the peopled corn-rich land?
If the great bear prowls alone in desolate wastes of ice,
Could it joy to range in herded power through a tropic
    Paradise?
If the vulture gorges on carrion and all abhorrent things, 25

34 THE DOOM OF A CITY

Would it rather slake with fruits and wine the rush of its
obscene wings?

. . . . . .

'We sought through the archives of Fate, through all the
records of Doom,
Records of noontide refulgence, records of lightning-seared
gloom:
And lo, we have never found while the highth and the depth
we explored,
We have never yet traced out Punishment or Reward.   30

. . . . . .

'Peace may be happy and sweet; bitter and heart-rending
Strife;
Sin is corruption and death, Virtue is health and life:
But every being is placed in that sphere, in that crisis, that spot,
Which alone its own nature demands and asserts for its lot:
As itself from itself its web the spider spins out,   35
Doth each all the net of relations which weave it about:
The Sun shines the Sun by the lustre he lavishes forth;
For his might and his life and his light circles round him the
earth:
All the World—this infinite azure robe sphere-spangled
sublime,
In which God walks forth revealed and veiled to the creatures 40
of Space and Time,
Is all interwoven in one (each atom, each star, as each soul,
Evolving so duly the threads of its work for its part in the
Whole):
With a woof and warp of might and light and mysteries all is
wrought,
For the many-figured, many-hued being and passion and
thought.

. . . . . .

'Here hath a spirit full bliss to breathe ever-bland golden air; 45
Here hath a spirit wild hurrying storms of doubt, dread,
anguish, despair:
For the world-realms are swept on their path for ever, through
day and night;
And their course is advanced no less, no more, in the gloom
than in the light:
And the journey is infinite truly,—through every various clime
Do the countless myriads wander on, through every season of   50
time;
Cool water for him in the desert-blaze, red fire for him in the
frost,
Languor for him in the summer peace, fierce heart for the
tempest-tost:

While all whence they know not whither they know not wend;
Who appraiseth the means and progress, who conceiveth the
    End?
But we swear by the Life Eternal, we swear by Eternal Death,   55
We swear by the Fate supreme which rules in every pulse and
    breath;
That strong or weak, simple or wise, polluted or most holy,
Each each day is fed with the food befitting him fully and
    solely.'

III

Again deep peace, again the stars and moon:
   I stood between the theatre and square,   60
   Beholding as before the statues there
Unstirred and silent in the lethal swoon.

Lo! in the empyréan grew a light—
   A great and awful Splendour, through its shroud
   Of fold on fold of massy thunder-cloud   65
Intensely burning down with steadfast might.

Wherefrom a Voice descended vast and lone;
   Of thunder-dreadfulness, of sea-fierce anger,
   Yet in its lofty silver-volumed clangour
Chanting an unimpassioned monotone: 70

'WHEN ALL THE WINE IS POISONED, IT MUST BE DESTROYÈD
    UTTERLY;
THE VESSELS ALSO WHICH CONTAINED IT MUST
    BE BURNED AND GROUND TO DUST.'

Instantly shudderings shook the stony crowd:
   Some rigid arms with writhing spasms were lifted,   75
   Some dungeon-throats with frenzy-spasms rifted
By hideous strangled voices shrieking loud:

      'Abominable Fate,
      We hurl thee back thy hate!
      The poison and the wine—   80
      Our sins and souls are thine!
      Ah! pangs of utter death
         Stifle our breath—
   Hear us; we plead; hear us; oh, wait!'

No answer came save trumpet-voices blaring   85
Death and destruction as in furious fray;
And while those forms gasped out their cry despairing,
They sank down crumbling into dusty spray.
Then, as the trumpet clamours died away,

Did crash on crash in clear succession sound,
Like lingering peals of thunder; each the knell
Of house or column falling to the ground
In sudden ruin, as those statues fell.

And next, as if the solid hills were all
Disseated now to glide tremendously
Over the town and plunge athwart the sea,
A mass of gloom enveloped in its pall
Temple and palace, basement, dome and spire;
Then o'er the marble crowd submerging came:
Its black oppression burned throughout my frame,
A torture of intolerable fire.
Yet when at length its ponderous bulk was rolled
Over the shrinking waters out of sight,
The City and the steadfast statues white
Stood all unchanged about me; but, behold,
The uttered condemnation had been wrought
Upon the ruined fragments,— they were naught.

IV

That cloud-consuming fire still held the sky,
   Blotting its worlds out wholly; while the sphere
   Seemed listening breathless in an awful fear,
Till that great Voice again rang forth on high:

'WHEN NOW THE SAPLESS TREE BEARS BLOOM NOR FRUIT,
   WHY LINGER TRUNK AND ROOT?
LET IT BE HEWN AWAY AND FIRE-DESTROYED;
   AND IN ITS PLACE LEFT VOID
A LIVING TREE BE SET TO SPREAD AND RISE,
RESPONSIVE TO THE BOUNTY OF THE SKIES.'

The sentence smote some statues like a sword;
   With nerveless gestures pitiful to see
   They moaned their helpless hopeless litany,
'We lived, we lived, O great and dreadful Lord!'

Then as they crumbled into dust away,
The Answer speeded from the hills behind,—
A noise of rushing like a mighty wind.
The ashen fire-flood in a tempest grey
Hissed through the City and the wan array;
And hurrying o'er the sea, as if its might
With grim joy hasted to fulfil such trust,
Swept all the human and palatial dust
To irretrievable Chaos, Death and Night.

THE JUDGEMENTS

And when that deadly storm of fire was past,
A Voice came roaring like its final blast:

'Whose virtue cannot pay their Life's expense,
   Whose souls are lost in sense,
They are no more; themselves with God have willed,—   135
   Their æon is fulfilled.'

V

Once more that fire possessing sole the sky,
   Once more deep silence o'er the lessened throng
   Of waiting statues; and it lasted long
Ere that great Voice again pealed forth on high: 140

'When he who had a Palace and its power,
   Well-favoured for his dower,
Has proved unjust and proud, has spent its treasures
   On selfish pomps and pleasures;
He must descend from his exalted place: 145
   Yet, if in deep disgrace
   He do not sink still deeper, till his breath
   Be wholly quenched in death;
But learn to build again his kingly heart,
The throne awaits him and the kingly part.'   150

Ah, what a multitude of statues then
   Were shaken by the thunder of this doom!—
   'O Lord, all perish if Thou wilt consume
In justice! Lord have mercy on frail men!'

Ev'n as the crash of smitten structures roared   155
The answering Judgement-terrors filled the sky:
Inexorably swift it streamed and poured
A red fire-deluge from that cloud on high,
Which drowned the City and the multitude,
Devouring all the space from hills to sea.   160
Hissing and roaring the resistless flood
Plunged through the trembling earth, in haste to flee
With its vast ravage; and the earth gaped wide
To swallow in that cup of wrath amain,
Then gnashed her seared and riven jaws to hide   165
What shook her yet with shuddering throbs of pain.
How many had become the torrent's prey,
Swept down abrupt into some lower sphere!
But of the rest—Can vision cheat me here?
What forms are these amidst the wan array   170
Of human marble? Strange new stony forms—
These serpents, panthers, wolves, these apes and swine,

Vultures and hawks and owls, with sheep and kine,
And many others, brutes and birds and worms,
Couched in unutterably piteous rest,   175
The sorcery of that Judgement-fire attest.

VI

No more wild agonies shook the steadfast Earth;
   That night of cloud, unable to sustain
   Its soul of fire, was withering; when again
Upon the silence that great Voice flowed forth.   180

'WHEN HE WHO SHOULD HAVE TRAVELLED ALL THE DAY,
   HAS LINGERED ON HIS WAY
TO SPORT WITH IDLERS; OR IN COMMON FEAR
   OF LONE PATHS STEEP AND DREAR,
HAS TURNED ASIDE TO PACE DOWN CROWDED ROADS   185
   OF RICH AND GAY ABODES;
HE MUST PLOD THIS DAY'S JOURNEY ON THE MORROW
   WITH WEARY RUE AND SORROW,
ERE HE CAN WIN HIS HAPPY HOME, AND GREET
   THE DEAR FRIENDS WAITING FOR HIS LAGGARD FEET.'   190

Whereunto statue-voices low implored:
'Free human fellowship is very sweet;
Bitter with our own kind as foes to meet—
Heavy the load of uncompanioned life!
Alas, we are so weary-sick of strife!   195
Grant us awhile Thy perfect peace, O Lord!'

The humble plaining of that saddest prayer,
Relapsing into stony silentness,
So filled my heart that I was unaware,
Until surrounded by its sway and stress,   200
How the deep Ocean rushing from its lair
Bellowed against the hill-slopes planted broad;
Whilst fierce from sea-vast cloudglooms in the air,
Blazoned with dreadful sentences of God
In writhed and quivering lightnings wrought, the rain   205
Intense of swerveless thunderbolts streamed down,
Crashing amidst the ruins of the town,
And shrieking through the loud inundent main.

VII

The flood below, the flood above ebbed soon
Completely; fair and still the green earth lay,   210
Beneath a heaven surcharged with tenfold day,
More holy-sweet of lustre than the moon.
I gazed: the statues stood there as before,

Like dateless boulders by the old sea-shore:
But of the City's vast palatial pride 215
Of all the works of Man on every side—
The theatre's stupendous cirque of tiers,
The pharos and the galleons and the piers,
Remained no vestige; save that here and there,
Bathed in the sea of crystal-lucent air, 220
Some fragment wall, some column cleft stood dim,
More like strange rocks than structures reared by Him.
Had that swift deluge been the stream of Time,
And every billow some vast age sublime,
Over the vacant City flowing ever 225
Until a mind should swoon in the endeavour
Such infinite cycles of its course to mete,
ERASURE had been scarcely more complete.

VIII

The cloud was vanished from the perfect sky:
   Heaven, earth and sea all floated from my sight, 230
   Bathed in a dimness of exceeding light
Too pure, intense and calm for mortal eye.

And yet I saw as we may see in trance:
   Saw how a gradual change beatified
   The statues who had never yet replied 235
When those dread Judgements took dread utterance.

As Memnon woke to music with the dawn,
   They in the solemn splendour seemed to rouse
   From death to life, with glory on their brows;
A calm grand life, eyes shut and breath undrawn. 240

The crystal sea of sky then streamed away,
   The inmost Heavens revealed themselves abroad:
   A Throne ... the Vision of the Living God ...
Ravished and blind upon the earth I lay.

Once more a Voice descended vast and lone, 245
   The Voice of Infinite Love Omnipotent;
   Sweeter than life or death, it swelled and blent
The Universe all tuned into one tone:

'THE SOLDIER WHO HAS FOUGHT THE NOBLE FIGHT,
   PERSISTENT FOR THE RIGHT, 250
ENDURING ALL AND DARING ALL TO PROVE
   HIS GLAD UNPURCHASED LOVE
AND FAITHFULNESS, IN TRIUMPH AND DEFEAT:
   WHAT DOOM FOR HIM IS MEET?

The Battle, with the day it filled, is done; 255
  The field is lost or won:
Let night then greet him well with joy and rest
  By holy visions blest;
That on the Morrow he may rise up strong
  Hopeful and fresh and young, 260
His sharp wounds healed, to do and dare once more
  Heroic as before,—
But with a loftier rank, with nobler power,
  With far more generous dower.
And so for ever through the Nights and Days 265
While he remaineth lord of his own praise,
He may go on, exalted more and more,
Till final triumph crown the fateful war;
Till Love and Life and Bliss (which once was Faith)
Have vanquished wholly Evil, Falsehood, Death; 270
The loftiest station that his soul can fill,
The utmost sway commensurate with his will,
The All of Wisdom that he can believe,
Of Love and Goodness that he can receive,
Are then his dower from the reachless Throne 275
And Him who reigns eternally thereon.'

IX

I heard it all,—there prostrate on the ground;
  I floated in the Voice as in a sea,
  Or as a cloud may float dissolvingly
Within the sapphire noontide's burning bound. 280

And when it ebbed it left my shrinking soul
  To shudder back into its cave of clay,
  Blind, hopeless, one dead atom fallen astray
From vital union in and with the Whole.

After a time, from such fierce consciousness 285
  Of personal being as is lunacy—
  As not to know is perfectly to be—
I was withdrawn by human utterances:

'O Lord! let us be hidden, let us die!
  Thy love and wisdom are too infinite! 290
  We throb unpeaceful in Thy perfect light,
Star-specks of gloom no Sun can glorify.

'Were we less dark than our old midnight sphere,
  Transplant us not into Thy blinding day.
  Lord, we adore Thee, Perfect, Sole, for aye— 295
Our sins and weakness crush our spirits here!'

X

No answer sounded. I arose and stood.
  The gates of Heaven were shut, the Vision gone:
  But still undimmed miraculously shone
That tenfold noon of glareless sanctity.   300

They stood—the Spirits who had conquered Life;
  Erect—yet pleading, hands uplifted, there;
  Glorious—yet wan with that divine despair:
Was *this* the crowning issue of the strife?

The noble faces slowly turned to where   305
  The dim hills floated, exquisitely drawn
  Or interfused, like breathless streaks of dawn,
Upon the breathless ocean of wide air.

Thereon uplifted stood a lofty band;
  Some burning with the glory of their wings;   310
  Some golden-crowned and purpled-robed like Kings;
Some clad in white, a palm-branch in the hand;

Some like stern warriors armed with shield and sword;
  Some swaying crystal cups in which the fire
  Of red wine quivered; while a radiant quire   315
Striking their harps sang loud with sweet accord.

XI

  'Dear Friends, come! we wait for you;
  Strong and wise and pure and true.
  Why, alas, ascend so few?

'Where are the myriads that should now be here?   320
  How have they wasted all the lavish dower
With which God fitted them to rule their sphere—
  The Passion and the Vision and the Power?
For ever hoping, disappointed ever,
  We know too well the constant tragic doom: 325
Vision hath seen, with scarce a work-endeavour,
  Then closed its eyes for more voluptuous gloom;
Passion hath disenshrined the awful soul,
  Its large heart tempting fatal fleshly lusts;
And Power hath shaken off divine control,   330
  To gorge itself with universal trusts.

  'For the undone Many, ruth,
  Ye have conquered, true to truth;
  Dare our wine of Joy and Youth.

'The tree whose trunk and branches dark and bare 335
  Withstood the storms of Winter, planted strong,
Doth glorify itself in summer's air
  With leaf and fruit and nested bird's blithe song:
The earth-realm labouring blind and dumb and cheerless,
  Yet ever onward, through the reign of night, 340
Leaps forth with joy majestically fearless
  Into the pure new heaven of morning light.
Again stern Winter with its storms shall come,
  But find the tree grown stronger 'gainst its wrath;
Again the night-gloom, weary, blind and dumb, 345
  But find the realm far forward on its path.

   'Then, dear Friends, come, come away!
   Now is Summer, now is Day;
   Joy assumes imperial sway!'

XII

As when the warm spring-breezes overblow 350
  Some silent, frozen, melancholy main,
  Its waters heave and throb and rend their chain,
And singing in the sunbeams flash and flow:

So with the breathing of that gracious song
  Those Spirits burst their trance of silent sadness; 355
  Their bosoms heaved with glorious life and gladness;
Clear-eyed, erect, full-voiced, advanced their throng:

'O Brothers of this Heaven supreme and glorious!
  O Sisters of this greeting full of love!
Into what a dawn of perfect day victorious, 360
  Do ye usher us, and welcome us above!
The World o'erflows with life serene and tender;
  The air, the light is all celestial wine;
Our inmost soul is interfused with splendour
  And harmony divine! 365

'As birds the boundless azure sky-deep winging,
  As breezes flowing round and round the earth,
As flowers into the vernal welcome springing,
  As fountains leaping seawards bright with mirth;
Our thoughts throughout Infinity float chainless, 370
  Our souls encompass spheres of life sublime,
Our beings thrill and glow with new life stainless,
  Our swift joy laughs at Time!

'The worlds go wheeling far their cycled courses,—
  From the fathomless Unbirth of the Abyss, 375

THE JUDGEMENTS

By golden laws attuning counter-forces
    Built up into the noonday Heaven of Bliss:
And pervading all, sustaining all, enwreathing
    With Its infinite embrace beneath, above,
The Æther—the Divine eternal breathing   380
    Of Life and Light and Love!'

XIII

So singing, they advanced with measured pace;
    And like a silver morning-mist were drawn
    Slow-floating up the hillside wood and lawn,
Unto that high seraphical embrace.   385

All stood triumphant, beautiful, divine,
    Between the heaven and earth; all stood there bright,
    Informed, transfigured with the holy light
As crystal cups with sacramental wine.

I would have stood there evermore and gazed   390
    Entranced in adoration, consciousless,
    Upon that beauty of all holiness
In human forms embodied and upraised.

Alas! the universal light too soon
    Was fading, flowing backward to its fount,   395
    Until they stood upon that sombre mount
Sole-shining o'er the dark earth as a moon.

And still the glory-stream flowed back to God;
    And they with it were floated up the sky;
    Whose gates shut blank against my straining eye,   400
And left the earth a dark and soulless clod—

Left all the earth like some most desolate shore
    Wherefrom has ebbed the free and living tide;
    And left me stranded on its dark waste wide,
A wreck to be recovered nevermore.   405

O Life! this is thy deepest woe of all—
    That as a soul regains its heaven of birth,
    The body drags it swooning back to earth,
Stunned, hopeless, blind with its tremendous fall.

XIV

When I arose, the ever-ancient Night   410
    Filled with his sombre pomp the earth and sky:
No memories of that doom of dire affright
Perturbed the calm; and undismayed on high
    The moon and stars where they had shone before

Shone on in cold and stern sublimity. 415
The hills loomed dark upon the silent shore,
　Round which the waves in thoughtful monotone
Rolled their old voice of *Ever—evermore.*
A royal City dwelt upon this throne,—
　And what now left of all its wealth and pride? 420
A few strange groups of pallid-gleaming stone!
But Nature cares not for the ruin wide,
　Her dreaming beauty glows in perfect bloom:
Most cold, imperial, unlamenting Bride,
　Her Lord and Bridegroom scarcely in the tomb... 425
　　The moon sank slowly down from heaven's crest;
Pale radiance lined and flecked the eastern gloom;
　A stir, a breathing thrilled the world's deep rest;
　　No wakening bird, half-wakened, here and there
Uttered uncertain warning from its nest; 430
But spread a cold and fresh and fragrant air,
　That seemed with lifeful breath to cleanse away
The grosser shades and vapours everywhere,
And all memorials of the night's dismay,
　That pure and odorous the earth might greet 435
The first divine embraces of the Day,
　Now hurrying up the heavens with fiery feet,
　　The crown of burning gold upon his head,
Cloud-robed with gold and purple, light and heat. . . .
Ages on ages in their course have shed 440
　Ruin of fire and tempest on the earth,
Uncounted æons of her sons are dead;
Yet she exults with aboriginal mirth,
　Nor feels her frame grow weak, her blood grow cold,
But pure and strong and young as at her birth 445
When first God's hand her glorious path out-rolled:
　For day by day He seals her with His sign—
Night's tomb is rent, the gates of heaven unfold
To let the ever-youngest Dawn divine
　Bathe her in balms of sempiternal youth. 450
I think no human soul which here doth pine
In personal anguish and with general ruth,
　Without these Dawn-evangels fresh from God
Could feel its immortality a truth.
Dear are all dawns: but this that coming trod 455
　The eastern heavens to kiss the earth's pale brow
With heavenly benedictions, when the rod
Of the Avenging Justice was but now
　Withdrawn from penal smitings dire!—what speech
That mortals use, what words of lofty vow 460
Or soaring chant can emulate and reach

The awe, the bliss, the gratitude, the love,
That saving dawn brought with it from above?

XV
What a dawn ascendeth fair through the pure and silent air,
   Fain to greet with holy rapture what a glorious virgin Earth!   465
From her sins and fears and woes, from her memories, by the
    throes
   Of a fierce regeneration born anew in perfect birth!
But what forms, what forms are they, there between the sea-
    loved bay
   And the spiritual hills with the woods that clothe their feet;
Human forms erect in power, beasts that crouch and birds   470
    that cower,
   But all wrought in fadeless marble, white and shining, pure
    and sweet?
Lo! as ever more and more broadening out the dawn doth soar,
   Kindling emerald purple golden quivering splendours round
    her way;
What a flush—as if of Life kindling with triumphant strife
   Through the torpid marble—fires them, though they all so   475
    steadfast stay!
Lo, as ever more and more music with the dawn doth soar,
   Breezes whisper, leaflets murmur, waters warble joy for day;
What a thrill—as if of Life stirring with triumphant strife
   Through the rigid marble—heaves them, though they all so
    silent stay!
These are forms that couch and stand, still as marble fountains   480
    grand,
   Still in meek victorious patience, till the Sea of Life arise;
Till the World-sustaining Sea, Soul of all Eternity,
   Once more fill them with its waters of the Life that never
    dies.
When the royal Sun shall leap glorious on the eastern steep,
   Gazing grand athwart this province of his measureless   485
    domains;
Straightway at that conquering sign, straightway at that
    glance divine,
   Soul shall fill them, stone incarnate, life-blood gush through
    all their veins.
And this Nature which doth dream in Titanic sloth supreme,
   Hill and river, wood and meadow, heaven of azure, care-
    less sea,
Shall have all its want fulfilled, strength employed and bosom   490
    thrilled
   By a lordly domination—soul and thought and passion free.
Oh, that these who in this hour shall attain such solemn dower,

Consecrated Lords and Bridegrooms wedding this fair virgin
      Earth,
Have such holy strength of will, love, faith, truth unquench-
      able,
  Wisdom, justice, making concord of inheritance and worth,   495
  As shall give a nobler being from the blissful marriage birth!

XVI

  As one who in the morning-shine
      Reels homeward, shameful, wan, adust,
  From orgies wild with fiery wine
      And reckless sin and brutish lust: 500
  And sees a doorway open wide,
      And then the grand Cathedral space;
  And hurries in to crouch and hide
      His trembling frame, his branded face.

  The organ-thunders surge and roll   505
      And thrill the heights of branching stone;
  They shake his mind, they crush his soul,
      His heart knells to them with a moan:
  He hears the voice of holy prayer,
      The chanting of the fervent hymn;   510
  They pierce his depths of sick despair,
      He trembles more, his eyes are dim.

  He sees the world-wide morning flame
      Through windows where in glory shine
  The saints who fought and overcame,   515
      The martyrs who made death divine:
  He sees pure women bent in prayer,
      Communing low with God above:—
  Too pure! what right has *he* to share
      Their silent feast of sacred love?   520

  How can he join the songs of praise?
      His throat is parched, his brain is wild:
  How dare he seek the Father's gaze,
      Thus hopeless, loveless and defiled?
  How taint the pureness—though he yearn   525
      To join such fellowship for aye?
  He creeps out pale—May he return
      Some time when he shall dare to stay!

  As he within that holy fane,
      Was I upon that solemn shore;   530
  One murky cloud, one spoiling stain,
      One jarring note,—all these and more:

A Spectre from the wicked Past,
　　Familiar with the buried years;
The joys that fade, the griefs that last,　　　535
　　The baffled hopes, the constant fears;

The fair, fair dawn of many a day
　　That sinks in storm clouds red and wild;
The souls that in their huts of clay
　　Are crushed and buried, all defiled;　　　540
The Lusts that rage like savage steeds,—
　　While Will with reinless hand sleeps on,
And drunken Thought but goads their speeds,—
　　Then one mad plunge, and all is gone;

The Moods that strew palm-branches now　　　545
　　And with Hosannas fill the sky,
Then shortly crown with thorns the brow,
　　And mock and scourge and crucify;
The error, guile and infamy,
　　The waste of foul and bloody strife,　　　550
The unforeseen catastrophe,
　　That make the doleful drama, Life.

Ah, what had I to do with these
　　Young lovely souls serene and clear,
Awaking up by fine degrees　　　555
　　To life unsullied as its sphere?
The Spectre that has roamed forlorn,
　　Sin-restless, through the sombre night,
Must creep to its old grave at morn,
　　Nor blot the world of life and light.　　　560

XVII

Where I had left it, on the lonely strand,
　　Uninjured lay my boat, and lovely; seeming
　　Some fair sea-creature, of the mid-sea dreaming
To light foam-whispers on the yellow sand.

While yet we skimmed the wavelets of the bay,　　　565
　　Methought there rose, ev'n as the sun arose,
　　A vehement Chorus hurrying to its close—
Fresh as the breath of the awakened day.

With vital fires the morning seemed to glow
　　While it rang onward like a trumpet-blast　　　570
　　Of keen reveillé crying: NIGHT IS PAST!
AROUSE YE DREAMERS, TO THE DAY AND FOE!

The stars for ever sweep through space, surrounding
  Their sun-kings and God's central hidden Throne
With splendour and deep music far-resounding,   575
  Though heard by pure celestial ears alone:
Their music chants His lofty praise for ever,
  Their splendours burn to Him—the Light Divine;
In their grand uneager motions pausing never,
  They live and sing and shine.   580

Eternally they sweep on their vast courses,
  With solemn joy fulfilling His behest;
While the balance of stupendous counter-forces
  Buildeth up a stable Infinite of rest.
And the Æther, breathing life through vast pulsations,   585
  Thrills with rapture to their God-supported flight;
And its waves against the rushing constellations
  Break in the foam called light.

Each world-sphere groweth grandly through the ages
  From its lifeless weltering unsubstantial birth,   590
Through unnumbered fiery throes and cyclic stages
  Till it shines in heaven a life-abounding earth;
Till its vapours are green fields and glorious oceans,
  Till with countless living beings it is rife:
By harmony constraining dread commotions   595
  It is crowned and thronged with life.

Until conscious, doubting, worshipping Immortals,
  As they journey on their infinite Life-way,
Passing through its Birth and Death mysterious portals
  Inform with spirit-fire the clothing clay: 600
And the dead, spectral, consciousless Material
  Is a dwelling-place for essences divine;
Throbs with thought and passion deathlessly ethereal,
  A Heaven-honoured shrine.

All spirits from their infancy's bland sleeping   605
  Must struggle to a strong and noble prime
Through sins, dangers, anguish, terrors,—ever reaping
  Costly fruits in every season of swift Time:
From their fountain in its deepest dark foundation,
  Glory-shrouded in the shadow of God's Throne,   610
Through all worlds to their highest-soaring station
  By unrest all have grown.

Life *is* only by perpetual on-flowing;
  Torpid rest is the true life-devouring death;
Through stern struggles all things ever are upgrowing;   615

Sighs and moanings prove a vital-throbbing breath.
One alone—Eternal, Infinite, All-holy,
Is in changeless rest; the Perfect grows nor grew:
Finite souls and all things live by progress solely,
All *are* but what they *do*. 620

Part IV

THE RETURN

I

Long tranquil days one more than seven
    The beamless sun from out the main
Went burning through the vault of heaven,
    And circled to the deep again:
While day by day in dreamful ease 5
We glided o'er the glistening seas.

Long calm autumnal nights just seven
    The moon with all her starry train
Went shining through the vault of heaven,
    And circled to the deep again: 10
While night by night in dreamful ease
We glided o'er the glimmering seas.

Long days so rich in rest, so still;
    As warm as love, as calm as truth;
Long nights which did those days fulfil, 15
    As some sweet girl a fervent youth:
While day and night in dreamful ease
We floated o'er the silent seas.

Time set within his circled sky
    A topaz sun, a diamond moon, 20
And thick star-pearls, and made thereby
    A marriage-ring of blissful boon;
With which in ever-dreamful ease
We floated o'er the happy seas.

Did Nature sleep, and dream in sleep 25
    Of all the Spring and Summer toil
Her children were about to reap—
    The wealth of corn and wine and oil:
As day and night in dreamful ease
We floated o'er the sleeping seas? 30

Or was it her deep-thoughted mood;
    A little sad, such loss had been;

  And grieved, the dear Past seemed so good;
  Yet proud, triumphant and serene:
  As day and night in dreamful ease
  We floated o'er the solemn seas?

  I lay in one long trance of rest
   And contemplation,—free from thought
  Of Future issue, worst or best,
   To be from Past and Present wrought:
  While day and night in dreamful ease
  We glided o'er the trancèd seas.

II

Before me, in the drowsy night outspread,
The City whence in anguish I had fled
  A vast dark Shadow loomed:
  So still, so black it gloomed,
It seemed the darkness of a great abyss
  Gulfed in a desert bare;
  Around whose precipice
Dim lamps burnt yellow in the vacant air,
Lifted on high portentous. Yet to me
Its dark suggestions were of Life, not Death;
Its awful mass of life oppressed my soul:
The very air appeared no longer free,
But dense and sultry in the close control
Of such a mighty cloud of human breath.
The shapeless houses and the monstrous ships
Were brooding thunderclouds that could eclipse
  The burning sun of day;
Surcharged with storms of such electric life,
Keen as the lightning to its chosen prey,
Curbless and dreadful when aroused to strife. . .
Who once has gazed upon the face of Death
Confounds no more its calm with calmest Sleep;
The terror of that beauty shadoweth
His spirit with an influence too deep.

III

And while I gazed upon the sleeping City,
And pondered its unnumbered destinies,
A flood of awe and fear, and love and pity
Swelled in my heart and overflowed my eyes
  With unexpected tears.
The burden of the message I had brought
From that great City far across the Sea
Lay heavy on my soul; as if for years

THE RETURN

And years I had been wandering wearily 75
In travail with it: now the time was spent;
Now, as a cloud with fire and thunder fraught,
I must give birth with throes of agony,
And perish in the bearing. So I leant
Back in the boat, all desolate and distraught, 80
Pangs shuddering through the faintness of cold fears:
Death passed his hand across my brow; but went
To lay its plenary pressure on some heart
That throbbed true life—'for this poor pulse,' thought he,
'Is not worth quelling'—Him I watched depart 85
Bearing all peace with him; when suddenly
That Spirit which will never be withstood
Came down, and shook and seized and lifted me,—
As men uplift a passive instrument
Through which to breathe whatever fits their mood, 90
Stately triumphal march or war-note dread,
Anthem, gay dance, or requiem for the dead:
And through my lips with irrepressible might
Poured forth its own stern language on the night.

IV

'Haughty and wealthy and great, mighty, magnificent, free, 95
Empress in thine own right of the earth-surrounding sea!
Broad and deep flows the river that feedeth thy mighty heart,
Bringing from all the zones to crowd thine imperial mart
Of all their produce the best—their silks, their gems, their gold,
Their fruits and corn and wine, their luxuries thousand-fold: 100
Thy merchants are palaced princes, thy nobles scorn great kings,
Thy meanest children swell with pride beneath thy shadowing wings;
And thy voice throughout the world, complacently serene,
Proclaims "Of all my Sisters, I am the rightful Queen!
This one is blind, this deaf, and that other is but a mute; 105
This one is fair indeed, but drunken and dissolute;
This is a very slave, dishonourèd long ago;
This one is dying of age, that other of want and woe;
This one is proud and great, but a heathen in her soul,
And subject to fatal frenzies, raging beyond control: 110
But I, I am rich and strong, I am wise and good and free;
Thronèd above them, Empress sole of the earth-surrounding Sea!"

'Yes, indeed thy power is great, but thy evil is great no less,
And thy wealth is poor to pay the debt of thy guiltiness;
And the world is judged with justice, and thou must pass 115
through that fire

Which hath tested so sternly the glitter of Venice and Carthage
   and Tyre:
For no wealth can bribe away the doom of the Living God,
No haughtiest strength confront the sway of His chastening rod.
Repent, reform, or perish! the Ages cry unto thee:
Listen, oh listen, ere yet it be late, thou swarthy Queen of the   120
   Sea!

'Thy heritage vast and rich is ample to clothe and feed
The whole of thy millions of children beyond all real need;
One of the two main wheels whereon thy Faith doth move
Is that each as he loves himself so shall he his neighbour love:
But thy chief social laws seem strictly framed to secure   125
That one be corruptingly rich, another bitterly poor,
And another just starving to death: thy fanes and mansions
   proud
Are beleaguered with filthy hovels wherein poor wretches
   crowd,
Pining in body and soul; untaught, unfed by those
Who are good if they merely dribble bland alms upon fatal   130
   woes—
Resigning scarcely aught of their pleasure and pride and
   content,
Nor dreaming that all their life is one huge embezzlement.

'The sumptuous web of thy trade encompassing all the globe
Is fretted by gambling greed like a moth-eaten robe,
Is slimed by creeping fraud, is poisoned by falsehood's breath,   135
Is less a garment of life than a shroud of rotting death.

'The mass of thy rulers live with scarcely one noble aim,
Scarcely one clear desire for a not inglorious fame;
"Slaves to a prudence base", idolaters unto Might,
Jailors of lofty zeal, infidels to pure Right,   140
Deaf to the holy voice of the Conscience of the World,
Blind to the banner of God when it floats in the storm unfurled;
They, and with them the array of thine actual Priesthood, thy
   proud
And numberless Father-confessors—ineffable crowd
Of scribes who by day and by night, unceasingly blatant,   145
   dictate
Thine every move in the contest with Time the Servant of Fate.

'Thy flaring streets each night affront the patient skies
With an holocaust of woes, sins, lusts and blasphemies;
When thy thousands of harlots abroad with the other thousands
   are met
Of those who made them first and who keep them harlots yet: 150

So dreadful, that thou thyself must sometimes look for the fire
That rained from heaven on Sodom to make thee one funeral
    pyre.

'Thy Church has long been becoming the Fossil of a Faith;
The Form of dry bones thou hast, but where are the blood and
    breath?
Dry bones, that seem a whole, with dead sinews binding the
    parts,
Inert save when bejuggled to ghastly galvanic starts:
Though thou swearest to thy people, "The King is but sick,
    not dead"—
Gaining the time while you choose you another in His stead;
Though thy scribes and thy placemen all, most of whom know
    the fact,
Vouchsafe in His name to write, pretend by His will to act:
Where are the signs of His life?—While living He never ceased
To thrill with the breath of His being thy realm from the West
    to the East;
While He lived He fought with sin, with fleshly lust and pride;
While He lived His poor and mean were wealthy and dignified;
While He lived His reign was freedom, faith, chastity, peace
    and love;
And the symbol borne on His banner was not the raven but
    dove;
While He lived there yawned a Hell with a Devil for His foes,
And a God-ruled Heaven of triumph before His followers rose;
While He lived the noblest of men were wholly devoted to Him,
The saints, the bards, the heroes, in soul and mind and limb,—
Who now without a Leader, mournful in silence wait,
Girding each one himself to his lonely fight with Fate.

'But thou, O Queen, art false: a liar, if He is dead
And becoming a mammoth fossil whose æon is wholly sped;
A traitor if still He lives and shall for ever reign,
For thou spurnest the laws most sacred of all He doth ordain,
Should Christ come now from Heaven, to reap the harvest sown
When He buried Himself in the earth, watered with blood of
    His own,
How many Christians indeed could He gather with strictest
    care
From thy two hundred myriads who claim in Him a share?
He agonised to save thee and thy children all;
And He saveth scarcely enough to delay thy deadly fall.

'For fall thou wilt, thou must, so proud as thy state is now,
Thou and thy sisters all, scarce better or worse than thou,
If ye do not all repent, and cleanse each one her heart

From the foulness circling with its blood to poison every part.
Woe to thy pampered rich in their arrogant selfishness;
Woe to thy brute-like poor who feel but their bread-distress;
Woe to thy people who dare not live without hope of wealth,
Who look but to fruits of the earth for their life and saving   190
    health;
Woe to thy rulers who rule for the good of themselves alone,
Fathers who give their children crying for bread a stone;
Woe to thy mighty men whose strength is unused or sold;
Thy sages who shut their eyes when Truth is stern to behold;
Woe to thy prophets who smile Peace, Peace, when it is a   195
    sword;
Thy poets who sing their own lusts instead of hymns of the
    Lord;
Thy preachers who preach the life of what they feel to be death;
Thy sophists who sail wild seas without the compass of faith;
Thy traders trading in lies and in human bodies and souls;
Thy good men cursing those better who strive on to loftier   200
    goals:—
The final Doom evolveth, burdened with woe on woe,
Sure as the justice of God while yet by His patience slow:
For the earth is pervaded wholly, through densest stone and
    clod,
With the burning fire of the law of the Truth of the Living God;
Consuming the falsehood, the evil, the pride, the lust, the   205
    shame,
With ever-burning, unrelenting, irresistible flame;
Until all save the purest spirit, eternal, of truth and love,
Be altogether consumed away, beneath as well as above.'

A CHANT

'WHILE the trees grow,
While the streams flow,
While the winds blow,
    We will be free:
Free as trees growing,
Free as streams flowing,
Free as winds blowing,
    Evermore free.'

LINES ON HIS TWENTY-THIRD BIRTHDAY

LAST evening's huge lax clouds of turbid white
    Grew dark and louring, burthened with the rain
Which that long wind monotonous all night
    Swept clashing loud through Dreamland's still domain,

LINES ON HIS TWENTY-THIRD BIRTHDAY

Until my spirit in fatigue's despite
   Was driven to weary wakefulness again:
With such wild dirge and ceaseless streaming tears
Died out the last of all my ill-used years.

The morn has risen pure and fresh and keen;
   Its perfect vault of bright blue heaven spreads bare
Above the earth's wide laughter twinkling green.
   The sun, long climbing up with lurid glare
Athwart the storm-rack's rent and hurrying screen,
   Leapt forth at dawn to breathe this stainless air;
The strong west wind still streams on full and high,
Inspiring fresher life through earth and sky.

Yon hazeless river flashes silver signs
   Of where it flows; how delicate and clear
The distant hills curve far their grey-blue lines,
   Steadfast amidst the rushing atmosphere:
With every blade distinct the green grass shines,
   Untouched by frost; those old trees dark or sere,
Swaying and soughing in the lifeful dawn,
Have every leaf and twig distinctly drawn.

This day my own particular year has birth;
   The general year is very old to-day:
Yet, with what healthful life o'er heaven and earth
   The death-bound monarch holdeth steadfast sway!
Not too austere for much of hearty mirth
   And energetic pleasure, nor so grey
But that he still can deck himself with flowers;—
Would that like his could be my dying hours!

Still dew-pearled fuchsias shine like pendent gems,
   While some lie purely on the deep-dark mould
Beneath their glossy leaves and ruddy stems;
   The thick chrysanthemums range white and cold;
Of all its wealth of marvellous anadems,
   That gleamed amidst their fruits of orange gold
Glowing red-hearted in the Autumn sun,
The passion-flower has still for me kept one.

I pace the garden in this genial morn,
   And meditate the dirge of my dead year,—
With even less of grief than sharp self-scorn.
   The retrospect in truth brings little cheer;
As if of one long-tired, who stares forlorn
   Across flat marshland, barren, gloomy, drear;
Where fields, nor home, nor church, his vision greet
Which he has toiled through with unsteady feet.

LINES ON HIS TWENTY-THIRD BIRTHDAY

He turns; before him, as behind, all round
    The pathless waste outstretches flat and bare; 50
From sullen pools amidst the dark heath-ground
    Frogs jar their croakings through the murky air,
Which up that vault of solid sky stone-bound
    Heaves huge dense glooms to shut on his despair.
Let him crawl on as he has crawled all day, 55
Till Night comes down upon his homeless way.

My golden morning hours, which should have brought
    Strength, wisdom, faith and love, or hope of all,
Have sunk and dribbled while I heeded not
    Into the slush of sloth beyond recall. 60
O nerveless hands, O brain of aimless thought,
    O slow dim eyes that never marked their fall—
Absorbed in dreams both waking and asleep
Our golden hours for ever lost, now weep.

All lost for ever! and the hours to come, 65
    Poor refuse! but our sole remaining wealth,
So much the likelier thence to share their doom!
    The brain unused to mark insidious stealth,
Short-sighted eyes long filled with mist and gloom,
    Lax hands uncustomed to the grasp of health, 70
That lost the fight in their best youth,—shall these
Victorious prove in languor and disease?

Oh, for the flushed excitement of keen strife!
    For mountains, gulfs and torrents in my way,
With peril, anguish, fear and strugglings rife! 75
    For friends and foes, for love and hate in fray,—
And not this lone base flat of torpid life!
    I fret 'neath gnat-stings, an ignoble prey,
While others with a sword-hilt in their grasp
Have warm rich blood to feed their latest gasp. 80

Wrathful and dangerous, restless, free, profound,
    With fair green islands shining o'er its verge,
The Sea of Life there heaves and roars around.
    To pierce its depths, to throb against its surge,
Breasting to gain the Happy Isles!—if drowned, 85
    The loser pays; he fought his game; no dirge!
But to be whelmed in torpor at the last,
As one with this dead crag which holds me fast!

Flushed grapes, full-charged with life's delirious wine,
    Brush my wan temples, hanging thick about: 90
Chained fast I cannot reach them, while I pine

To press their very inmost rapture out,
Flooding with fire these dust-dry lips of mine;
  Better wild drunkenness than hectic drought:
And torture breeds new tortures, in the dread
That ere they fall my power to drink be dead.

The prisoner loses other years than yearn
  Within the lifeless dungeon crusht and pent:
Late freedom frees dead ashes from their urn;
  His torture has become his element.
This Bride of Life for whom I waiting burn
  May grow a withered hag ere she relent,
Herself refused then; or our worn-out eld
In bridal chimings have its funeral knelled.

O pure West wind, strong life-breath of the day,
  Inspire my wasted heart with strength and hope!
Sweep thou its grievous doubts and fears away,
  Who swept far-scattering down the eastern slope
The brooding rain-clouds massed in dense array
  Till this green earth shone laughing to the cope
Of this pure heaven, whose naked form austere
Yet genial glows with sunshine warm and clear.

I hope, I feel that I can yet break free
  From this accursèd cage wherein I pine;
There comes a vision of the sounding sea,
  The all-sustaining, all-intombing brine:
Through want and peril, wretchedness and glee,
  Wrestling with lives more coarse and strong than mine,
I yet may woo its love and dare its strife;
By self-dependence earning careless life.

And so attaining strength! The crazy ship,
  Frigate or bumboat, slaver, mission ark,
Shall surely in the first squall heel and dip;
  The strong may hope to sail its voyage: and, mark,—
What of the ends, means, issues of its trip
  Knows holy vessel or Brazilian barque?
Through storm and calm it does its best to float;
For what? He knows who steers and rules the boat.

So much more strength, so much more life, I say;
  So much more love and thought, more soul and sense:
We pare our members bit by bit away,
  Because they're damning us with foul offence:
Cowards! be strong and force them to obey!
  Is virtue but a eunuch's continence?

Napoleon, ev'n, seems nobler than such saint 135
As eighteen centuries have learned to paint.

Thus Hope is born,—pale birth of grim Despair.
   Whether the Father shall his child devour,
Or this poor Babe, maturing strong and fair,
   Shall dispossess the parent of his power, 140
I know not: yet I think that I could dare
   A death-stern struggle with the fiercest hour,
Would foolish Wisdom's whirls of dreary thought
But leave my doubt-vexed spirit undistraught.

Meanwhile, then, let me wait and hope, and learn 145
   To curb with galling steel and ruthless hand
These strong and passionate impulses that burn
   To sweep me from my post of self-command,
Into the battle raging thick and stern,
   Into the desert's freedom vast and grand: 150
That horseman proves full strength, firm skill indeed,
Who holdeth statue-calm his savage steed.

A RECUSANT

The Church stands there beyond the orchard-blooms:
   How yearningly I gaze upon its spire!
Lifted mysterious through the twilight glooms,
   Dissolving in the sunset's golden fire,
Or dim as slender incense morn by morn 5
   Ascending to the blue and open sky.
For ever when my heart feels most forlorn
   It murmurs to me with a weary sigh,
How sweet to enter in, to kneel and pray
   With all the others whom we love so well! 10
All disbelief and doubt might pass away,
   All peace float to us with its Sabbath bell.
Conscience replies, There is but one good rest,
Whose head is pillowed upon Truth's pure breast.

THE LORD OF THE CASTLE OF INDOLENCE

Nor did we lack our own right royal king,
   The glory of our peaceful realm and race.
By no long years of restless travailing,
   By no fierce wars or intrigues bland and base,
   Did he attain his superlofty place; 5
But one fair day he lounging to the throne
   Reclined thereon with such possessing grace

That all could see it was in sooth his own,
That it for him was fit and he for it alone.

He there reclined as lilies on a river,
   All cool in sunfire, float in buoyant rest;
He stirred as flowers that in the sweet south quiver;
   He moved as swans move on a lake's calm breast,
   Or clouds slow gliding in the golden west;
He thought as birds may think when 'mid the trees
   Their joy showers music o'er the brood-filled nest;
He swayed us all with ever placid ease
As sways the thronèd moon her world-wide wandering seas.

Look, as within some fair and princely hall
   The marble statue of a god may rest,
Admired in silent reverence by all;
   Soothing the weary brain and anguished breast,
   By life's sore burthens all-too-much oppressed,
With visions of tranquillity supreme;
   So, self-sufficing, grand and bland and blest,
He dwelt enthroned, and whoso gazed did seem
Endowed with death-calm life in long unwistful dream.

While others fumed and schemed and toiled in vain
   To mould the world according to their mood,
He did by might of perfect faith refrain
   From any part in such disturbance rude.
   The world, he said, indeed is very good,
Its Maker surely wiser far than we;
   Feed soul and flesh upon its bounteous food,
Nor fret because of ill; All-good is He,
And worketh not in years but in Eternity.

How men will strain to row against the tide,
   Which yet must sweep them down in its career!
Or if some win their way and crown their pride,
   What do they win? the desert wild and drear,
   The savage rocks, the icy wastes austere,
Wherefrom the river's turbid rills downflow:
   But he upon the waters broad and clear,
In harmony with all the winds that blow,
'Mid cities, fields and farms, went drifting to and fro.

The king with constant heed must rule his realm,
   The soldier faint and starve in marches long,
The sailor guide with sleepless care his helm,
   The poet from sick languors soar in song:
   But he alone amidst the troubled throng

THE LORD OF THE CASTLE OF INDOLENCE

In restful ease diffused beneficence;
   Most like a mid-year noontide rich and strong,
That fills the earth with fruitful life intense,
And yet doth trance it all in sweetest indolence.

When summer reigns the joyous leaves and flowers 55
   Steal imperceptibly upon the tree;
So stole upon him all his bounteous hours,
   So passive to their influence seemed he,
   So clothed they him with joy and majesty;
Basking in ripest summer all his time, 60
   We blessed his shade and sang him songs of glee;
The dew and sunbeams fed his perfect prime,
And rooted broad and deep he broadly towered sublime.

Thus could he laugh those great and generous laughs
   Which made us love ourselves, the world, and him; 65
And while they rang we felt as one who quaffs
   Some potent wine-cup dowered to the brim,
   And straightway all things seem to reel and swim,—
Suns, moons, earth, stars sweep through the vast profound,
   Wrapt in a golden mist-light warm and dim, 70
Rolled in a volume of triumphant sound;
So in that laughter's joy the whole world carolled round.

The sea, the sky, wood, mountain, stream and plain,
   Our whole fair world did serve him and adorn,
Most like some casual robe which he might deign 75
   To use when kinglier vesture was not worn.
   Was all its being by his soul upborne,
That it should render homage so complete?
   The day and night, the even and the morn,
Seemed ever circling grateful round his feet, 80
'With Thee, through Thee we live this rich life pure and
      sweet!'

For while he loved our broad world beautiful,
   His placid wisdom penetrated it,
And found the lovely words but poor and dull
   Beside the secret splendours they transmit, 85
   The Heavenly things in earthly symbols writ:
He knew the blood-red sweetness of the vine,
   Yet did not therefore at the revel sit;
But straining out the very wine of wine,
Lived calm and pure and glad in drunkenness divine. 90

Without an effort the imperial sun
   With ever ample life of light doth feed

The spheres revolving round it every one:
  So all his heart and soul and thought and deed
  Flowed freely forth for every brother's need;   95
He knew no difference between good and ill,
  But as the sun doth nourish flower and weed
With self-same bounty, he too ever still
Lived blessing all alike with equal loving will.

The all-bestowing sun is clothed with splendour,   100
  The all-supporting sun doth reign supreme;
So must eternal justice ever render
  Each unsought payment to its last extreme:
  Thus he most rich in others' joy did seem,
And reigned by servitude all-effortless;   105
  For heaven and earth must vanish like a dream
Ere such a soul divine can know distress,
Whom all the laws of Life conspire to love and bless.

A REAL VISION OF SIN

Like a soaking blanket overhead
Spongy and lax the sky was spread,
Opaque as the eye of a fish long dead.

Like trees in a drawing gummed together
Some trees stood dim in the drizzling weather;   5
Sweating mere blood-flowers gloomed the heather.

Like a festering gash left gaping wide
That foul canal, long swooned from tide,
The marshy moorland did divide.

In a slushy hollow near its bank,   10
Where noisome weeds grew thick and dank,
And the very soil like an old corpse stank,

They cowered together, the man and crone,
Two old bags of carious bone;
They and a mangy cur alone: 15

Ragged, haggard, filthy, both;
Viewing each the other loath;
Growling now and then an oath.

She at length with a spasm raised
Her strong grey eyes, still strong tho' glazed;   20
And thus her meditations phrased:

'No mite left of all our treasure;
Sin itself has no more pleasure:
Drained out, drained out, our full measure!'

He quavered back: 'It does seem so:
The sun 'e died out long ago;
The earth and the sky are a-rottin' slow?'

She writhed her thick brows, dirty grey:
'Then take at once my easy way
Of swamping misery from our clay.

'No trembling, dear red-rat-eyes! Come!
We slip together through that green scum,
And then with the world here rot on dumb.'

He sat still, nipping spiteful blows
On the snarling cur's amorphous nose;
Relishing faintly her propose.

'Well *you* look lovely, so you do,
To call *me* names: a-drownin' you
Would go to spoil this pleasant view!

'This 'ere damned life is bad enough;
But, say we smother in that stuff,
Our next life's only worse, you muff!'

The woman thereto coldly sneered:
'Of course, as usual all afeared,
Old slaver-dewy stubble-beard.

'Idiot and coward! hell-flames feed
On certain fuel; but, indeed,
A used-up soul won't sate their greed.

'When Earth once gets us cold and stark
She'll keep us safely in the dark:
No fear of rousing with the lark!

'Full long ago in grim despair,
She growled, *How those two witch-fires flare!
They'll get no second chance I swear!*'

She laught this truth out 'gainst the man;
Who shuffling, ill at ease, began:
'You can be devilish sore, you can.

'Suppose you're right; this life's a one
That's cursèd bad, but better than none. . . .
I wish they'd light another Sun.

'We used to spree and we don't spree now;
A screw is loose in the world, allow,
We didn't make it, anyhow.

'Say Life's hard-up, No-life's more glum:
Just think—a lashing lot of rum,
And a night with you and a cool old chum!'

She fingered a toad from its love-work sweet,
And flung to the cur with a 'Mangy, eat;
They say there's poison in the meat;

'And so the next time you bite this dear
He'll die off mad; for else I fear
He'd fester for ever and ever here.'

Its loose fangs squashed through the nectarous lump;
Then it went and crouched on a doddered stump,
With an evil eye on the Male Sin's hump.

He blinked and shuffled and swore and groaned:
Rasping the bristly beard she owned,
She thought drear thoughts until she too moaned.

'I see the truth,' with a scornful laugh,
'I have starved abroad on the swine-fouled draff,
While sleek at home sucked the fatt'ning calf.

'Too late, too late! Yet it's good to see,
If only damnation, thoroughly;
My Life has never met with me.

'And *you*, you never loved me, *you!*
A heart that never once beat true,
How could it love? I loved for two.

'This dirty crumpled rag of a breast
Was globed with milk once; I possest
The means of being grandly blest!

'Did the babe of mine suck luscious sips,
Soothing the nipple with rose-soft lips
While her eyes drooped mild in a dear eclipse?

'A babe!—could I now squeeze out three drops
Between that poor cur's ulcerous chaps,   95
He'd die as livid as yon tree-tops.

'You know where it rests, that child-dream gone?
Come, grope in this charming water-lawn,
Through ooze and slime and filth and spawn:

'Perhaps we shall find a shudderous feel,   100
Neither of eft, nor toad, nor eel;
May hear a long long stifled squeal:

'Touch the rotten bones of a murdered brat
Whose flesh was daynt to the water-rat,—
If it *does* gnaw flesh, it would relish that!'   105

He ventured, 'Curse all memory!
It's more than thirty years:' but she
Continued fierce, unheedingly.

'Come, and this loathsome life out-smother,
No fear that we'll ever have another: 110
The rain may beat and the wind may wuther,

'But we shall rot with the rotting soil,
Safe in sleep from the whole sad coil;
Sleep's better than corn and wine and oil.

'Here's a kiss; now at once!' effused the witch,   115
And dragged the wildered male to the ditch,
And plunged there prone by a bladdery bitch.

Drowned dead, stone dead . . . and still her grasp
Clawed *him:* but with a frenzied gasp
He shuddered off the scranny clasp.   120

Up the soddened bank in a fury of funk
He sprawled: 'She's awful! but she's sunk;
I daren't die except dead drunk.'

He managed at length the hollow to win;
And was gulping down with a pang-writhed grin   125
The black bottle's last of vitriol gin,

When his gorge was choked by a sudden blight:
The cur growled mad with venom and fright,
And its blotches of hair all bristled upright.

Its frenzy burst out in a wolfish yell;
It leapt at his throat like an imp of hell;
In a spasm of horror the bottle fell:

It griped up his flaccid throat with a force
That made his terrorment gurgle hoarse,
While he turned as blue as a cholera-corse.

It haled him into the festering dike;
So all sank dead in its clam alike,—
The Man, the Woman, the virtuous Tyke.

And the dense rain crooned in its sullen flow
From the sodden sky-stretch drooping low
To the sodden earth; and to and fro

Crept a maundering wind too weak to blow;
And the dim world murmured dismal woe:
For the earth and the sky *were* a-rotting slow.

MATER TENEBRARUM

In the endless nights, from my bed, where sleepless in anguish I lie,
I startle the stillness and gloom with a bitter and strong cry:
O Love! O Belovèd long lost! come down from thy Heaven above,
For my heart is wasting and dying in uttermost famine for love!
Come down for a moment! oh, come! Come serious and mild
And pale, as thou wert on this earth, thou adorable Child!
Or come as thou art, with thy sanctitude, triumph and bliss,
For a garment of glory about thee; and give me one kiss,
One tender and pitying look of thy tenderest eyes,
One word of solemn assurance and truth that the soul with its love never dies!

In the endless nights, from my bed, where sleepless in frenzy I lie,
I cleave through the crushing gloom with a bitter and deadly cry:
Oh! where have they taken my Love from our Eden of bliss on this earth,
Which now is a frozen waste of sepulchral and horrible dearth?
Have they killed her indeed? is her soul as her body, which long
Has mouldered away in the dust where the foul worms throng?
O'er what abhorrent Lethes, to what remotest star

Is she rapt away from my pursuit through cycles and systems far?
She is dead, she is utterly dead; for her life would hear and speed
To the wild imploring cry of my heart, that cries in its dreadful need. 20

In the endless nights, on my bed, where sleeplessly brooding I lie,
I burden the heavy gloom with a bitter and weary sigh:
No hope in this worn-out world, no hope beyond the tomb;
No living and loving God, but blind and stony Doom.
Anguish and grief and sin, terror, disease and despair: 25
Why throw not off this life, this garment of torture I wear,
And go down to sleep in the grave in everlasting rest?
What keeps me yet in this life, what spark in my frozen breast?
A fire of dread, a light of hope, kindled, O Love, by thee;
For thy pure and gentle and beautiful soul, it must immortal be. 30

THE 'MELENCOLIA' OF ALBRECHT DÜRER

She sits, a Woman like a Titaness:
    Her clench't left hand, the elbow on its knee,
Supports her cheek with concentrative stress;
    The unremembered right unconsciously
Still holds the sphere-describing compasses; 5
    And strown about the narrow floor we see
The instruments with which she lately wrought
To carve material symbols of her thought.

But, Oh, the stern, strong, swarthy countenance!
    Oh, the intensely fixt sole-thoughted eyes 10
Gazing athwart the sullen sea's expanse,
    Wherein the sun is drowning from the skies!
A Sphynx thus gazes in eternal trance
    Athwart the desert's gloomy mysteries,
Thus images a soul beyond the scope 15
Of all fond frailties of fear and hope.

A bat is floating in the waste of air,
    Its uncouth wings outspread to spread the scroll
Whereon—perchance imprinted by the glare
    Of those fierce eyes instinct with fiery soul— 20
One word is legible; one word, yet ne'er
    In volume heaped on volume was the whole
Of any nature more completely writ:
This 'Melencolia' comprehends all wit.

  Lo! she has set herself with fierce intent 25
    Of never-quailing will and desperate pride,
  Alike unloving and unreverent,
    To clutch the inmost mysteries that hide
  In Nature's being and God's government;
    And she has found but Fate—God petrified— 30
  And not a single word or sign can wring
    From the tremendous, dumb, blind, crushing **Thing**.

  Therefore she sits thus sternly desolate;
    Therefore the fruitless thoughts that vex her brain
  Have blossomed outwardly to mock her state 35
    With such a fragile wreath adust and vain;
  Therefore the hopeless consciousness of Fate
    Imprisoning her soul is pictured plain
  In the metallic polished rigidness
    Of the voluminous indented dress. 40

  Those compasses could measure out no arc
    Concentric with the measureless round sweep
  Of Heaven and Earth; that globe was ever dark
    And could not mirror in its crystal sleep
  One vision of the secret powers which mark 45
    (Working mysterious in the central deep)
  Time's progress on the world's broad **dial-face**
  With grand unlingering, unhurrying pace.

SONNET

THROUGH foulest fogs of my own sluggish soul,
  Through midnight glooms of all the wide world's guilt,
Through sulphurous cannon-clouds that surge and roll
  Above the steam of blood in anger spilt;
Through all the sombre earth-oppressing piles 5
  Of old cathedral temples which expand
Sepulchral vaults and monumental aisles,
  Hopeless and freezing in the lifeful land;
I gaze and seek with ever-longing eyes
  For God, the Love-Supreme, all-wise, all-good: 10
Alas! in vain; for over all the skies
  A dark and awful shadow seems to brood,
A numbing, infinite, eternal gloom:
I tremble in the consciousness of Doom.

TO OUR LADIES OF DEATH[1]

'Tired with all these, for restful death I cry.'
SHAKESPEARE: *Sonnet* 66.

WEARY of erring in this desert Life,
    Weary of hoping hopes for ever vain,
Weary of struggling in all-sterile strife,
    Weary of thought which maketh nothing plain,
I close my eyes and calm my panting breath,   5
And pray to Thee, O ever-quiet Death!
    To come and soothe away my bitter pain.

The strong shall strive,—may they be victors crowned;
    The wise still seek,—may they at length find Truth;
The young still hope,—may purest love be found   10
    To make their age more glorious than their youth.
For me; my brain is weak, my heart is cold,
My hope and faith long dead; my life but bold
    In jest and laugh to parry hateful ruth.

Over me pass the days and months and years   15
    Like squadrons and battalions of the foe
Trampling with thoughtless thrusts and alien jeers
    Over a wounded soldier lying low:
He grips his teeth, or flings them words of scorn
To mar their triumph: but the while, outworn,   20
    Inwardly craves for death to end his woe.

Thus I, in secret, call, O Death! to Thee,
    Thou Youngest of the solemn Sisterhood,
Thou Gentlest of the mighty Sisters Three
    Whom I have known so well since first endued   25
By Love and Grief with vision to discern
What spiritual life doth throb and burn
    Through all our world, with evil powers and good.

The Three whom I have known so long, so well,
    By intimate communion, face to face,   30
In every mood, of Earth, of Heaven, of Hell,
    In every season and in every place,
That joy of Life has ceased to visit me,
As one estranged by powerful witchery,
    Infatuate in a Siren's weird embrace.   35

---

[1] The Three Ladies suggested by the sublime sisterhood of Our Ladies of Sorrow, in the 'Suspiria de Profundis' of De Quincey.

First Thou, O priestess, prophetess, and queen,
  Our Lady of Beatitudes, first Thou:
Of mighty stature, of seraphic mien,
  Upon the tablet of whose broad white brow
Unvanquishable Truth is written clear,
  The secret of the mystery of our sphere,
  The regnant word of the Eternal Now.

Thou standest garmented in purest white;
  But from thy shoulders wings of power half-spread
Invest thy form with such miraculous light
  As dawn may clothe the earth with: and, instead
Of any jewel-kindled golden crown,
The glory of thy long hair flowing down
  Is dazzling noonday sunshine round thy head.

Upon a sword thy left hand resteth calm,
  A naked sword, two-edged and long and straight;
A branch of olive with a branch of palm
  Thy right hand proffereth to hostile Fate.
The shining plumes that clothe thy feet are bound
By knotted strings, as if to tread the ground
  With weary steps when thou wouldst soar elate.

Twin heavens uplifted to the heavens, thine eyes
  Are solemn with unutterable thought
And love and aspiration; yet there lies
  Within their light eternal sadness, wrought
By hope deferred and baffled tenderness:
Of all the souls whom thou dost love and bless,
  How few revere and love thee as they ought!

Thou leadest heroes from their warfare here
  To nobler fields where grander crowns are won;
Thou leadest sages from this twilight sphere
  To cloudless heavens and an unsetting sun;
Thou leadest saints into that purer air
Whose breath is spiritual life and prayer:
  Yet, lo! they seek thee not, but fear and shun!

Thou takest to thy most maternal breast
  Young children from the desert of this earth,
Ere sin hath stained their souls, or grief opprest,
  And bearest them unto an heavenly birth,
To be the Vestals of God's Fane above:
And yet their kindred moan against thy love,
  With wild and selfish moans in bitter dearth.

Most holy Spirit, first Self-conqueror;
  Thou Victress over Time and Destiny
And Evil, in the all-deciding war   80
  So fierce, so long, so dreadful!—Would that me
Thou hadst upgathered in my life's pure morn!
Unworthy then, less worthy now, forlorn,
  I dare not, Gracious Mother, call on Thee.

Next Thou, O sibyl, sorceress and queen,   85
  Our Lady of Annihilation, Thou!
Of mighty stature, of demoniac mien;
  Upon whose swarthy face and livid brow
Are graven deeply anguish, malice, scorn,
Strength ravaged by unrest, resolve forlorn   90
  Of any hope, dazed pride that will not bow.

Thy form is clothed with wings of iron gloom;
  But round about thee, like a chain, is rolled,
Cramping the sway of every mighty plume,
  A stark constringent serpent fold on fold: 95
Of its two heads, one sting is in thy brain,
The other in thy heart; their venom-pain
  Like fire distilling through thee uncontrolled.

A rod of serpents wieldeth thy right hand;
  Thy left a cup of raging fire, whose light   100
Burns lurid on thyself as thou dost stand;
  Thy lidless eyes tenebriously bright;
Thy wings, thy vesture, thy dishevelled hair
Dark as the Grave; thou statue of Despair,
  Thou Night essential radiating night.   105

Thus have I seen thee in thine actual form;
  Not thus can see thee those whom thou dost sway,
Inscrutable Enchantress: young and warm,
  Pard-beautiful and brilliant, ever gay;
Thy cup the very Wine of Life, thy rod   110
The wand of more voluptuous spells than God
  Can wield in Heaven; thus charmest thou thy prey.

The selfish, fatuous, proud, and pitiless,
  All who have falsified life's royal trust;
The strong whose strength hath basked in idleness,   115
  The great heart given up to worldly lust,
The great mind destitute of moral faith;
Thou scourgest down to Night and utter Death,
  Or penal spheres of retribution just.

O mighty Spirit, fraudful and malign, 120
    Demon of madness and perversity!
The evil passions which may make me thine
    Are not yet irrepressible in me;
And I have pierced thy mask of riant youth,
And seen thy form in all its hideous truth: 125
    I will not, Dreadful Mother, call on Thee.

Last Thou, retirèd nun and throneless queen,
    Our Lady of Oblivion, last Thou:
Of human stature, of abstracted mien;
    Upon whose pallid face and drooping brow 130
Are shadowed melancholy dreams of Doom,
And deep absorption into silent gloom,
    And weary bearing of the heavy Now.

Thou art all shrouded in a gauzy veil,
    Sombrous and cloudlike; all, except that face 135
Of subtle loveliness though weirdly pale.
    Thy soft, slow-gliding footsteps leave no trace,
And stir no sound. Thy drooping hands infold
Their frail white fingers; and, unconscious, hold
    A poppy-wreath, thine anodyne of grace. 140

Thy hair is like a twilight round thy head:
    Thine eyes are shadowed wells, from Lethe-stream
With drowsy subterranean waters fed;
    Obscurely deep, without a stir or gleam;
The gazer drinks in from them with his gaze 145
An opiate charm to curtain all his days,
    A passive languor of oblivious dream.

Thou hauntest twilight regions, and the trance
    Of moonless nights when stars are few and wan:
Within black woods; or over the expanse 150
    Of desert seas abysmal; or upon
Old solitary shores whose populous graves
Are rocked in rest by ever-moaning waves;
    Or through vast ruined cities still and lone.

The weak, the weary, and the desolate, 155
    The poor, the mean, the outcast, the opprest,
All trodden down beneath the march of Fate,
    Thou gatherest, loving Sister, to thy breast,
Soothing their pain and weariness asleep;
Then in thy hidden Dreamland hushed and deep 160
    Dost lay them, shrouded in eternal rest.

O sweetest Sister, and sole Patron Saint
   Of all the humble eremites who flee
From out life's crowded tumult, stunned and faint,
   To seek a stern and lone tranquillity 165
In Libyan wastes of time: my hopeless life
With famished yearning craveth rest from strife;
   Therefore, thou Restful One, I call on Thee!

Take me, and lull me into perfect sleep;
   Down, down, far-hidden in thy duskiest cave; 170
While all the clamorous years above me sweep
   Unheard, or, like the voice of seas that rave
On far-off coasts, but murmuring o'er my trance,
A dim vast monotone, that shall enhance
   The restful rapture of the inviolate grave. 175

Upgathered thus in thy divine embrace,
   Upon mine eyes thy soft mesmeric hand,
While wreaths of opiate odour interlace
   About my pulseless brow; babe-pure and bland,
Passionless, senseless, thoughtless, let me dream 180
Some ever-slumbrous, never-varying theme,
   Within the shadow of thy Timeless Land.

That when I thus have drunk my inmost fill
   Of perfect peace, I may arise renewed;
In soul and body, intellect and will, 185
   Equal to cope with Life whate'er its mood;
To sway its storm and energise its calm;
Through rhythmic years evolving like a psalm
   Of infinite love and faith and sanctitude.

But if this cannot be, no less I cry, 190
   Come, lead me with thy terrorless control
Down to our Mother's bosom, there to die
   By abdication of my separate soul:
So shall this single, self-impelling piece
Of mechanism from lone labour cease, 195
   Resolving into union with the Whole.

Our Mother feedeth thus our little life,
   That we in turn may feed her with our death:
The great Sea sways, one interwoven strife,
   Wherefrom the Sun exhales a subtle breath, 200
To float the heavens sublime in form and hue,
Then turning cold and dark in order due
   Rain weeping back to swell the Sea beneath.

One part of me shall feed a little worm,
    And it a bird on which a man may feed;
One lime the mould, one nourish insect-sperm;
    One thrill sweet grass, one pulse in bitter weed;
This swell a fruit, and that evolve in air;
Another trickle to a springlet's lair,
    Another paint a daisy on the mead:

With cosmic interchange of parts for all,
    Through all the modes of being numberless
Of every element, as may befall.
    And if earth's general soul hath consciousness,
Their new life must with strange new joy be thrilled,
Of perfect law all perfectly fulfilled;
    No sin, no fear, no failure, no excess.

Weary of living isolated life,
    Weary of hoping hopes for ever vain,
Weary of struggling in all-sterile strife,
    Weary of thought which maketh nothing plain,
I close my eyes and hush my panting breath,
And yearn for Thee, divinely tranquil Death,
    To come and soothe away my bitter pain.

TWO SONNETS

I

'Why are your songs all wild and bitter-sad
    As funeral dirges with the orphans' cries?
Each night since first the world was made hath had
    A sequent day to laugh it down the skies.
Chant us a glee to make our hearts rejoice,
    Or seal in silence this unmanly moan.'
My friend, I have no power to rule my voice:
    A spirit lifts me where I lie alone,
And thrills me into song by its own laws;
    That which I feel, but seldom know, indeed
Tempering the melody it could not cause.
    The bleeding heart cannot for ever bleed
Inwardly solely: on the wan lips too
    Dark blood will bubble ghastly into view.

II

Striving to sing glad songs, I but attain
    Wild discords sadder than Grief's saddest tune;
As if an owl with his harsh screech should strain
    To over-gratulate a thrush of June.

The nightingale upon its thorny spray 5
  Finds inspiration in the sullen dark;
The kindling dawn, the world-wide joyous day
  Are inspiration to the soaring lark;
The seas are silent in the sunny calm,
  Their anthem-surges in the tempest boom; 10
The skies outroll no solemn thunder-psalm
  Till they have clothed themselves with clouds of gloom.
My mirth can laugh and talk, but cannot sing;
My grief finds harmonies in everything.

ON GEORGE HERBERT'S POEMS

WHAT are these leaves dark-spotted and acerb?
  'A very holy *herb*.'
To what good use may I this herb convert?
  'Press it on thy soul's *hurt*.'
When *herb* unto the *hurt* I thus apply? 5
  '*Herb-ert* is sanctity.'

SIX SONNETS
TO JOSEPH AND ALICE BARNES

I

MY dear, dear Friends, my heart yearns forth to you
  In very many of its lonely hours;
Not sweetlier comes the balm of evening dew
  To all-day-drooping in fierce sunlight flowers,
Than to this weary withered heart of mine 5
  The tender memories, the moonlight dreams
Which make your home an ever-sacred shrine,
  And show your features lit with heavenly gleams.
I have with some most noble friends been blest;
  I wage no quarrel with my human kin,— 10
Knowing my misery comes from my own breast,
  At war with Fate by chance and God by sin:
But of all living friends you claim in me
The love most sanctified by memory.

II

When too, too conscious of its solitude,
  My heart plains weakly as a widowed dove,
The forms of certain women sweet and good,
  Whom I have known and loved with reverent love,
Rise up before me; then my heart grows great 5
  With tearful gratitude, and no more pines.

You lovely souls that fitly consecrate
   The whiteness of your alabaster shrines!
You tender lives of purest good, that leaven
   The monstrous evils of our mortal birth!
There are no female angels up in Heaven,
   Because they all are women here on earth:
As once God's sons, God's daughters now come down,
But these to share, not lose, the heavenly crown.

III

Of all these women fair and wise and good,
   Of all save only her who died so young,
Thou art in this angelic womanhood,
   Whose solemn praises bards have seldom sung,
Supreme to me—most lovely and most pure,
   O second Mother of my orphaned youth:
Thou patient heart to suffer and endure,
   Thou placid soul to mirror heavenly truth,
Thou gracious presence wheresoe'er you go
   To gladden pleasure, or to chasten strife,
Thou gentlest friend to sympathise with woe,
   Thou perfect Mother and most perfect Wife,
Whose priceless goodness shed on worthless me
Makes gratitude itself half agony.

IV

A man of genial heart and liberal mind,
   A man most rich in that rare common-sense,
Whose common absence in its name we find;
   A man of nature scorning all pretence,
And honest to the core, yet void of pride
   Whose vice upon that virtue most attends;
A man of joyous humour, unallied
   With malice, never making foes but friends;
As such all know you, knowing you at all:
   But I, dear Guide and Teacher of my youth,
When deeply shamed yet strengthened I recall
   Your goodness, patience, constant loyal truth
In love for one whose life's a long defeat,
Say—Souls like this keep human nature sweet.

V

When I trace back from this my death-in-life,
   Through years of sensual sin and nerveless sloth,
And weary thought with Earth and Heaven at strife,
   And dull decay preventing natural growth;—
Trace back until that period I attain

When still stirred in me living seeds of good—
Some faith in soul, some active power in brain,
   Some love in heart, some hopefulness in mood;
I always reach at last that little room
   Wherein we lived a life so sweet and mild,   10
When he who now lies sleeping in the tomb
   Was but an infant, and your only child:
The happy Child! thus saved, still pure in soul,
From our false world of sin and strife and dole.

VI

Indeed you set me in a happy place,
   Dear for itself, and dearer much for you,
And dearest still for one life-crowning grace—
   Dearest, though infinitely saddest too:
For there my own Good Angel took my hand,   5
   And filled my soul with glory of Her eyes,
And led me through the love-lit Faerie Land
   Which joins our common world to Paradise.
How soon, how soon, God called Her from my side,
   Back to Her own celestial sphere of day!   10
And ever since She ceased to be my Guide,
   I reel and stumble on Life's solemn way;
Ah, ever since Her eyes withdrew their light,
I wander lost in blackest stormy night.

THE THREE THAT SHALL BE ONE

Love on the earth alit,
Come to be Lord of it;
Looked round and laughed with glee,
Noble my empery!
Straight ere that laugh was done   5
Sprang forth the royal sun,
Pouring out golden shine
Over the realm divine.

Came then a lovely may,
Dazzling the new-born day,   10
Wreathing her golden hair
With the red roses there,
Laughing with sunny eyes
Up to the sunny skies,
Moving so light and free   15
To her own minstrelsy.

Love with swift rapture cried,
Dear Life, thou art my bride!
Whereto, with fearless pride,
Dear Love, indeed thy bride!
All the earth's fruit and flowers,
All the world's wealth are ours;
Sun, moon, and stars gem
Our marriage diadem.

So they together fare,
Lovely and joyous pair;
So hand in hand they roam
All through their Eden home;
Each to the other's sight
An ever-new delight:
Blue heaven and blooming earth
Joy in their darlings' mirth.

Who comes to meet them now,—
She with the pallid brow,
Wreathing her night-dark hair
With the red poppies there,
Pouring from solemn eyes
Gloom through the sunny skies,
Moving so silently
In her deep reverie?

Life paled as she drew near,
Love shook with doubt and fear.
Ah, then, she said, in truth
(Eyes full of yearning ruth),
Love, thou would'st have this Life,
Fair may! to be thy wife?
Yet at an awful shrine
Wert thou not plighted mine?

Pale, paler poor Life grew;
Love murmured, It is true!
How could I thee forsake?
From the brief dream I wake.
Yet, O belovèd Death,
See how *she* suffereth;
Ere we from earth depart
Soothe her, thou tender heart!

Faint on the ground she lay;
Love kissed the swoon away;

Death then bent over her,
Death the sweet comforter!
Whispered with tearful smile,
Wait but a little while,
Then I will come for thee;
We are one family.

SUNDAY AT HAMPSTEAD

AN IDLE IDYLL BY A VERY HUMBLE MEMBER OF
THE GREAT AND NOBLE LONDON MOB

I

This is the Heath of Hampstead,
There is the dome of Saint Paul's;
Beneath, on the serried house-tops,
A chequered lustre falls:

And the mighty city of London,
Under the clouds and the light,
Seems a low wet beach, half shingle,
With a few sharp rocks upright.

Here will we sit, my darling,
And dream an hour away:
The donkeys are hurried and worried,
But we are not donkeys to-day:

Though all the weary week, dear,
We toil in the murk down there,
Tied to a desk and a counter,
A patient stupid pair!

But on Sunday we slip our tether,
And away from the smoke and the smirch;
Too grateful to God for His Sabbath
To shut its hours in a church.

Away to the green, green country,
Under the open sky;
Where the earth's sweet breath is incense
And the lark sings psalms on high.

On Sunday we're Lord and Lady,
With ten times the love and glee
Of those pale and languid rich ones
Who are always and never free.

They drawl and stare and simper,
So fine and cold and staid, 30
Like exquisite waxwork figures
That must be kept in the shade:

We can laugh out loud when merry,
We can romp at kiss-in-the-ring,
We can take our beer at a public, 35
We can loll on the grass and sing. . . .

Would you grieve very much, my darling,
If all yon low wet shore
Were drowned by a mighty flood-tide,
And we never toiled there more? 40

Wicked?—there is no sin, dear,
In an idle dreamer's head;
He turns the world topsy-turvy
To prove that his soul's not dead.

I am sinking, sinking, sinking; 45
It is hard to sit upright!
Your lap is the softest pillow!
Good night, my Love, good night!

II

How your eyes dazzle down into my soul!
   I drink and drink of their deep violet wine,
And ever thirst the more, although my whole
   Dazed being whirls in drunkenness divine.

Pout down your lips from that bewildering smile 5
   And kiss me for the interruption, Sweet!
I had escaped you: floating for awhile
   In that far cloud ablaze with living heat:

I floated with it through the solemn skies,
   I melted with it up the Crystal Sea 10
Into the Heaven of Heavens; and shut my eyes
   To feel eternal rest enfolding me. . . .

Well, I prefer one tyrannous girl down here,
   You jealous violet-eyed Bewitcher, you!
To being lord in Mohammed's seventh sphere 15
   Of meekest houris three score ten and two!

III

Was it hundreds of years ago, my Love,
  Was it thousands of miles away,
That two poor creatures we know, my Love,
  Were toiling day by day;
    Were toiling weary, weary, 5
    With many myriads more,
    In a City dark and dreary
    On a sullen river's shore?

Was it truly a fact or a dream, my Love?
  I think my brain still reels, 10
And my ears still throbbing seem, my Love,
  With the rush and the clang of wheels;
    Of a vast machinery roaring
    For ever in skyless gloom;
    Where the poor slaves peace imploring, 15
    Found peace alone in the tomb.

Was it hundreds of years ago, my Love,
  Was it thousands of miles away?
Or was it a dream to show, my Love,
  The rapture of to-day? 20
    This day of holy splendour,
    This Sabbath of rich rest,
    Wherein to God we render
    All praise by being blest.

IV

Eight of us promised to meet here
And tea together at five:
And—who would ever believe it?—
We are the first to arrive!

Oh, shame on us, my darling; 5
It is a monstrous crime
To make a tryst with *others*
And be before our time!

Lizzie is off with William,
Quite happy for her part; 10
Our sugar in her pocket,
And the sweet love in her heart.

Mary and Dick so grandly
Parade suburban streets;
His waistcoat and her bonnet 15
Proving the best of treats.

And Fanny plagues big Robert
With tricks of the wildest glee:
O Fanny, *you'll* get in hot water
If you do not bring us our tea!

Why, bless me, look at that table,
Every one of them there!—
'Ha, here at last we have them,
The always behindhand pair!

'When the last trumpet-solo
Strikes up instead of the lark,
They'll turn in their sleep just grunting
Who's up so soon in the dark?'

Babble and gabble, you rabble,
A thousand in full yell!
And this is your Tower of Babel,
This not-to-be-finished Hotel.[1]

'You should see it in the drawing,
You'd think a Palace they make,
Like the one in the *Lady of Lyons*,
With this pond for the lovely lake!'

'I wish it wasn't Sunday,
There's no amusement at all:
Who was here Hot-cross-bun-day?
We had such an open-air ball!

'The bands played polkas, waltzes,
Quadrilles; it was glorious fun!
And each gentleman gave them a penny
After each dance was done.'

'Mary is going to chapel,
And what takes her there, do you guess?
Her sweet little duck of a bonnet,
And her new second-hand silk dress.'

'*We* went to Church one Sunday,
But felt we had no right there;
For it's only a place for the grand folk
Who come in a carriage and pair.

---

[1] Since finished, in a fashion. The verses were written in 1863.

'And I laughed out loud,—it was shameful!
But Fanny said, *Oh, what lives!*
He must have been clever, the rascal, 55
To manage seven hundred wives!'

'Suppose we play Hunt-the-Slipper?'
'We can't, there's the crinoline!'—'Phew!
Bother it, always a nuisance!'
'Hoop-de-dooden-do!' 60

'I think I've seen all the girls here,
About a thousand, or more;
But none of them half so pretty
As our own loving four.'

'*Thank* you! and I've been listening 65
To lots of the men, the knaves;
But none of them half such humbugs
As our devoted slaves.'

'Do you see those purple flushes?
The sun will set in state: 70
Up all! we must cross to the heath, friends,
Before it gets too late.

'We will couch in the fern together,
And watch for the moon and the stars;
And the slim tree-tops will be lighted, 75
So the boys may light their cigars.

'And while the sunset glory
Burns down in crimson and gold,
LAZY shall tell us a story
Of his wonderful times of old.' 80

V

Ten thousand years ago, ('*No more than that?*')
Ten thousand years, ('*The age of Robert's hat!*'—
'*Silence you gods!*'—'*Pinch Fanny!*'—'*Now we're good.*')
This place where we are sitting was a wood,
Savage and desert save for one rude home 5
Of wattles plastered with stiff clay and loam;
And here, in front, upon the grassy mire
Four naked squaws were squatted round a fire:
Then four tall naked wild men crushing through
The tangled underwood came into view; 10
Two of them bent beneath a mighty boar,
The third was gashed and bleeding, number four

Strutted full-drest in war-paint, ('*That was Dick!*')
Blue of a devilish pattern laid on thick.
The squaws jumped up to roast the carcass whole;
The braves sank silent, stark 'gainst root and bole.
The meat half-done, they tore it and devoured,
Sullenly ravenous; the women cowered
Until their lords had finished, then partook.
Mist rose; all crept into their cabin-nook,
And staked the mouth; the floor was one broad bed
Of rushes dried with fox and bearskins spread.
Wolves howled and wild cats wailed; they snored; and so
The long night passed, shedding a storm of snow;
This very night ten thousand years ago.

VI

Ten thousand years before, ('*Come, draw it mild!
Don't waste Conk-ology like that, my child!*')
From where we sit to the horizon's bound
A level brilliant plain was spread all round,
As level and as brilliant as a sea
Under the burning sun; high as your knee
Aflame with flowers, yellow and blue and red:
Long lines of palm-trees marked out there the bed
Of a great river, and among them gleamed
A few grey tents. Then four swift horsemen streamed
Out of the West, magnificent in ire,
Churning the meadow into flakes of fire,
Brandishing monstrous spears as if in fight,
They wheeled, ducked, charged, and shouted fierce delight:
So till they reach the camp: the women there
Awaiting them the evening meal prepare;
Milk from the goats and camels, dates plucked fresh,
Cool curds and cheese, millet, sweet broiled kid's flesh.
The spear struck deep hath picketed each barb;
A grave proud turbaned man in flowing garb
Sups with a grave meek woman, humbly proud,
Whose eyes flash empire. Then the solemn crowd
Of stars above, the silent plain below,
Until the East resumes its furnace-glow;
This same night twenty thousand years ago.

VII

Ten thousand years before, ('*But if you take
Such mouthfuls, you will soon eat up Time's cake!*')
Where we are sitting rose in splendid light
A broad cool marble palace; from the height
Broad terrace-gardens stairlike sank away

Down to the floor of a deep sapphire bay.
Where the last slope slid greenly to the wave,
And dark rich glossy foliage shadow gave,
Four women—or four goddesses—leaned calm,
Of mighty stature, graceful as the palm:
One stroked with careless hand a lion's mane,
One fed an eagle; while a measured strain
Was poured forth by the others, harp and voice,
Music to make the universe rejoice.
An isle was in the offing seen afar,
Deep-purple based, its peak a glittering star;
Whence rowed a galley (drooped the silken sails),
A dragon-barque with golden burning scales.
Then four bronzed giants leapt to land, embraced
The glorious women, chanting: 'Did we haste?
The Cavern-Voice hath silenced all your fears;
Peace on our earth another thousand years!'
On fruits and noble wine, with song's rich flow,
They feasted in the sunset's golden glow;
This same night thirty thousand years ago.

VIII

Ten thousand years before, (*'Another ten!*
Good Lord, how greedy are these little men!')
This place where we are sitting (*'Half asleep.'*)
Was in the sea a hundred fathoms deep:
A floor of silver sand so fine and soft,
A coral forest branching far aloft;
Above, the great dusk emerald golden-green;
Silence profound and solitude serene.
Four mermaids sit beneath the coral rocks,
Combing with golden combs their long green locks,
And wreathing them with little pearly shells;
Four mermen came from out the deep-sea dells,
And whisper to them, and they all turn pale:
Then through the hyaline a voice of wail,
With passionate gestures, 'Ever alas for woe!
A rumour cometh down the Ocean-flow,
A word calamitous! that we shall be
All disinherited from the great sea:
Our tail with which like fishes we can swim
Shall split into an awkward double-limb,
And we must waddle on the arid soil,
And build dirt-huts, and get our food with toil,
And lose our happy, happy lives!' And so
These gentle creatures wept 'Alas for woe!'
This same night forty thousand years ago.

IX

'*Are you not going back a little more?*
What was the case ten thousand years before?'
Ten thousand years before 'twas Sunday night;
Four lovely girls were listening with delight,
Three noble youths admired another youth
Discoursing History crammed full of truth:
They all were sitting upon Hampstead Heath,
And monstrous grimy London lay beneath.
'The stupidest story LAZY ever told;
I've no more faith in his fine times of old.'
'How do you like our prospects now, my dears?
We'll all be mermaids in ten thousand years.'
'Mermaids are beautiful enough, but law!
Think of becoming a poor naked squaw!'
'But in these changes, sex will change no doubt;
We'll all be men and women turn about.'
'Then these four chaps will be the squaws?—that's just;
With lots of picaninnies, I *do* trust!'
'If changes go by fifty thousand, yes;
But if by ten, they last were squaws, I guess!'
'Come on; we'll go and do the very beers
We did this night was fifty thousand years.'
Thou prophet, thou deep sage! we'll go, we'll go:
The ring is round, Life naught, the World an O;
This night is fifty thousand years ago!

X

As we rush, as we rush in the Train,
   The trees and the houses go wheeling back,
But the starry heavens above the plain
   Come flying on our track.

All the beautiful stars of the sky,
   The silver doves of the forest of Night,
Over the dull earth swarm and fly,
   Companions of our flight.

We will rush ever on without fear;
   Let the goal be far, the flight be fleet!
For we carry the Heavens with us, Dear,
   While the Earth slips from our feet!

XI

Day after day of this azure May
The blood of the Spring has swelled in my veins;
Night after night of broad moonlight
A mystical dream has dazzled my brains.

A seething might, a fierce delight,
The blood of the Spring is the wine of the world;
My veins run fire and thrill desire,
Every leaf of my heart's red rose uncurled.

A sad sweet calm, a tearful balm,
The light of the Moon is the trance of the world;
My brain is fraught with yearning thought,
And the rose is pale and its leaves are furled.

O speed the day, thou dear, dear May,
And hasten the night I charge thee, O June,
When the trance divine shall burn with the wine
And the red rose unfurl all its fire to the Moon!

XII

O mellow moonlight warm,
Weave round my Love a charm;
O countless starry eyes,
Watch from the holy skies;
O ever-solemn Night,
Shield her within thy might:
    Watch her, my little one!
    Shield her, my darling!

How my heart shrinks with fear,
Nightly to leave thee, dear;
Lonely and pure within
Vast glooms of woe and sin:
Our wealth of love and bliss
Too heavenly-perfect is:
    Good night, my little one!
    God keep thee, darling!

VERSIFICATION OF THOMAS COOPER'S ARGUMENT

IN A DEBATE ON THE EXISTENCE OF GOD BETWEEN THAT GENTLEMAN AND CHARLES BRADLAUGH

My poor friends, I come to you kindly,
  With a brotherly kiss, not a rod;
For I know that sincerely, though blindly,
  You look up in vain for a God.
For a very long time I have sought you—
  Since we met last the years are now seven—
And here I have found you, and brought you
  My Ladder for climbing to Heaven.

My wonderful Ladder, that reaches
    From Self here to God (be not vext);   10
Though its rungs are so few, and though each is
    A quite simple step from the next.
For five years and eight months precisely
    It has borne me to either extreme,
As cleverly, safely, and nicely   15
    As those angels of Jacob's sweet dream.

You have seen a lamp-lighter at work, friends?
    Well, just in his fashion I'll stop,
Set my Ladder, mount quick, give a jerk, friends,
    And light up a God at the top.   20
And Bradlaugh, this ignorant fellow,
    May pelt at my lamp as he likes
(Young fools often do so when mellow);
    I wager no stone of his strikes.

I plant it on *I;* you can never   25
    Persuade me *I* am not, now, here:
But as I have not been for ever,
    I must have a Cause—that is clear.
And as *I* am a personal being,
    Intelligent, conscious, I claim   30
That the stupidest cannot help seeing
    My Cause must be ditto—the same.

Take another neat step: there is nowhere
    Where Nothing at all can be found;
Wherever our thoughts go, they go where   35
    Unlimited Something's around:
And the Cause of this infinite Something
    Must be certainly infinite too;
For it would be a monstrous and rum thing
    To fancy a finite would do.   40

So ourselves and the whole world of Matter
    Have *one* Cause—for who would explore
(Without he was mad as a hatter)
    Still backwards forever for more?
One cause, without cause, thus eternal;   45
    And infinite, therefore the power
Of His will uncontrolled is supernal—
    Omnipotence must be His dower.

And this all-wise, all-good, and almighty
    Creator of spirit and clod,   50
At the top of my Ladder of light, He

It is whom we worship as God.
O my friends, is the climbing not easy?
And are not the steps safe and strong?
And how should my Ladder not please ye 55
When *I*'ve trusted to it so long?

O my luminous, logical Ladder,
  My natural musical scale,
Whose notes swell up gladder and gladder
  In glory and triumph—all hail! 60
The Cross, though a very good notion,
  And on the whole rather divine,
Inspires no such fervid devotion
  As doth this grand Ladder of mine.

P.S. penn'd for such as Truelove there 65
  And Bradlaugh: My God in the sky
Is the little round dot up above there
  Perfecting this neat little *i*:
For *i* wants the dot for completion,
  But no dot is wanted by *u*:— 70
O Plato, much lecturing Grecian,
  The Metempsychosis is true!

THE FIRE THAT FILLED MY HEART OF OLD

I

The fire that filled my heart of old
  Gave lustre while it burned;
Now only ashes grey and cold
  Are in its silence urned.
Ah! better was the furious flame, 5
  The splendour with the smart:
I never cared for the singer's fame,
  But, oh! for the singer's heart
    Once more—
  The burning fulgent heart! 10

II

No love, no hate, no hope, no fear,
  No anguish and no mirth;
Thus life extends from year to year,
  A flat of sullen dearth.
Ah! life's blood creepeth cold and tame, 15
  Life's thought plays no new part:
I never cared for the singer's fame,
  But, oh! for the singer's heart
    Once more—
  The bleeding passionate heart! 20

FROM THE MIDST OF THE FIRE

From the midst of the fire I fling
   These arrows of fire to you:
If they sing, and burn, and sting,
   You feel how I burn too;
But if they reach you there   5
   Speed-spent, charred black and cold,
The fire burns out in the air,
   The Passion will not be told.

VANE'S STORY
Prologue

This is the story
(To God be the glory!)
Which Vane, found in bed
When a splash of fierce red
From the sunset made strange   5
The street's opposite range,
Told me; who, astonished,
Had firstly admonished,
Then asked him outright,
'On the spree all last night?'   10
   Pale looked he, and queer;
But his speech calm and clear,
And his voice, sweet and strong,
So swayed me ere long,
That I almost or quite   15
Believed him that night.
He named not the hall
Where he went to the ball;
Of his friends I could trace
None who knew of the case,   20
Nor the Jones, nor the Brown—
There are myriads in town!
The landlord avows
He went out with his spouse
After tea; slept at Bow,   25
At her sister's.
          And so,
Shall we trust Vane? or deem
Him the dupe of a dream?
Let who will decide.   30
The next week he died,
And thus ended his story.
(To God be the glory!)

The Story

One flamelet flickered to and fro
Above the clear vermilion glow;
The house was silent, and the street
Deserted by all echoing feet;
And that small restless tongue of light
Possest my ear and mocked my sight,
While drowsy, happy, warm, I lay
[1]Upon the couch at close of day,
And drowsy, dreamy, more and more,
I floated from the twilight shore
Over the vague vast sea of sleep,
Just conscious of the rest so deep;
Not sinking to the under caves,
But rocking on the surface waves.
When fitfully some muffled sound
Came from the crowded streets around,
It brought no thought of restless life
With wakeful care and passionate strife;
But seemed the booming of a bell
Sweetly ringing tumult's knell,
Slowly chiming far away
The euthanasia of the day.
And then unsummoned by my will
Came floating through this mood so still
The scenes of all my life's past range,
In perfect pictures, fair and strange,
As flowers limned in purest light
Upon a background such as might
Expand beneath some forest-screen
After the sunset, goldbrowngreen.
And then I heard on every side
The shadowy rustling slow and wide
Of night's dim curtains softly drawn
To hush the world asleep till dawn.
I heard the rustling, and my eyes
Were curtained with the curtained skies;
And I lay wrapt as in a fleece
Of warmth and purity and peace;
While consciousness within the stream
Of rippling thought and shadowy dream
Sank slowly to the deepest deep,
Lured by the murmuring Siren, sleep;
When suddenly a little thrill
Of splendour pricked both mind and will,

---

[1] Here for decorum be it said,
This couch was sofa and not bed.

And brought me tidings grand and strange;
I did not stir with outward change,
But felt with inward royal mirth,
On all this dusk of heaven and earth
The moon may rise or not to-night;
But in my soul she rises bright!

   The globe of glory swelling rose
In mighty pulses, solemn throes;
And filled and overfilled me soon
With light and music, with the swoon
Of too much rapture and amaze,
A murmurous hush, a luminous haze.
How long in this sweet swoon I lay,
What hours or years, I cannot say;
Vast arcs of the celestial sphere
Subtend such little angles here.
But after the ineffable,
This first I can remember well:
A Rose of Heaven, so dewy-sweet
Its fragrance was a soul complete,
Came, touched my brow, caressed my lips,
And then my eyes in their eclipse;
And still I stirred not, though there came
A wine of fire through all my frame,
An ecstasy of joy and love,
A vision of the throne above,
A myriad-voiced triumphant psalm
Upswelling through a splendour calm;
Then suddenly, as if a door
Were shut, veiled silence as before.

   The sweetest voice said, 'True it is!
He does not waken at my kiss!'

   I smiled: 'Your kisses three and four
Just gave me Heaven, no less, no more;
I held me still, eyes shut, lest bliss
Should overflow and waste a kiss.'

   Then dreamily my lids I raised,
And with grand joy, small wonder, gazed,
Although the miracle I saw
Might well have made me wan with awe.
'Why have you left your golden hair,
These gorgeous dusky braids to wear?
Why have you left your azure eyes,
To gaze through deep dark mysteries?

Why have you left your robe of white,
And come in cloudy lace bedight?   90
Or did you think that I could fail
To know you through whatever veil?
As bird or beast, as fish or worm,
In fiendish or angelic form,
As flower or tree, as wave or stone,   95
Be sure I recognise My Own!'

    The sweet sad voice was sad no more,
But sweeter, tenderer, than before;
'Oh, ask no questions yet,' said she,
'But answer me, but answer me.   100

    'I now have listened very long
To catch some notes of that great song
Your youth began to sing so well;
Oh, why have none yet reached me? tell!'
'And why is any lamp not bright,   105
With no more oil to feed its light?
Why does a robe moth-eaten fade
When she is gone whom it arrayed?
Great songs must pulse with lifeful breath,
No hymns mark time for timeless death;   110
One long keen wail above the bier,
Then smothered moans, then stillness drear.'

    'I long have listened, all aflame,
For some full echoes of the fame
Youth pledged ripe manhood to achieve: 115
Why must I, hearing none, still grieve?'
'And why should he who cannot spend
Not make of gold his life's chief end?
O Love, the jewels of renown,
So priceless in a monarch's crown,   120
What are they when his realm is lost,
And he must wander like a ghost
Alone through wilds of rocky dearth,
But pretty pebbles nothing worth?
And would you have our love's proclaim   125
In shouts and trumpet-peals of fame;
Or whispered as I whisper here,
In this little pink-shell ear
Still full of echoes from the sea
Of fathomless Eternity?'   130

    'I do not seek thy fame because
Enamoured of the world's applause,

Though even its most reckless shout
Involves some true love-praise no doubt:
But, Dearest, when fame's trumpets blare 135
Great hearts are battling with despair:
Better the tumult of the strife
Than stillness of lone-wasting life.
If you were working out God's will,
Could all the air around be still?' 140

'But I am working out God's will
Alike when active and when still;
And work we good or work we ill,
We never work against His will. . . .
All work, work, work! Why must we toil 145
For ever in the hot turmoil?
God wrought six days, and formed the world;
Then on the seventh His power refurled,
And felt so happy that He blest
That Sabbath day above the rest; 150
And afterwards, we read, He cursed
The work He thought so good at first;
And surely Earth and Heaven evince
That He has done but little since.

[1]"Well, I, who am a puny man, 155
And not a God who all things can,
Have also worked: not six short days
Of work refulgent with self-praise,
Of work 'all-good' whose end was blest
With infinite eternal rest: 160
No, I have worked life after life
Of sorrow, sufferance and strife,
So many ages, that I ask
To rest one lifetime from the task,
To spend these years (forlorn of thee) 165
Sequestered in passivity;
Observing all things God hath made,
And of no ugliest truth afraid,
But having leisure time enough
To look at both sides of the stuff. . . . 170
With Shelley to his ocean-doom,
With Dante to his alien tomb;
With Wallace, Raleigh, Sidney, Vane,
All to the axe's bloody stain;
With Socrates until the cup 175

---

[1] The last chapter of George Sand's *Lélia* may seem to be the source of the following section: in fact, however, I chanced to read that work just after, and not before, this section was written.

Of hemlock lifted calmly up,
With Jesus to the fatal tree
After the garden's agony,
With Mohammed in flight and fight,
With Burns in all his fate's deep night,　　　　180
With Joan to the fiery screen,
With Charlotte to the guillotine,
With Campanella all the while
And Tasso in their dungeons vile,
With Swift slow-dying from the top,　　　　185
With Rabelais to the curtain's drop,
Cervantes prisoner and slave,
Columbus on the unknown wave,
And Luther through his lifelong war;
With these, and with how many more,　　　　190
Since poor Eve fell, and as she fell
Of course pulled Adam down as well,—
In these, and in how many more,
Have I outbattled life's stern war,
Endured all hardships, toiled and fought,　　　　195
Oppressed, sore-wounded, and distraught,
While inwardly consumed with thought;
How long! how long!—Mankind no whit
The better for the whole of it!
And *I*, look at me, do I need　　　　200
The little rest I claim, indeed,
With body dwindled, brain outworn,
Soul's pith dried up, and heart forlorn? . . .
And so I rest me, half-content
That all my active power is spent:　　　　205
No new campaign till after cure!
Meanwhile I passively endure
The wounds bequeathed by so much strife,
The hopelessness of present life:
And this is much; what further can　　　　210
Be looked for from a wreck of man?
I bear in silence and alone
What maddened me at first, I own.'

'*The wounds bequeathed by so much strife,*
The hopelessness of present life.'　　　　215
She dwelt upon these words again
With such a look of wistful pain
As made my heart all creep and stir
With pity, not for self, for her.
'O my true Love!' she said (the while　　　　220
Her poor lips sought and failed to smile),
'O Love! your laugh is like a knell;

Your phantasy is horrible,
Thus calmly plunged a glittering knife
Into the core of your own life!' 225
And there she broke down; all the grief,
Love, pity powerless for relief,
Yearning to suffer in my stead,
Revulsion against fatal dread,
Long swelling mighty in her soul 230
O'erflooded now beyond control.
She gave a little laughing cry,
Choked sharply off; then heavily
Flung herself down upon my breast
With passionate weeping unreprest; 235
A night-dark cloud upon some bleak
And thunder-furrowed mountain peak
Pouring itself in rain and fire;
For now through all the black attire
Heaving about her heaving frame 240
Fermented flashes of swift flame;
Not tempest-lightnings, but indeed
Auroral splendours such as speed
Battling with gloom before the day,
And herald its triumphant sway. 245
Her instincts in that mighty hour
Of insurrection grasped at power;
And her true self arrayed in light,
Azure and golden, dazzling-bright,
Was struggling through the mask of night. 250

  The mask remained,—for some good cause
Well emphasised by Heavenly laws;
She sobbed herself to self-control,
Represt the heavings of her soul;
Then stood up, pallid, faint, distraught, 255
Facing some phantom of dread thought.

  'Another spasm like this,' I said,
'Will kill me! When we both are dead
I'll use my very first new breath
To thank you for the blissful death, 260
The torture-rapture utterless,
You dear life-giving murderess!'
I laughed; and yet the while I gazed
Upon her standing wan and dazed:
Would I had bitten out my tongue 265
Ere any word of mine had stung
With such an unforeboded smart
That purest and most loving heart!

'And do you never kneel and pray
For comfort on your lonely way?
And have you no firm trust in God
To lighten your so-heavy load?'
The voice how strange and sad! the mien
How troubled from its pure serene!
'You good Child! I beseech no more
That one and one may make up four,
When one and one are my assets
And four the total of my debts:
Nor do I now with fervour pray
To cast no shadow in broad day:
Nor even ask (as I asked once)
That laws sustaining worlds and suns
In their eternal path should be
Suspended, that to pleasure me
Some flower I love,—now drooping dead,
May be empowered to lift its head.'

'Ah, good pure souls have told me how
You laughed at prayer as you laugh now,
And turned all holy things to mirth,
And made a mock of heaven and earth;
And sometimes seemed to have no faith
In God, in true life after death.'
'But God exists, or not, indeed,
Quite irrespective of our creed;
We live, or live not, after death,
Alike whatever be our faith;
And not a single truth, in brief,
Is modified by our belief.
And if God *does* subsist and act,
Though some men cannot learn the fact,
Who but Himself has made mankind,
Alike the seërs and the blind?
It may be that for some good cause
He loves to rest deep-veiled in laws;
And better likes us who don't ask
Or seek to get behind the mask,
Than those our fellow-insect fry
Who creep and hop and itch and pry,
The Godhead's lice, the swarming fleas
In Jove's great bed of slumbrous ease?'

'They said you scorned all wise restraints,
And loved the sinners, not the saints;
And mocking these, still dwelt with those
The friends who are the worst of foes.'

'They told you something like the truth,
These dear tale-bearers full of ruth.
How proffer mere coarse human love
To hearts sole-set on things above?
And furthermore, although of old
Wolves ravaged dreadfully the fold,
Yet now Christ's tender lambs indeed
Securely frisk, unstinted feed.
To us poor goats they freely give
The dreariest tracts, but they—they live
In pastures green, by rivers clear,
Quite sleek and happy even here:
And when these lambs that frisk and leap
Are all staid, stout, and well-clothed sheep,
The shepherd, having taken stock,
Will lead away the whole white flock
To bleat and batten in galore
Of Heavenly clover evermore!
The dear saints want no earthly friend,
Having their Jesus: but, perpend;
What of the wild goats? what of us,
A hundred times more numerous,
Poor devils, starving wretched here
On barren tracts and wild rocks drear,
And in the next life (as they tell)
Roasted eternally in Hell?'

'But when you join the multitude
Of sinners, is it for their good;
To hale them from the slough of sin,
Or but to plunge your own soul in?'
'And what they are, must I not be?
The dear Lord made them Who made me?
If God *did* make us, this is sure,
We all are brothers, vile and pure.
I've known some brilliant saints who spent
Their lives absorbed in one intent,
Salvation each of his own soul;
The race they ran had just one goal,
And just one modest little prize,
A wicket-gate in Paradise,
A sneaking-in there through the wall
To bliss eternal; that was all.
Some of them thought this bliss would too
Be spiced by the contrasting view
Of Hell beneath them surging crammed
With all the tortures of the damned.
Their alms were loans to poor God lent,

Interest infinity-per-cent.,
(And God must be hard-up indeed
If of such loans He stands in need);
Their earnest prayers were coward cries,   365
Their holy doctrines blasphemies;
Their faith, hope, love, no more, no less,
Than sublimated selfishness.

  'Now my gross, earthly, human heart
With man and not with God takes part;   370
With men, however vile, and not
With Seraphim I cast my lot:
With those poor ruffian thieves, too strong
To starve amidst our social wrong,
And yet too weak to wait and earn   375
Dry bread by honest labour stern;
With those poor harlots steeping sin
And shame and woe in vitriol-gin:
Shall these, so hardly dealt with here,
Be worse off in a future sphere;   380
And I, a well-fed lounger, seek
To "cut" them dead, to cringe and sneak
Into that bland *beau monde* the sky,
Whose upper circles are so high? . .
If any human soul at all   385
Must die the second death, must fall
Into that gulph of quenchless flame
Which keeps its victims still the same,
Unpurified as unconsumed,
To everlasting torments doomed;   390
Then I give God my scorn and hate,
And turning back from Heaven's gate
(Suppose me got there!) bow, *Adieu!*
Almighty Devil, damn me too!"[1]

  As lightnings from dusk summer skies,   395
Mirth dazzled from her brow and eyes;
A charming chiming silvery laughter
Accompanied my speech, and after
Still tinkled when the speech was done
Its symphony of faëry fun: 400
And then her lips superbly smiled.
'*You* are the child, the naughty child,
Screaming and kicking on its back,

---

[1] This was written before Mr. J. S. Mill published a similar declaration. It will be noticed, however, that while the philosopher treated the matter with his habitual lofty earnestness, the flippant rhymester but makes it a subject for mockery and laughter.

And choking with convulsions black,
At these old-bogey tales of Hell 405
Its hard-pressed priestly nurses tell!'
And gaylier, sweetlier yet she laughed,
Till I was drunken, dizzy, daft.
'You wicked holy one!' I cried,
'You changeling seraph! you black-eyed 410
Black-hearted scoffer! Heaven itself
Has only made you worse, mad elf,[1]

. . . .

Well, I confess that I deserve
Your arrowy laugh, your lip's grand curve,
For foaming out in such a rage 415
Of boyish nonsense at my age,
Anent this stupid Hell and Heaven
Some half-believe one day in seven.
Let all who stickle for a Hell
Have it; they deserve it well. . . . 420
Not often in these latter years
Am I, my darling, moved to tears
Or joyous laughter or hot scorn,
While plodding to the quiet bourne;
'Tis you have brought me back a part 425
Of my old youthful passionate heart.'

'And do you feel no bitter grief
Of penitence for unbelief?
No stings of venomous remorse
In tracing backward to its source 430
This wicked godless lifetime's course?'

'I half remember, years ago,
Fits of despair that maddened woe,
Frantic remorse, intense self-scorn,
And yearnings harder to be borne 435
Of utter loneliness forlorn;
What passionate secret prayers I prayed!
What futile firm resolves I made!
As well a thorn might pray to be
Transformed into an olive-tree; 440
As well a weevil might determine
To grow a farmer hating vermin;
The *I am that I am* of God
Defines no less a worm or clod.
My penitence was honest guile; 445
My inmost being all the while

---

[1] [For lines which Thomson omitted here, see Notes.]

Was laughing in a patient mood
At this externe solicitude,
Was waiting laughing till once more
I should be sane as heretofore; 450
And in the pauses of the fits
That rent my heart and scared my wits,
Its pleasant mockery whispered through—
*Oh, what can Saadi have to do
With penitence? and what can you?* 455
Are Shiraz roses wreathed with rue?

'Now tell me, ere once more we turn
To things which us alone concern,
Of all the prosperous saints you see
Has none a kindly word for me?' 460
'First SHELLEY, parting for above,
Left you a greeting full of love.'

'The burning Seraph of the Throne!
Not for my worship deep and lone
Of him, but for my love of you, 465
He loves and greets me; in his view
I stand all great and glorified,
The bridegroom worthy of the bride
For whom the purest soul in Heaven
Might wait and serve long lifetimes seven, 470
And other seven when these were past,
Nor deem the service long at last,
Though after all he failed for ever
In his magnificent endeavour.'

'Then that dear Friend of yours, who came 475
Uncouthly shrinking, full of shame,
Hopeless and desolate, at first,
Dismayed that he was not accurst;
But when his essence shone out clear
Was found the noblest of our sphere; 480
Beautiful, faithful, valiant, wise,
With tenderest love that may suffice
When once with equal power unfurled
To sway and bless a whole bad world:
Is it for my own sake that *he* 485
Bows down, Sir, half-adoring me?'

'The great deep heart of purest gold,
Ever o'erflowing as of old
From the eternal source divine
With Heaven's most rich and cordial wine! 490

Enough: the loneliest on earth,
Famishing in affection's dearth,
Who found but two such friends above
Would banquet evermore on love.'

'Now ask me what you wish to ask;
Your slave is eager for her task.'
'Then, firstly, I who never mix
With our vile nether politics,
Have also ceased for many years
To study those of your high spheres.
Who now is, under God and Fate,
The Steward of the world-estate,
The Grand Vizier, Prime Minister,
Or (if you will) sole Manager
Of this bewildering Pantomime
Whose scenes and acts fill Space and Time?'

'I have heard many and many a name;
The laws seem evermore the same,
The operation of the laws
Reveals no variance in the cause.'

'A learned politician, you!
Well, any name perchance will do;
And we will take an old one, say
That Demiurgos still bears sway.
I want a prayer to reach his throne,
And you can bear it, you alone;
For neither God nor fiend nor man
(Nay, scarcely any woman) can
Resist that voice of tenderest pleading,
Or turn away from it unheeding.
Not in this mystic mask of night,
But in your dazzling noonday light;
Not with this silent storm of hair,
But crowned with sunbeams you shall fare,
Not with these darkest Delphian eyes,
But with your luminous azure skies;
For powers of solemn awe and gloom
Love loveliness and joy and bloom.
Only your voice you must not change;
It is not, where all else is, strange;
The sweetest voice in all the world,
The soul of cosmic music furled
In such a little slender sound,
Delighting in its golden bound;
The evening star of melody,

The morning star of harmony;
When I can catch its faintest tone
In sighing breeze, in dim wave's moan,
I feel you near, my Love, my Own.'

'And who shall guide me to the throne 540
Whose place is unto all unknown?'
'By one at least the path is known:
[1]To Demogorgon's awful throne,
Down, down, through all the mysteries
He led the Oceanides: 545
Where Demogorgon dwelleth deep
There Demiurgos watch doth keep,
Though Vesta sleeps æonian sleep:
SHELLEY himself shall be your guide,
Since I must still on earth abide: 550
Down, down, into the deepest deep;
Down, down, and through the shade of sleep;
Down, down, beyond the cloudy strife
Of interwoven death and life;
Down, down, unto the central gloom 555
Whose darkness radiates through the tomb
And fills the universal womb.

'Then he shall leave thee lonely there,
And thou shalt kneel and make thy prayer,
A childish prayer for simple boon: 560
That soon and soon and very soon
Our Lady of Oblivious Death
May come and hush my painful breath,
And bear me thorough Lethe-stream,
Sleeping sweet sleep without a dream; 565
And bring you also from that sphere
Where you grow sad without me, Dear;
And bear us to her deepest cave
Under the Sea without a wave,
Where the eternal shadows brood 570
In the Eternal Solitude,
Stirring never, breathing never,
Silent for ever and for ever;
And side by side and face to face,
And linked as in a death-embrace, 575
Leave us absorbing thus the balm
Of most divinely perfect calm,
Till ten full years have overflowed
For each wherein we bore the load

[1] *Prometheus Unbound*, act ii., scene 3, *et seq.*

Of heavy life upon this earth 580
From birth to death from death to birth:
That when this cycle shall be past
We may wake young and pure at last,
And both together recommence
The life of passion, thought and sense, 585
Of fear and hope, of woe and bliss;—
But in another world than this.

   'For I am infinitely tired
With this old sphere we once admired,
With this old earth we loved too well; 590
Disgusted more than words can tell,
And would not mind a change of Hell.
The same old stolid hills and leas,
The same old stupid patient trees,
The same old ocean blue and green, 595
The same sky cloudy or serene;
The old two-dozen hours to run
Between the settings of the sun,
The old three hundred sixty-five
Dull days to every year alive; 600
Old stingy measure, weight and rule,
No margin left to play the fool;
The same old way of getting born
Into it naked and forlorn,
The same old way of creeping out 605
Through death's low door for lean and stout;
Same men with the old hungry needs,
Puffed up with the old windy creeds;
Old toil, old care, old worthless treasures,
Old gnawing sorrows, swindling pleasures: 610
The cards are shuffled to and fro,
The hands may vary somewhat so,
The dirty pack's the same we know
Played with long thousand years ago;
Played with and lost with still by Man,— 615
Fate marked them ere the game began;
I think the only thing that's strange
Is our illusion as to change.

   'This is the favour I would ask:
Can you submit to such a task?' 620

   'All you have told me I will do,
Rejoicing to give joy to you:
Oh, I will plead, will win the boon,
That we may be united soon. . . .

But sameness palls upon you so, 625
That to relieve you I will go.'

'By no means! wait a little, Dear!
The change is in your being here.
Besides, I have not finished yet—
How stupid of me to forget! 630
Sh! I shall think of it just now. . . .
Your kiss, my Angel, on my brow!
Your kiss that through the dullest pain
Flashed inspiration on my brain!'

Her face was fulgent with clear bliss; 635
She bent down o'er me with the kiss
As bends a dawn of golden light
To kiss away the earth's long night.
The splendour of her beauty made
Me blind, and in the rapturous shade 640
From head to foot my being thrilled
As if with mighty music filled,
To feel that kiss come leaning down
Upon me like a radiant crown.
Her royal kiss was on my brow 645
A burning ruby, burning now
As then, and burning evermore;
A Star of Love above the roar
And fever of this life's long war:
And suddenly my brain was bright 650
With glowing fire and dancing light,
A rich intoxicating shine
Like wave on wave of noble wine,
The Alcahest of joy supreme
Dissolving all things into dream. 655

So when at length I found a tongue
Bell-clear and bold my voice outrung:
'Dearest, all thanks were out of place
For this thine overwhelming grace.
The kiss of tenderness, the kiss 660
Of truth, you gave me erst; but this
Is consecration; to the man
Who wears this burning talisman
The veil of Isis melts away
To woven air, the night is day, 665
That he alone in all the shrine
May see the lineaments divine:
And Fate the marble Sphinx, dumb, stern,
Terror of Beauty cold, shall yearn

And melt to flesh, and blood shall thrill 670
The stony heart, and life shall fill
The statue: it shall follow him
Submissive to his every whim,
Ev'n as the lion of the wild
Followed pure Una, meek and mild. 675

'Now, I can tell you what we two
Before we part this night will do.
There is a dance—I wish it were
Some brilliant night-fête rich and rare,
With gold-and-scarlet uniforms 680
Far-flashing through the music-storms;
Some Carnival's last Masquerade,
Wherein our parts were fitly played.
This is another sort of thing,
The mere tame weekly gathering 685
Of humble tradesmen, lively clerks,
And fair ones who befit such sparks:
Few merry meetings could look duller;
No wealth, no grandeur, no rich colour.
Yet they enjoy it: give a girl 690
Some fiddle-screech to time her twirl,
And give a youth the limpest waist
That wears a gown to hold embraced;
Then dance, dance, dance! both girl and boy
Are overbrimmed and drunk with joy; 695
Because young hearts to love's own chime
Beat passionate rhythms all the time.

'This is the night, and we will go,
For many of the *Class* I know;
Young friendly fellows, rather rough, 700
But frank and kind and good enough
For this bad world: how all will stare
To see me with a dark Queen there!
I went last winter twice or thrice,
As dull as lead, as cold as ice, 705
Amidst the flushed and vivid crowd
Of youths and maidens laughing loud;
For thought retraced the long sad years
Of pallid smiles and frozen tears
Back to a certain festal night, 710
A whirl and blaze of swift delight,
When we together danced, we two!
I live it all again! . . . Do you
Remember how I broke down quite
In the mere polka? . . . Dressed in white, 715

A loose pink sash around your waist,
Low shoes across the instep laced,
Your moonwhite shoulders glancing through
Long yellow ringlets dancing too,
You were an Angel then; as clean   720
From earthly dust-speck, as serene
And lovely and beyond my love,
As now in your far world above.

'You shall this night a few more hours
Be absent from your heavenly bowers;   725
With leave or not, 'tis all the same,
I keep you here and bear the blame.
Your Star this night must take its chance
Without you in the spheral dance,
For you shall waltz and whirl with me   730
Amidst a staider companie;
The Cherubim and Seraphim
And Saintly Hosts may drown their hymn
With tenfold noise of harp and lyre;
The sweetest voice of all the quire   735
Shall sing to me, shall make my room,
This little nutshellful of gloom,
A Heaven of Heavens, the best of all,
While I am dressing for the Ball! . . .

'What book is this I held before,   740
The gloaming glooming more and more,
Eyes dreamed and hand drooped on the floor?
The *Lieder*—Heine's—what we want!
A lay of Heine's you shall chant;
Our poor Saint Heinrich! for he was   745
A saint here of the loftiest class,
By martyrdom more dreadly solemn
Than that of Simeon on the column.
God put him to the torture; seven
Long years beneath unpitying heaven,   750
The body dead, the man at strife
With all the common cares of life:
A living Voice intense and brave
Issuing from a Mattress-grave.
At length the cruel agony wrung   755
Confessions from that haughty tongue;
Confessions of the strangest, more
Than ever God had bargained for;
With prayers and penitential psalms
That gave the angels grinning qualms,   760
With jests when sharp pangs cut too deep

That made the very devils weep.
Enough of this! the Monarch cried;
Fear gave what Mercy still denied;
Torture committed suicide
To quench that voice; the victim died
Victorious over Heaven and Doom;
The Mattress-grave became a tomb
Deep in our Mother's kindly womb,
Oblivion tranced the painful breath,
The Death-in-Life grew perfect Death.'

'Is it the mere quaint German type,
Or is it from some blackened pipe?
The volume seems without a joke
A volume of tobacco-smoke!'

'The choice is difficult in sooth;
But sing that song of love and ruth
The Princess Ilse sang his youth:
And sing it very softly sweet,
As not to ravish all the street;
And sing it to what air you will,
Your voice in any tune must thrill. . . .
Yet stay, there was a certain hymn
Which used at Sunday School to brim
Our hearts with holy love and zeal,
Our eyes with tears they yearned to feel:
Mild Bishop Heber shall embrace
Wild Heine by sweet music's grace,
The while you sing the verses fair
To *Greenland's icy mountains*' air;
A freezing name! but icy mountains
Were linked with Afric's sunny fountains.'

Ich bin die Prinsessin Ilse,
Und wohne im Ilsenstein;
Komm mit nach meinem Schlosse,
Wir wollen selig sein.
'Dear Princess, I will come with thee
Into thy cavern's mystery,
And both of us shall happy be.'

In meinen weissen Armen,
An meiner weissen Brust,
Da sollst du liegen und träumen
Von alter Märchenlust.
'In your white arms, on your white breast,
I'll lie and dream in perfect rest,
With more than faëry blessings blest.'

Es bleiben todt die Todten,
Und nur der Lebendige lebt;
Und ich bin schön und blühend,
Mein lachendes Herze bebt.   810
'Yes, dead the dead for ever lie;
But you my Love and your Love I
Are of the souls that cannot die.'

Doch dich soll mein Arm umschlingen,
Wie er Kaiser Heinrich umschlang;—   815
Ich hielt ihm zu die Ohren,
Wenn die Trompet erklang.
'Roll drum, plead lute, blare trumpet-call;
Our ears shall be fast closed to all,
Beneath divine Oblivion's pall.'   820

Oh what a quaintly coupled pair
The poem and the music were!
The Sunday School's old simple air,
The heathen verses rich and rare!
. . . . .

Wan ghosts have risen from the grave   825
To flit across the midnight wave;
Pale phantoms started from the tomb
To hurry through the wildwood gloom;
Cold corpses left their wormy bed
To mingle in high feasts, 'tis said;   830
But never since old Noah's flood
Turned Eden into sand and mud,
(Relieving thus the Heavenly guard
From its long spell of duty hard?)[1]
Has any Angel left the sphere   835
Of Heaven to dance with mortals here:
Though earthly angels crowd each ball,
Since women are such angels all.

My partner was no icy corse,
No phantom of a wild remorse,   840

---

[1] The Holy Bible unfortunately tells us nothing of this. Readers may, however, refer to our auxiliary Bible, 'Paradise Lost,' Book xi, Michael's prophecy of the Flood. But Milton was really too careless about the fate of the guard. Was it recalled in time, or did it perish at its post? Did the deluge sweep over that gate, 'With dreadful faces thronged, and fiery arms?' Let us hope not. It would be sad to think that the 'flaming sword' was extinguished with a hiss; and that the 'Cherubim' were drowned like the other animals, without even the salvation of a single live specimen in the Ark. Probably, however, being abundantly and superabundantly furnished with wings, they all flew away to Heaven when the waters began sweeping the Mount of Paradise 'Down the great river to the opening gulf.'

No Lamia of delirious dream,
No nymph of forest, sea, or stream:
A soul of fire, a lovely form
Lithe to the dance and breathing warm;
A face that flushed with cordial pleasure, 845
Dove-feet that flew in perfect measure;
A little hand so soft and fine,
Whose touch electric thrilled through mine;
A heart that beat against my breast
Full pulses of triumphant zest; 850
Deep eyes, pure eyes, as dark as night,
Yet full of liquid love and light
When their moon-soul came floating through
The clouds of mystery into view,
And myriad star-rays glittering keen 855
Were tempered in its mystic sheen;
Soft lips full curved in ruddy glow,
And swift as young Apollo's bow,—
What arrowy laughters flashing free
With barbs of pleasant mockery 860
Pierced through and through the whirling rout,
And let thought in where life flew out,
And made the world a happy dream
'Where nothing is, but all things seem!'

   The splendid beauty of her face, 865
Her dancing's proud and passionate grace,
Her soul's eternal life intense
Lavishly poured through every sense,
Intoxicated all the air,
Inspiring every dancer there: 870
Never again shall that old Hall
Spin round with such another Ball;
The human whirlwind might have whirled
It through the heights of air and hurled
It down at last into the sea, 875
Nor yet disturbed the revelry.
The violin and the violoncello,
The flute that withered little fellow,
The red-faced cornet always mellow,
Our noble Orchestra of four, 880
Played as they never played of yore,
Played as they will play nevermore,
As if the rushing air were cloven
By all the legions of Beethoven.

   In one of the eternal trances 885
(Five minutes long) between two dances,

The Brown whom one meets everywhere
Came smug and grinning to me there,
And 'May I have the pleasure,—honour?'
A glance (encouraging) upon her.   890

'My dear good Brown, you understand
This lady's from a foreign land,
And does not comprehend a word
You speak so well: nay, I have heard
That one may search all England through,   895
And not find twenty scholars who
Can speak or write her language clearly,
Though once our great men loved it dearly.
The little of it I know still
(Read well, write badly, speak so ill!)   900
I first learnt many years ago
From her, and one you do not know,
A restless wanderer, one of these
You call damned doubtful refugees,
Enthusiasts, whom while harboured here   905
All proper folk dislike and fear.'

  Brown muttered, 'I've a little knowledge
Of French,—the Working Man's New College.'

'Ah, yes; your French is doubtless good,
And French we know is understood   910
By polished people everywhere;
But then her land though rich and fair
Lies far beyond the continents
Of civilised accomplishments;
And she could sooner learn to speak   915
Persian or Sanskrit, Norse or Greek,
Than this delightful brilliant witty
Tongue of delightful Paris city
[1](*The devils' paradise, the hell*

[1]"Mich ruft der Tod. . . .
 .   .   .   .
Glaub mir, mein Kind, mein Weib, Mathilde,
Nicht so gefährlich ist das wilde
Erzürnte Meer und der trotzige Wald,
Als unser jetzige Aufenthalt!
Wie schrecklich auch der Wolf und der Geier,
Haifische und sonstige Meerungeheuer:
Viel grimmere, schlimmere Bestien enthält
Paris, die leuchtende Hauptstadt der Welt,
Das singende, springende, schöne Paris,
Die Hölle der Engel, der Teufel Paradies—
Das ich dich hier verlassen soll,
Das macht mir verrückt, das macht mir toll!'
  LETZTE GEDICHTE: *Babylonische Sorgen.*

Of angels,—Heine loved it well!). 920
And finally, my dearest Brown,
The customs of her folk would frown
Austere rebukes on her if she
Dared dance with any one but me!'

    Brown went and whispered strange remarks 925
To eager girls and staring clerks. . . .
We are caught up and swept away
In the cyclone-gallop's sway
And round and round and round and round
Go whirling in a storm of sound. 930

    But in the next brief perfect trance
That followed the impassioned dance,
The Jones whom one too rarely sees
Came rushing on me like a breeze;
'What miracle! what magic might!— 935
But have you seen yourself to-night?'

    'Oh yes! twin-mirrored in the skies
Of these my Lady's glorious eyes!
In our rude days of kingly fear,
If any monarch drawing near 940
The palace saw so bright and clear
His picture in the windows shine,
He well might say, *Auspicious sign
That still this noble home is mine!*'

    'But you are half as tall again, 945
And stately as a King of Men;
And in the prime of health and youth,
Younger by twenty years, in sooth;
Your face, the pale and sallow, glows
As fresh as any morning rose; 950
Your voice rings richly as a bell,

   The title suggests, and may have been specially suggested by, that great verse of Jeremiah li. 7: 'Babylon hath been a golden cup in the Lord's hand, that made all the earth drunken: the nations have drunken of her wine; therefore the nations are mad.'
   So Béranger, in his *Jean de Paris:*
                  'Quel amour incroyable,
                    Maintenant et jadis,
                    Pour ces murs dont le diable
                    A fait son paradis!'
   And he who knew his Paris best, Balzac the Terrible: 'Cette succursale de l'enfer.' *Melmoth Reconcilié.*
   Again, 'Paris a été nommé un enfer. Tenez ce mot pour vrai.' *La Fille aux Yeux d'or.* (*Histoire des Treize.*)
   And yet again, 'Ce Paris qualifié d'antichambre de l'enfer.' *Balzac, to the Abbé Aglé.*

Resonant as a trumpet-swell;
Your dull and mournful dreamy eyes
Now dazzle, burn, and mesmerise:
Thus gazed, thus spoke, thus smiled, thus trod, 955
Apollo the immortal God!'

'Dear Jones, as usual, you are right;
I stand revealed Myself to-night,
The God of Poesy, Lord of Light. . . .
But you would learn now whence the change: 960
Listen; it is and is not strange.

'There was a Fountain long ago,
A fountain of perpetual flow,
Whose purest springlets had their birth
Deep in the bosom of the earth. 965
Its joyous wavering silvery shaft
To all the beams of morning laughed,
Its steadfast murmurous crystal column
Was loved by all the moonbeams solemn;
From morn to eve it fell again 970
A singing many-jewelled rain,
From eve to morn it charmed the hours
With whispering dew and diamond showers;
Crowned many a day with sunbows bright,
With moonbows halo'd many a night; 975
And so kept full its marble urn,
All fringed with fronds of greenest fern,
O'er which with timeless love intent
A pure white marble Goddess leant:
And overflowing aye the urn 980
In rillets that became a burn,
It danced adown the verdant slope
As light as youth, as gay as hope,
And "wandered at its own sweet will;"
And here it was a lakelet still, 985
And there it was a flashing stream;
And all about it was a dream
Of beauty, such a Paradise
As rarely blooms beneath our skies;
The loveliest flowers, the grandest trees, 990
The broadest glades, the fairest leas;
And double music tranced the hours,—
The countless perfumes of the flowers,
The countless songs of swift delight
That birds were singing day and night. 995

'But suddenly there fell a change;
So suddenly, so sad, so strange!
The fountain ceased to wave its lance
Of silver to the spheral dance;
The runnels were no longer fed,   1000
And each one withered from its bed;
The stream fell stagnant, and was soon
A bloated marsh, a pest-lagoon;
The sweet flowers died, the noble trees
Turned black and gaunt anatomies;   1005
The birds all left the saddened air
To seek some other home as fair;
The pure white Goddess and her urn
Were covered with the withered fern,—
The red and yellow fans outworn,   1010
And red and yellow leaves forlorn,
Slow drifting round into a heap
Till the fair shapes were buried deep:
The happy Eden rich and fair
Became a savage waste, a lair   1015
Where Silence with broad wings of gloom
Brooded above a nameless tomb. . . .
And thus it was for years and years;
And only there were bitter tears
Beneath those dark wings shed alway   1020
Instead of the bright fountain's play,
And in the stead of sweet bird-tones
Low unheard solitary moans.

'Ah, sudden was that ruin sad;
As sudden, resurrection glad!   1025
Unheralded one quiet night
There came an Angel darkly bright,
An Angel from the Heavenly Throne,
Or else that Goddess carved in stone
Enraptured into life by power   1030
Of her most marvellous beauty's dower:
And from her long robe's sweeping pride
The dead leaves all were scattered wide;
And from a touch of her soft hand,
Without one gesture of command,   1035
All suddenly was rolled away
A mighty stone, whose broad mass lay
Upon the urn, as on a tomb
There lies a stone to seal its gloom:
And straightway sprang into the night   1040
That joyous Fountain's shaft of light,
Singing its old unwearied tune

Of rapture to the quiet moon,
As strong and swift and pure and high
As ere it ever seemed run dry: 1045
For never since that Long-ago
Had its deep springlets ceased to flow;
But shut down from the light of day
Their waters sadly oozed away
Through pores of the dim underearth, 1050
Bereft of splendour, speed, and mirth;
Yet ever ready now as then
To leap into the air again.'

'Ah yes,' said Jones, 'I understand.'
Then with his smile of sadness bland, 1055
'*My* fountain never got a chance
To spring into the sunlight's glance,
And wave its mystic silver lance
In time with all the starry dance;
Yet I believe 'tis ever there 1060
Heart-pulsing in its secret lair,
Until the Goddess some fine day
Shall come and roll the stone away. . . .
Nor have you startled me; I knew
Quite well it was a Goddess too.' 1065

'Because so well you know and speak
Her esoteric Persian-Greek.'

'Or shall we say (a truth of wine,
If falsehood in the nectar-shine),
Because a beauty so divine 1070
Has stirred no envy, grudge, or pine
In any girl's or woman's breast,
But only love and joyous zest?—
For if the beauty dazzling thus
Were nubile and not nebulous?' 1075

'This beauty is more real far
Than all the other beauties are;
And such a beauty's bridal kiss
Transcends all other bridal bliss;
And such a marriage-love will last 1080
When all the other loves are past.
You know this well, dear friend of mine,
When drinking nectar and not wine.'

'I know it,—know it not: we rhyme
The petals of the Flower of Time; 1085
And rhyming strip them off, perplext

For every leaflet by the next
Is contradicted in its turn;
And thus we yearning ever yearn,
And ever learning never learn;   1090
For while we pluck, from hour to hour
New petals spring to clothe the flower,
And till we strip the final one
Can final answer fall to none. . . .
To strip and strip the living bloom,   1095
Nor learn the oracle of Doom
Until the fulgent Flower o' the Day
Is altogether stripped away;
Then with the dead stem leave the light,
And moulder in eternal night!'   1100

'The sad old truth of earthly wine;
The joyous fable in the shine
Of nectar at the feast divine! . . .
Love a near maid, love a far maid,
But let Hebe be your barmaid;   1105
When she proffers you the cup,
Never fear to drink it up;
Though you see her crush her wine
From a belladonna vine,
Drink it, pouring on the clods   1110
Prelibation to the gods.
Reck this rede unto the end:
It is my good night, good friend.'

.   .   .   .   .

The music 'gan again arise;
A music of delicious sighs,
A music plaintive with a grief   1115
More exquisite than all relief;
Music impassioned, but subdued
To a sweet sad dreamy mood. . . .
And now a swift and sudden stream   1120
Of melody breaks through the dream:
The still air trembles, and the whole
Night-darkness fills with life and soul,
And keen stars listen throbbing pale
The drama of the nightingale. . . .   1125
The nightingale is now a thrush. . . .
And now a soaring skylark . . . . Hush!
Never a song in all the world!
But low clouds floating soft and furled,
And rivers winding far away,   1130
And ripples weaving faëry spray,
And mists far-curving swelling round

Dim twilight hills that soon are drowned,
And breezes stirring solemn woods,
And seas embracing solitudes;
Interminable intervolving,
Weaving webs for redissolving;
The intertwining, interblending
Of spirals evermore ascending;
The floating hither, wheeling thither,
Without a whence, without a whither;
And still we whirl and wheel and float,
But how the dancers are remote!

'Is that the wonderful waltz-tune,
Or is it the full-shining moon?
And are those notes, so far and far?
Each seems to me a brilliant star!
Can we be dancing in the ball,
And yet not see the earth at all? . . .
The starry notes are round us whirling,
Beneath the great moon-waltz is twirling;
And thus without our own endeavour
May we float and float for ever?'

'When six long days of toil are past,
The holy Sabbath comes at last.'

Oh better than a battle won,
And better than a great deed done,
And better than a martyr's crown,
And better than a king's renown,
And better than a long calm life
With lovely bairns and loving wife,
And better than the sweetest thought
That tearful Memory ever brought
From searching with her rapturous woe
Within the moonlit Long-ago,
And better than the stillest sleep
To him who wakes to moan and weep,
And better than the trance of death
To him who yearning suffereth;
Better than this, than these, than all
That mortals joys and triumphs call,
Was last night's Meeting, last night's Ball!

. . . . .

The tongue of flame had ceased to play,
The steadfast glow long died away;
The house was grave-still, and the street
Re-echoed to no wandering feet;

And still and chill as any stone
¹I lay upon the couch alone,
Drest to the white kid-gloves in all
The dress I put on for the Ball: 1180
And there, that glorious flower you see,
She fixed it in my breast for me;
Could such a flower of flowers have birth
Upon our worn-out frigid earth?
That golden-hearted amethyst 1185
Her own hand held, her own mouth kissed.

   The clocks struck one and two and three,
And each stroke fell as aimed at me;
For none should muse or read or write
So late into the awful night, 1190
None dare awake the deep affright
That pulseth in the heart of night,
None venture save sleep-shrouded quite
Into the solemn dead of night,
None wander save in dreams of light 1195
Through the vast desert of black night;
And none at three be dressed at all,
Unless mere night-clothes dress you call
Or underlinen of a pall;
Therefore, my friend, in bidding you 1200
And all the rest a long adieu,
For I am weary, Alleleu!—
Yourself and all I re-advise,
Early to bed and early to rise,
Is the way to be healthy, wealthy, and wise! 1205

Epilogue

(Grossness here indeed is regnant,
But it is the grossness pregnant;
HEINE growled it, ending thus
His wild *Book of Lazarus;*
Modern swansong's final note, 5
Hoarse death-rattle in the throat.
Swan was white or black?—*Our* candour!
Black or white no swan's a gander.)

   'Glory warms us in the grave!
Stupid words, that sound so brave! 10
Better warmth would give to us
Molly Seagrim amorous,

---

¹ It may not be amiss to vouch
   The previous note anent this couch.

Slobbering kisses lips and tongue,
And yet reeking from the dung.[1]
Better warmth would likewise dart 15
Through the cockles of one's heart,
Drinking mulled wine, punch, or grog,
Until helpless as a log,
In the lowest den whose crowd is
Thieves and drabs and ragged rowdies, 20
Mortgaged to the gallows-rope,
But who meanwhile breathe and hope,
And more enviable far
Than the son of Thetis are.
Yes, Pelides was a judge;— 25
Better live the poorest drudge
In the upper world, than loom
On the Stygian shore of gloom
Phantom-Leader, bodiless roamer,
Though besung by mighty Homer.' 30

VERSICLES

WHEREVER on this round earth
Your shaft may enter,
Strike it straight, and never fear
But you'll reach at last the centre.

EACH doth by his birth belong 5
To some sphere wherein he's strong;
Nine of ten with passion seek
Alien spheres wherein they're weak;
Whence in almost every man
Such incongruous *Will* and *Can*. 10

DEAR Mother Earth, tell us, tell us, tell us!
What is the meaning of all the things we see?—
Oh, what a family of funny little fellows,
Calling me always, *Tellus*, *Tellus*, *Tellus!*
Eat your bread, drink your wine, snatch at all you see; 15
But I am very busy, do not bother me.

THE old man moans, saints' eyes with tears are wet;
Wherefore? this real earthly human life
Offered to all, is the Socratic wife;
Had or had not, the issue is regret. 20

---

[1] *Eine Kuh-magd*—Any farm-wench; but Heine, who knew Fielding, probably had Molly Seagrim in his mind.

LOW LIFE
AS OVERHEARD IN THE TRAIN

THAT jolly old gentleman, bless his white hat!
Wouldn't come in to spoil our chat;
We are alone and we can speak,—
What have you done, Miss, all the week?

'Oh, all the day it's been fit and shew,
And all the night it's been trim and sew,
For the ladies are flocking to Exeter Hall
In lovely light dresses fit for a ball.'

Under your eye a little dark streak,
And a point of red on the top of your cheek,
And your temples quite dim against your hair;
This sha'n't last very much longer I swear.

And what is the news from the workroom now?
'The week began with a bit of a row;
Emmy Harley married young Earl
Just in the busy time!'—sensible girl!

'That was on Monday; Missis said
It was very ungrateful, very ill-bred,
And very unkind to us when she knew
The work so heavy, the hands so few.

'But this was nothing: the minute we woke
On Wednesday, before it seemed any one spoke,
We knew that poor Mary Challis was dead;
Kate Long had been sleeping in the same bed.

'Mary worked with us till twelve, when tea
Was brought in to keep us awake, but she
Was so ill then, Miss Cooper sent her to bed;
And there in the morning they found her dead;

'With Kate fast asleep by her side: they had come
To see how she was, and the sight struck them dumb:
At last they roused Kate and led her away;
She was sick and shuddering all the day.

'Kate says when she went up at four to their room
She was stupid with sleep; but she marked a faint bloom
On Mary's pale face, and she heard her breathe low—
A light fluttering breath now quick and now slow;

'And feared to disturb her, for *she* had a cough,
But the moment she laid her head down she was off,
And knew nothing more till they stood by the side
Of the bed: p'r'aps Mary slept on till she died.   40

'They buried her yesterday. Kate was there,
And she was the only one Missis could spare;
Some dresses were bound to be finished by night,
For the ladies to go in to Church all right.

'Poor Mary! she didn't fear dying, she said,   45
Her father drinks and her mother is dead;
But she hoped that in Heaven the white garments wear
For ever; no fashions and dressmaking There.'

My Love, if the ladies most pious of all
Who flock to the Church and to Exeter Hall   50
Find Heaven has but one dress for rich as for poor,
And no fashions, they'll very soon cut it I'm sure.

I saw you ten minutes on Tuesday night,
Then I took the 'bus home for I had to write;
And I wrote and I wrote like an engine till five,   55
When my fingers were dead and the letters alive.

A fair Bill of Costs from a deuce of a draft
In our Cashier's worst scrawl like Chinese run daft;
With entries between, on the margin, the back,
And figures like short-hand marks put to the rack.   60

But our Common-law Clerk is going away,
And the Gov'nor had me in yesterday,
And said he would try me, he thought I might do;
And I jumped at the chance, for this child thinks so too.

Just fancy, each morning a jolly good walk,   65
And instead of the copying, bustle and talk!
And if I do well—and well I will do—
A couple of sovs. a week for my screw!

And then when I'm free of the desk and the stool,
Do you think you will keep to the nunnery rule   70
Of the shop, till you go off like Mary some night
Smothered in work from the air and the light?

We'll use our professional talents, my dear:
You shall make such a wedding-dress, best of the year!
And a wonderful marriage-deed I will draw   75
With magnificent settlements perfect in law.

Thus doing our duties in those states of life
In which it has pleased God to call us, *my wife!*
'And how much a year will you settle on me?'
My body and soul and—what we shall see. 80

POLYCRATES ON WATERLOO BRIDGE

 Let no mortals dare to be
 Happier in their lives than we:
 Thus the jealous gods decree.

 This decree was never heard,
 Never by their lips averred, 5
 Yet on high stands registered.

 I have read it, and I fear
 All the gods above, my Dear,
 All must envy us two here.

 Let us, then, propitiate 10
 These proud satraps of sole Fate;
 Our hearts' wealth is all too great.

 Say, what rich and cherished thing
 Can I to the river fling
 As a solemn offering? 15

 O belovèd Meerschaum Pipe,
 Whose pink bloom would soon be ripe,
 Must thou be the chosen type?

 Cloud-compeller! Foam o' the Sea,
 Whence rose Venus fair and free 20
 On some poet's reverie!

 In the sumptuous silken-lined
 Case where thou hast lain enshrined
 Thou must now a coffin find!

 And, to drag thee surely down, 25
 Lo! I tie my last half-crown:
 We shall have to walk through town.

 Penny toll is paid, and thus
 All the bridge is free to us;
 But no cab, nor even a 'bus! 30

Far I fling thee through the gloom;
Sink into thy watery tomb,
O thou consecrate to Doom!

May no sharp police, while they track
Spoils thrown after some great 'crack,'   35
Ever, ever bring thee back!

No mudlarkers, who explore
Every ebb the filthy floor,
Bring thee to the day once more!

No sleek cook—I spare the wish;   40
Dead dogs, cats, and suchlike fish,
Surely are not yet a dish? . . .

Gods! the dearest, as I wis,
Of my treasures offered is;
Pardon us our heavenly bliss!   45

What Voice murmurs full of spleen?
Not that Pipe, but—Ssss! how mean
All the gods have ever been!

ONCE IN A SAINTLY PASSION

ONCE in a saintly passion
  I cried with desperate grief:
O Lord, my heart is black with guile,
  Of sinners I am chief!
Then stooped my guardian-angel   5
  And whispered from behind:
'Vanity, my little man,
  You're nothing of the kind.'

ON THE TERRACE AT RICHMOND

FIXED to a tall stem like a mast,
  A board with certain rhymes
Here overlooked the vale and stream:
  Where is it in these times?

The lines were scarcely of the best;   5
  Not one can I recall;
The board looked like a board of rules
  Against a workhouse wall.

Yet they were meant to honour one
    Who honour merited;
A gentle heart and free from guile,
    A poet long since dead.

My great-great-grandfather he was,
    Although no child had he;
Yet as the lineal heir I'm blessed
    With all the property:—

The Castle hight of Indolence,
    And all the rich domain
Which to that Castle and its Lords
    Doth ever appertain;

Thereto a noble royalty
    Of rhymes and various verse,—
The quantity is now much less
    The quality much worse.

The Castle is so beautiful,
    The land so rich and wide;
Such sweet birds sing, such sweet flowers spring,
    Such silver streamlets glide!

The Landlord and the Tenants all
    Are far too indolent
For that which troubles most estates,
    The payment of a rent.

II

You're not quite sure you ever heard
    This pleasant poet's name?
But you will like him womanlike
    Since someone bears the same?

I'm sure you never read a page
    Of anything he wrote;
I'm sure for all his books of verse
    You would not care a groat.

Were I to read you some, of course
    You'd make a fine pretence,
How pretty! pleased to see me pleased,
    Not caring for the sense.

And you are right: Doth Lycidas
  Leave Milton's tome and urge
Young Adonais to recite 15
  His supramortal dirge?

Do roses gaze on pictured walls
  Where scentless roses bloom?
Do stars read sonnets where we praise
  Their shining through the gloom? 20

Sweet living Poem! Why should you
  Read dull dead words that shrine
Dim echoes of your voice, rude hints
  Of your own grace divine?

III

The Castle hight of Indolence
  Holds many pictures fair;
And many portraits with his own
  The Architect placed there.

But one grand portrait lacked, alack! 5
  And in his secret Will
He gave his heirs a solemn charge
  This mighty void to fill.

The Portrait of the very Lord
  Of all the Lords who sway 10
The Castle and its happy realms
  Was wanting to this day!

He ever lives, this Lord supreme,
  In many a quaint disguise;
Full hard to meet, and then when met 15
  Full hard to recognise.

I met him, knew him, loved him well;
  For me he dropped his mask;
To place his portrait in our Hall
  Has been my pleasant task. 20

Here is the sketch,—how thin and blurred!
  He dreams, beyond desire,
Clothed with the ninefold robes of verse
  Loved by our Eastern Sire.

SUNDAY UP THE RIVER
AN IDYLL OF COCKAIGNE

> En allant promener aux champs,
> J'y ai trouvé les blés si grands,
> Les aubépines florissant.
>   En vérité, en vérité,
> C'est le mois, le joli mois,
> C'est le joli mois de mai.
>
>   .   .   .   .
>
> Dieu veuill' garder les vins, les blés,
> Les jeunes filles à marier,
> Les jeun' garçons pour les aimer!
>   En vérité, en vérité,
> C'est le mois, le joli mois,
> C'est le joli mois de mai.
> <div align="right"><i>Carol of Lorraine.</i> [1]</div>

I

I LOOKED out into the morning,
  I looked out into the west:
The soft blue eye of the quiet sky
  Still drooped in dreamy rest;

The trees were still like clouds there,
  The clouds like mountains dim;
The broad mist lay, a silver bay
  Whose tide was at the brim.

I looked out into the morning,
  I looked out into the east:
The flood of light upon the night
  Had silently increased;

The sky was pale with fervour,
  The distant trees were grey,
The hill-lines drawn like waves of dawn
  Dissolving in the day.

I looked out into the morning;
  Looked east, looked west, with glee:
O richest day of happy May,
  My Love will spend with me!

II

'Oh, what are you waiting for here, young man?
  What are you looking for over the bridge?'
A little straw hat with the streaming blue ribbons
  Is soon to come dancing over the bridge.

---

[1] From Victor Fournel's charming book, '*Ce qu'on voit dans les rues de Paris.*'

Her heart beats the measure that keeps her feet dancing,
    Dancing along like a wave o' the sea;
Her heart pours the sunshine with which her eyes glancing
    Light up strange faces in looking for me.

The strange faces brighten in meeting her glances;
    The strangers all bless her, pure, lovely, and free:
She fancies she walks, but her walk skips and dances,
    Her heart makes such music in coming to me.

Oh, thousands and thousands of happy young maidens
    Are tripping this morning their sweethearts to see;
But none whose heart beats to a sweeter love-cadence
    Than hers who will brighten the sunshine for me.

'Oh, what are you waiting for here, young man?
    What are you looking for over the bridge?'
A little straw hat with the streaming blue ribbons;
    —And here it comes dancing over the bridge!

ART

I

What precious thing are you making fast
    In all these silken lines?
And where and to whom will it go at last?
    Such subtle knots and twines!

I am tying up all my love in this,
    With all its hopes and fears,
With all its anguish and all its bliss,
    And its hours as heavy as years.

I am going to send it afar, afar,
    To I know not where above;
To that sphere beyond the highest star
    Where dwells the soul of my Love.

But in vain, in vain, would I make it fast
    With countless subtle twines;
For ever its fire breaks out at last,
    And shrivels all the lines.

II

If you have a carrier-dove
    That can fly over land and sea;
And a message for your Love,
    'Lady, I love but thee!'

And this dove will never stir
    But straight from her to you,
And straight from you to her;
    As you know and she knows too.

Will you first ensure, O sage,
    Your dove that never tires
With your message in a cage,
    Though a cage of golden wires?

Or will you fling your dove:
    'Fly, darling, without rest,
Over land and sea to my Love,
    And fold your wings in her breast'?

III

Singing is sweet; but be sure of this,
Lips only sing when they cannot kiss.

Did he ever suspire a tender lay
While her presence took his breath away?

Had his fingers been able to toy with her hair
Would they then have written the verses fair?

Had she let his arm steal round her waist
Would the lovely portrait yet be traced?

Since he could not embrace it flushed and warm
He has carved in stone the perfect form.

Who gives the fine report of the feast?
He who got none and enjoyed it least.

Were the wine really slipping down his throat
Would his song of the wine advance a note?

Will you puff out the music that sways the whirl,
Or dance and make love with a pretty girl?

Who shall the great battle-story write?
Not the hero down in the thick of the fight.

Statues and pictures and verse may be grand,
But they are not the Life for which they stand.

A POLISH INSURGENT (1863)

WHAT would you have? said I;[1]
'Tis so easy to go and die,
'Tis so hard to stay and live,
In this alien peace and this comfort callous,
Where only the murderers get the gallows,   5
Where the jails are for rogues who thieve.

'Tis so easy to go and die,
Where our Country, our Mother, the Martyr,
Moaning in bonds doth lie,
Bleeding with stabs in her breast,   10
Her throat with a foul clutch prest,
Under the thrice-accursed Tartar.

But Smith, your man of sense,
Ruddy, and broad, and round—like so!
Kindly—but dense, but dense,   15
Said to me: 'Do not go:
It is hopeless; right is wrong;
The tyrant is too strong.'

Must a man have *hope* to fight?
Can a man not fight in despair?   20
Must the soul cower down for the body's weakness,
And slaver the devil's hoof with meekness,
Nor care nor dare to share
Certain defeat with the right?

They do not know us, my Mother!   25
They know not our love, our hate!
And how we would die with each other,
Embracing proud and elate,
Rather than live apart
In peace with shame in the heart.   30

No hope!—If a heavy anger
Our God hath treasured against us long,
His lightning-shafts from His thunder-clangour
Raining a century down:
We have loved when we went most wrong;   35
He cannot for ever frown.

---

[1] Some time after writing this I found that the great BALZAC, in *La Cousine Bette*, dwells on this very phrase, 'Que voulez-vous?' as characteristic of the gallant and reckless Poles.

No hope!—We can haste to be killed,
That the tale of the victims get filled;
The more of the debt we pay,
The less on our sons shall weigh: 40
This star through the baleful rack of the cope
Burns red; red is our hope.

O our Mother, thou art noble and fair!
Fair and proud and chaste, thou Queen!
Chained and stabbed in the breast, 45
Thy throat with a foul clutch prest;
Yet around thee how coarse, how mean,
Are these rich shopwives who stare!

Art thou moaning, O our Mother, through the swoon
Of thine agony of desolation? 50
'Do my sons still love me? or can they stand
Gazing afar from a foreign land,
Loving more peace and gold—the boon
Of a people strange, of a sordid nation?'

O our Mother, moan not thus! 55
We love you as you love us,
And our hearts are wild with thy sorrow:
If we cannot save thee, we are blest
Who can die on thy sacred bleeding breast.—
    So we left Smith-Land on the morrow, 60
    And we hasten across the West.

MR. MACCALL AT CLEVELAND HALL
(April 15, 1866)

    Mr. Maccall at Cleveland Hall,
    Sunday evening—date to fix—
    Fifteenth April, sixty-six,
    Speech reported and redacted
    By a fellow much distracted. 5

Who lectures? No mere scorner;
  Clear-brained, his heart is warm.
She sits at the nearest corner
  Of I will not say what form.

The Conflict of Opinions 10
  In the Present Day, saith Chair.
What muff in the British dominions
  Could dispute that she is fair?

Mammon-worship is horrid,
    Plutocracy is base.
Dark hair from a fine small forehead;
    I catch but the still side-face.

We wallow in mere dimension,
    The Big to us is Great.
If she stood at her utmost tension
    She *might* pass four feet eight.

We lay on colour in splashes,
    With a mop, or a broom for brush.
How dark are her long eyelashes!
    How pure is her cheek's slight flush!

But we have no perception
    For form—the divinest—now.
Each curve there is perfection,
    In nostril, chin, and brow.

Our women are good kind creatures,
    But they cannot dress at all.
Does her bonnet grace her features?—
    Clear blue with a black lace fall.

Low Church—very low—in the gutter;
    High Church—as ven'son high.
O'er the flower of her face gleams the flutter
    Of a smile like a butterfly.

Herder, Wieland, Lessing;
    Bossuet, Montalembert.
Fine names, but the name worth guessing
    Is the name of the sweet girl there.

The individual; true man;
    Individuality.
A man's but one half; some woman
    The other half must be.

Persistent valour the sternest,
    With love's most gentle grace.
How grand is the eye fixed earnest
    In the half-seen up-turned face!

'How did you like the lecture?   50
  Was it not beautiful?'
I should think *she was!* 'I conjecture
  That your brains have been gathering wool!'

                 P.S.
The Chairman was a rare man;
  At every telling point   55
He smiled at his post like a jolly host
  Carving rich cuts from the joint;
Which the name he bore was Richard Moore
  Whom Heaven with grace anoint!

      That conflict of opinion   60
        It had its counterpart
      In conflict for dominion
        Between my head and heart.

              LIFE'S HEBE

      In the early morning-shine
      Of a certain day divine,
      I beheld a Maiden stand
      With a pitcher in her hand;
      Whence she poured into a cup   5
      Until it was half filled up
      Nectar that was golden light
      In the cup of crystal bright.

      And the first who took the cup
      With pure water filled it up;   10
      As he drank then, it was more
      Ruddy golden than before:
      And he leapt and danced and sang
      As to Bacchic cymbals' clang.

      But the next who took the cup   15
      With the red wine filled it up;
      What he drank then was in hue
      Of a heavy sombre blue:
      First he reeled and then he crept,
      Then lay faint but never slept.   20

      And the next who took the cup
      With the white milk filled it up;
      What he drank at first seemed blood,

Then turned thick and brown as mud:
And he moved away as slow
As a weary ox may go.

But the next who took the cup
With sweet honey filled it up;
Nathless that which he did drink
Was thin fluid black as ink:
As he went he stumbled soon,
And lay still in deathlike swoon.

She the while without a word
Unto all the cup preferred;
Blandly smiled and sweetly laughed
As each mingled his own draught.

And the next who took the cup
To the sunshine held it up,
Gave it back and did not taste;
It was empty when replaced:
First he bowed a reverent bow,
Then he kissed her on the brow.

But the next who took the cup
Without mixture drank it up;
When she took it back from him
It was full unto the brim:
He with a right bold embrace
Kissed her sweet lips face to face.

Then she sang with blithest cheer:
Who has thirst, come here, come here!
Nectar that is golden light
In the cup of crystal bright,
Nectar that is sunny fire
Warm as warmest heart's desire:
Pitcher never lacketh more,
Arm is never tired to pour:
Honey, water, milk, or wine
Mingle with the draught divine,
Drink it pure, or drink it not;
Each is free to choose his lot:
Am I old? or am I cold?
Only two have kissed me bold!

She was young and fair and gay
As that young and glorious day.

DAY

WAKING one morning
In a pleasant land,
By a river flowing
Over golden sand:—

Whence flow ye, waters,
O'er your golden sand?
We come flowing
From the Silent Land.

Whither flow ye, waters,
O'er your golden sand?
We go flowing
To the Silent Land.

And what is this fair realm?
A grain of golden sand
In the great darkness
Of the Silent Land.

NIGHT

HE cried out through the night:
  'Where is the light?
  Shall nevermore
  Open Heaven's door?
  Oh, I am left
  Lonely, bereft!'

He cried out through the night:
  It spread vaguely white,
  With its ghost of a moon
  Above the dark swoon
  Of the earth lying chill,
  Breathless, grave-still.

He cried out through the night:
  His voice in its might
  Rang forth far and far,
  And then like a star
  Dwindled from sense
  In the Immense.

He cried out through the night:
  No answering light,
  No syllabled sound;
  Beneath and around
  A long shuddering thrill,
  Then all again still.

PHILOSOPHY

I

His eyes found nothing beautiful and bright,
Nor wealth nor honour, glory nor delight,
Which he could grasp and keep with might and right.

Flowers bloomed for maidens, swords outflashed for boys,
The world's big children had their various toys;   5
He could not feel their sorrows and their joys.

Hills held a secret they would not unfold,
In careless scorn of him the ocean rolled,
The stars were alien splendours high and cold.

He felt himself a king bereft of crown,   10
Defrauded from his birthright of renown,
Bred up in littleness with churl and clown.

II

How could he vindicate himself? His eyes,
That found not anywhere their proper prize,
Looked through and through the specious earth and skies.

They probed, and all things yielded to their probe;
They saw the void around the massy globe,   5
The raging fire within its flowery robe.

They pierced through beauty; saw the bones, the mesh
Of nerves and veins, the hideous raw red flesh,
Beneath the skin most delicate and fresh:

Saw Space a mist unfurled around the steep   10
Where plunge Time's waters to the blackest deep;
Saw Life a dream in Death's eternal sleep.

III

A certain fair form came before his sight,
Responding to him as the day to night:
To yearning, love; to cold and gloom, warm light.

A hope sprang from his breast, and fluttered far
On rainbow wings; beyond the cloudy bar,   5
Though very much beneath the nearest star.

His eyes drew back their beams to kindle fire
In his own heart; whose masterful desire
Scorned all beyond its aim, lower or higher.

This fire flung lustre upon grace and bloom, 10
Gave warmth and brightness to a little room,
Burned Thought to ashes in its fight with gloom.

IV

He said: Those eyes alone see well that view
Life's lovely surfaces of form and hue;
And not Death's entrails, looking through and through.

Bones, nerves, and veins, and flesh, are covered in
By this opaque transparency of skin, 5
Precisely that we should not see within.

The corpse is hid, that Death may work its vile
Corruption in black secrecy; the while
Our saddest graves with grass and fair flowers smile.

If you will analyse the bread you eat, 10
The water and the wine most pure and sweet,
Your stomach soon must loathe all drink and meat.

Life liveth but in Life, and doth not roam
To other realms if all be well at home:
'Solid as ocean-foam,' quoth ocean-foam. 15

If Midge will pine and curse its hours away
Because Midge is not Everything For-aye,
Poor Midge thus loses its one summer day;
Loses its all—and winneth what, I pray?

THE NAKED GODDESS

*Arcane danze
D'immortal piede i ruinosi gioghi
Scossero e l'ardue selve (oggi romito
Nido de' venti).* LEOPARDI

THROUGH the country to the town
Ran a rumour and renown,
That a woman grand and tall,
Swift of foot, and therewithal
Naked as a lily gleaming, 5
Had been seen by eyes not dreaming,
Darting down far forest glades,
Flashing sunshine through the shades.

With this rumour's swelling word
All the city buzzed and stirred; 10
Solemn senators conferred;

Priest, astrologer, and mage,
Subtle sophist, bard, and sage,
Brought their wisdom, lore, and wit,
To expound or riddle it: 15
Last a porter ventured—'We
Might go out ourselves to see.'

 Thus, upon a summer morn
Lo the city all forlorn;
Every house and street and square 20
In the sunshine still and bare,
Every galley left to sway
Silent in the glittering bay;
All the people swarming out,
Young and old a joyous rout, 25
Rich and poor, far-streaming through
Fields and meadows dark with dew,
Crowd on crowd, and throng on throng;
Chatter, laughter, jest, and song
Deafened all the singing birds, 30
Wildered sober grazing herds.

 Up the hillside 'gainst the sun,
Where the forest outskirts run;
On along the level high,
Where the azure of the sky, 35
And the ruddy morning sheen,
Drop in fragments through the treen
Where the sward surrounds the brake
With a lucid, glassy lake,
Where the ample glades extend 40
Until clouds and foliage blend;
Where whoever turneth may
See the city and the bay,
And, beyond, the broad sea bright,
League on league of slanting light; 45
Where the moist blue shadows sleep
In the sacred forest deep.

 Suddenly the foremost pause,
Ere the rear discern a cause;
Loiterers press up row on row, 50
All the mass heaves to and fro;
All seem murmuring in one strain,
All seem hearkening fixed and fain:
Silence, and the lifted light
Of countless faces gazing white. 55

THE NAKED GODDESS

Four broad beech-trees, great of bole,
Crowned the green, smooth-swelling knoll;
There She leant, the glorious form
Dazzling with its beauty warm,
Naked as the sun of noon,   60
Naked as the midnight moon:
And around her, tame and mild,
All the forest creatures wild—
Lion, panther, kid, and fawn,
Eagle, hawk, and dove, all drawn   65
By the magic of her splendour,
By her great voice, rich and tender,
Whereof every beast and bird
Understood each tone and word,
While she fondled and carest,   70
Playing freaks of joyous zest.

Suddenly the lion stood,
Turned and saw the multitude,
Swelled his mighty front in ire,
Roared the roar of raging fire: 75
Then She turned, the living light,
Sprang erect, grew up in height,
Smote them with the flash and blaze
Of her terrible, swift gaze;
A divine, flushed, throbbing form,   80
Dreadfuller than blackest storm.

All the forest creatures cowered,
Trembling, moaning, overpowered;
All the simple folk who saw
Sank upon their knees in awe   85
Of this Goddess, fierce and splendid,
Whom they witless had offended;
And they murmured out faint prayers,
Inarticulate despairs,
Till her haught and angry mien   90
Grew more gentle and serene.

Stood the high priest forth, and went
Halfway up the green ascent;
There began a preachment long
Of the great and grievous wrong   95
She unto her own soul wrought
In thus living without thought
Of the gods who sain and save,
Of the life beyond the grave:
Living with the beasts that perish,   100

Far from all the rites that cherish
Hope and faith and holy love,
And appease the thrones above:
Full of unction pled the preacher;
Let her come and they would teach her   105
Spirit strangled in the mesh
Of the vile and sinful flesh,
How to gain the heavenly prize,
How grow meet for Paradise;
Penance, prayer, self sacrifice,   110
Fasting, cloistered solitude,
Mind uplifted, heart subdued;
Thus a Virgin, clean and chaste,
In the Bridegroom's arms embraced.
Vestal sister's hooded gown,   115
Straight and strait, of dismal brown,
Here he proffered, and laid down
On the green grass like a frown.

Then stood forth the old arch-sage,
Wrinkled more with thought than age: 120
What could worse afflict, deject
Any well-trained intellect
Than in savage forest seeing
Such a full-grown human being
With the beasts and birds at play,   125
Ignorant and wild as they?
Sciences and arts, by which
Man makes Nature's poor life rich,
Dominates the world around,
Proves himself its King self-crowned,   130
She knew nothing of them, she
Knew not even what they be!
Body naked to the air,
And the reason just as bare!
Yet (since circumstance, that can   135
Hinder the full growth of man,
Cannot kill the seeds of worth
Innate in the Lord of Earth),
Yet she might be taught and brought
To full sovranty of thought,   140
Crowned with reason's glorious crown.
So he tendered and laid down,
Sober grey beside the brown,
Amplest philosophic gown.

Calm and proud she stood the while   145
With a certain wondering smile;

When the luminous sage was done
She began to speak as one
Using language not her own,
Simplest words in sweetest tone:
'Poor old greybeards, worn and bent!
I do know not what they meant;
Only here and there a word
Reached my mind of all I heard;
Let some child come here, I may
Understand what it can say.'

So two little children went,
Lingering up the green ascent,
Hand in hand, but grew the while
Bolder in her gentle smile;
When she kissed them they were free,
Joyous as at mother's knee.
'Tell me, darlings, now,' said she,
'What they want to say to me.'
Boy and girl then, nothing loth,
Sometimes one and sometimes both,
Prattled to her sitting there
Fondling with their soft young hair:
'Dear kind lady, do you stay
Here with always holiday?
Do you sleep among the trees?
People want you, if you please,
To put on your dress and come
With us to the City home;
Live with us and be our friend:
Oh, such pleasant times we'll spend! . . .
But if you can't come away,
Will you let us stop and play
With you and all these happy things
With hair and horns and shining wings?'

She arose and went half down,
Took the vestal sister's gown,
Tried it on, burst through its shroud,
As the sun burns through a cloud:
Flung it from her split and rent;
Said: 'This cerement sad was meant
For some creature stunted, thin,
Breastless, blighted, bones and skin.'

Then the sage's robe she tried,
Muffling in its long folds wide
All her lithe and glorious grace:

'I should stumble every pace!
This big bag was meant to hold
Some poor sluggard fat and old,
Limping, shuffling wearily,   195
With a form not fit to see!'
So she flung it off again
With a gesture of disdain.

    Naked as the midnight moon,
Naked as the sun of noon,   200
Burning too intensely bright,
Clothed in its own dazzling light;
Seen less thus than in the shroud
Of morning mist or evening cloud;
She stood terrible and proud   205
O'er the pallid quivering crowd.

    At a gesture ere they wist,
Perched a falcon on her wrist,
And she whispered to the bird
Something it alone there heard;   210
Then she threw it off: when thrown
Straight it rose as falls a stone,
Arrow-swift on high, on high,
Till a mere speck in the sky;
Then it circled round and round,   215
Till, as if the prey were found,
Forth it darted on its quest
Straight away into the West. . . .
Every eye that watched its flight
Felt a sideward flash of light,   220
All were for a moment dazed,
Then around intently gazed:
What had passed them? Where was She,
The offended deity?
O'er the city, o'er the bay,   225
They beheld her melt away,
Melt away beyond their quest
Through the regions of the west;
While the eagle screamed rauque ire,
And the lion roared like fire.   230

    That same night both priest and sage
Died accursed in sombre rage.
Never more in wild wood green
Was that glorious Goddess seen,
Never more: and from that day   235
Evil hap and dull decay

Fell on countryside and town;
Life and vigour dwindled down;
Storms in Spring nipped bud and sprout,
Summer suns shed plague and drought,   240
Autumn's store was crude and scant,
Winter snows beleaguered want;
Vines were black at vintage-tide,
Flocks and herds of murrain died;
Fishing boats came empty home,   245
Good ships foundered in the foam;
Haggard traders lost all heart
Wandering through the empty mart:
For the air hung thick with gloom,
Silence, and the sense of doom.   250

But those little children she
Had caressed so tenderly
Were betrothed that self-same night,
Grew up beautiful and bright,
Lovers through the years of play   255
Forward to their marriage-day.
Three long moons of bridal bliss
Overflowed them; after this,
With his bride and with a band
Of the noblest in the land,   260
Youths and maidens, wedded pairs
Scarcely older in life's cares,
He took ship and sailed away
Westward Ho from out the bay:
Portioned from their native shrine   265
With the Sacred Fire divine,
They will cherish while they roam,
Quenchless 'mid the salt sea foam,
Till it burns beneath a dome
In some new and far-off home.   270

As they ventured more and more
In that ocean without shore,
And some hearts were growing cold
At the emprise all too bold,
It is said a falcon came   275
Down the void blue swift as flame;
Every sunset came to rest
On the prow's high curving crest,
Every sunrise rose from rest
Flying forth into the west;   280
And they followed, faint no more,
Through that ocean without shore.

Three moons crescent fill and wane
O'er the solitary main,
When behold a green shore smile: 285
It was that Atlantic isle,
Drowned beneath the waves and years,
Whereof some faint shadow peers
Dubious through the modern stream
Of Platonic legend-dream. 290
High upon that green shore stood
She who left their native wood;
Glorious, and with solemn hand
Beckoned to them there to land.
Though She forthwith disappeared 295
As the wave-worn galley neared,
They knew well her presence still
Haunted stream and wood and hill.
There they landed, there grew great,
Founders of a mighty state: 300
There the Sacred Fire divine
Burned within a wondrous shrine
Which Her statue glorified
Throughout many kingdoms wide.
There those children wore the crown 305
To their children handed down
Many and many a golden age
Blotted now from history's page;
Till the last of all the line
Leagued him with the other nine 310
Great Atlantic kings whose hosts
Ravaged all the Mid Sea coasts:
Then the whelming deluge rolled
Over all those regions old;
Thrice three thousand years before 315
Solon questioned Egypt's lore.[1]

TWO LOVERS[2]

THEIR eyes met; flashed an instant like swift swords
　　That leapt unparrying to each other's heart,
Jarring convulsion through the inmost chords;
　　Then fell, for they had fully done their part.

She, in the manner of her folk unveiled, 5
　　Might have been veiled for all he saw of her;
Those sudden eyes, from which he reeled and quailed;
　　The old life dead, no new life yet astir.

[1] Plato: the *Timæus* and the *Critias*.
[2] [See p. 151 for Thomson's note on his source.]

His good steed bore him onward slow and proud:
   And through the open lattice still she leant;
Pale, still, though whirled in a black rushing cloud,
   As if on her fair flowers and dreams intent.

Days passed, and he passed timid, furtive, slow:
   Nights came, and he came motionless and mute;
A steadfast sentinel till morning-glow,
   Though blank her window, dumb her voice and lute.

She loved: the Cross stretched rigid arms to scare
   Her soul from the perdition of that love;
She saw Christ's wounds bleed when she knelt in prayer,
   And frown abhorrent all the saints above.

He loved: the Crescent hung with sharp cold gleam,
   A scimitar to cleave such love in twain;
The Prophet menaced in his waking dream,
   Livid and swoln with wrath that great brow-vein.

Each sternly true to the immortal soul,
   Crushed down the passion of the mortal heart;
Which bled away beneath the iron control,
   But inwardly: they die; none sees the smart.

Thus long months went, until his time came round
   To leave that city terrible and dear;
To go afar on soulless business bound,
   Perchance for absence of a whole dead year.

No word: but as she knelt to pray one night,
   What was that silk thing pendant from the Cross?
Half of a talisman of chrysolite:
   Farewell! Full triumph stunned like fatal loss.

A sacred jewel-charm of sovereign power
   'Gainst demons haunting soul and sense and brain,
'Gainst madness: had it not until that hour
   Despite love's impious frenzy kept him sane?

Now let her look forth boldly day by day;
   He will not come to wound her with his eyes;
Now at the open lattice darkling stay,
   Only the stars are watching from the skies;

Now with clear spirit let her sing and pray;
   No human presence clouds her Lord's full light:
Now let her weep and moan and waste away,
   With broken heart a-bleeding day and night.

Thin as a spectre, haggard, taciturn,
   He reached his native city; there did all 50
He had to do: indifferent yet stern,
   As one whose task must end ere evening-fall.

Then sank, and knew that Azrael was near:
   The hard dull rage of impotent remorse
Burned into passion that consumed old fear: 55
   He loathed his unlived life, his unspent force.

'Must we be sundered, then, beyond the grave,
   By that which here has sundered us? Not so!
I can be lost with her I cannot save,
   And with these Christian dogs to deep Hell go.' 60

A priest baptized the sinking renegade,
   A priest assured him of the Heaven he spurned;
His wealth for many a mass thereafter paid;
   And many a Moslem his example turned.

A friend had sworn to do his last behest; 65
   To be his swift and faithful messenger:
His own half talisman from his true breast
   Would seal the truth of all things told to her.

The funeral over, while the stars yet shone
   Though pale in the new dawn, this friend forth-spurred; 70
Brief rests, long stages, hurried fiercely on;
   Hating the errand, loyal to his word.

Twenty days' travel done in thrice three days,
   He reached her city, found her mansion there;
A crowd before it busy with amaze, 75
   Cries from within it wounding the sweet air.

She was no more since that day's sun had set;
   But wonder outran grief; for ere she died
Infinite yearning, fathomless regret,
   Flooded her soul and drowned its faith and pride. 80

'Shall I be happy with the saints above,
   While he is burning in the paynim Hell?
Here I have cheated him of all my love,
   But there with him I can for ever dwell.'

So she renounced the Cross and threefold God, 85
   And died in Islam; whence the bruit was great.
Silent the friend his backward journey trod,
   Silent, and shrouded with the sense of Fate.

Thus in the very hour supreme of death
   These two great hearts first dared live perfect life;
Drew inspiration with their failing breath,
   Snatched victory as they sank down slain in strife.

And thus Fate mocked them, who when life was sweet
   Had kept apart, both famished to the core;
Let them draw near and in the death-point meet,
   But to diverge for ever, evermore.

Yet both died happy in self-sacrifice;
   A dolorous happiness, yet true and deep:
And Gods and Fate and Hell and Paradise
   Perchance are one to their eternal sleep.

Poor human hearts, that yearn beyond the tomb,
   Wherein you all must moulder into dust!
What has the blank immitigable gloom
   Of light or fervour to reward your trust?

Live out your whole free life while yet on earth;
   Seize the quick Present, prize your one sure boon;
Though brief, each day a golden sun has birth;
   Though dim, the night is gemmed with stars and moon.

Love out your cordial love, hate out your hate;
   Be strong to grasp a foe, to clasp a friend:
Your wants true laws are; thirst and hunger sate:
   Feel you have been yourselves when comes the end.

Let the great gods, if they indeed exist,
   Fight out their fight themselves; for they are strong:
How can we puny mortals e'er assist?
   How judge the supra-mortal right and wrong?

But if we made these gods, with all their strife,
   And not they us: what frenzy equals this;
To starve, maim, poison, strangle our poor life,
   For empty shadows of death's dark abyss?

This man and maiden claim a brother's tear,
   Martyrs of sweet love, killed by bitter faith;
Defrauded by the Gods of glad life here,
   And mocked by Doom in their heroic death.

IN THE ROOM
Ceste insigne fable et tragicque comedie. RABELAIS.

THE sun was down, and twilight grey
    Filled half the air; but in the room,
Whose curtain had been drawn all day,
    The twilight was a dusky gloom:
Which seemed at first as still as death,   5
    And void; but was indeed all rife
With subtle thrills, the pulse and breath
    Of multitudinous lower life.

In their abrupt and headlong way
    Bewildered flies for light had dashed   10
Against the curtain all the day,
    And now slept wintrily abashed;
And nimble mice slept, wearied out
    With such a double night's uproar;
But solid beetles crawled about   15
    The chilly hearth and naked floor.

And so throughout the twilight hour
    That vaguely murmurous hush and rest
There brooded; and beneath its power
    Life throbbing held its throbs supprest: 20
Until the thin-voiced mirror sighed,
    I am all blurred with dust and damp,
So long ago the clear day died,
    So long has gleamed nor fire nor lamp.

Whereon the curtain murmured back,   25
    Some change is on us, good or ill;
Behind me and before is black
    As when those human things lie still:
But I have seen the darkness grow
    As grows the daylight every morn;   30
Have felt out there long shine and glow,
    In here long chilly dusk forlorn.

The cupboard grumbled with a groan,
    Each new day worse starvation brings:
Since *he* came here I have not known   35
    Or sweets or cates or wholesome things:
But now! a pinch of meal, a crust,
    Throughout the week is all I get.
I am so empty; it is just
    As when they said we were to let.   40

IN THE ROOM

What is become, then, of our Man?
 The petulant old glass exclaimed;
If all this time he slumber can,
 He really ought to be ashamed.
I wish we had our Girl again,
 So gay and busy, bright and fair:
The girls are better than these men,
 Who only for their dull selves care.

It is so many hours ago—
 The lamp and fire were both alight—
I saw him pacing to and fro,
 Perturbing restlessly the night.
His face was pale to give one fear,
 His eyes when lifted looked too bright;
He muttered; what, I could not hear:
 Bad words though; something was not right.

The table said, He wrote so long
 That I grew weary of his weight;
The pen kept up a cricket song,
 It ran and ran at such a rate:
And in the longer pauses he
 With both his folded arms downpressed,
And stared as one who does not see,
 Or sank his head upon his breast.

The fire-grate said, I am as cold
 As if I never had a blaze;
The few dead cinders here I hold,
 I held unburned for days and days.
Last night he made them flare; but still
 What good did all his writing do?
Among my ashes curl and thrill
 Thin ghosts of all those papers too.

The table answered, Not quite all;
 He saved and folded up one sheet,
And sealed it fast, and let it fall;
 And here it lies now white and neat.
Whereon the letter's whisper came,
 My writing is closed up too well;
Outside there's not a single name,
 And who should read me I can't tell.

The mirror sneered with scornful spite
 (That ancient crack which spoiled her looks

Had marred her temper), Write and write!
    And read those stupid, worn-out books!
That's all he does, read, write, and read, 85
    And smoke that nasty pipe which stinks:
He never takes the slightest heed
    How any of us feels or thinks.

But Lucy fifty times a day
    Would come and smile here in my face, 90
Adjust a tress that curled astray,
    Or tie a ribbon with more grace:
She looked so young and fresh and fair,
    She blushed with such a charming bloom,
It did one good to see her there, 95
    And brightened all things in the room.

She did not sit hours stark and dumb
    As pale as moonshine by the lamp;
To lie in bed when day was come,
    And leave us curtained chill and damp. 100
She slept away the dreary dark,
    And rose to greet the pleasant morn;
And sang as gaily as a lark
    While busy as the flies sun-born.

And how she loved us every one; 105
    And dusted this and mended that,
With trills and laughs and freaks of fun,
    And tender scoldings in her chat!
And then her bird, that sang as shrill
    As she sang sweet; her darling flowers 110
That grew there in the window-sill,
    Where she would sit at work for hours.

It was not much she ever wrote;
    Her fingers had good work to do;
Say, once a week a pretty note; 115
    And very long it took her too.
And little more she read, I wis;
    Just now and then a pictured sheet,
Besides those letters she would kiss
    And croon for hours, they were so sweet. 120

She had her friends too, blithe young girls,
    Who whispered, babbled, laughed, caressed,
And romped and danced with dancing curls,
    And gave our life a joyous zest.

But with this dullard, glum and sour,
   Not one of all his fellow-men
Has ever passed a social hour;
   We might be in some wild beast's den.

This long tirade aroused the bed,
   Who spoke in deep and ponderous bass,
Befitting that calm life he led,
   As if firm-rooted in his place:
In broad majestic bulk alone,
   As in thrice venerable age,
He stood at once the royal throne,
   The monarch, the experienced sage:

I know what is and what has been;
   Not anything to me comes strange,
Who in so many years have seen
   And lived through every kind of change.
I know when men are good or bad,
   When well or ill, he slowly said;
When sad or glad, when sane or mad,
   And when they sleep alive or dead.

At this last word of solemn lore
   A tremor circled through the gloom,
As if a crash upon the floor
   Had jarred and shaken all the room:
For nearly all the listening things
   Were old and worn, and knew what curse
Of violent change death often brings,
   From good to bad, from bad to worse;

They get to know each other well,
   To feel at home and settled down;
Death bursts among them like a shell,
   And strews them over all the town.
The bed went on, This man who lies
   Upon me now is stark and cold;
He will not any more arise,
   And do the things he did of old.

But we shall have short peace or rest;
   For soon up here will come a rout,
And nail him in a queer long chest,
   And carry him like luggage out.
They will be muffled all in black,
   And whisper much, and sigh and weep:

But he will never more come back,
And some one else in me must sleep.

Thereon a little phial shrilled,
    Here empty on the chair I lie:
I heard one say, as I was filled,
    With half of this a man would die.
The man there drank me with slow breath,
    And murmured, Thus ends barren strife:
O sweeter, thou cold wine of death,
    Than ever sweet warm wine of life.

One of my cousins long ago,
    A little thing, the mirror said,
Was carried to a couch to show
    Whether a man was really dead.
Two great improvements marked the case:
    He did not blur her with his breath,
His many-wrinkled, twitching face
    Was smooth old ivory: verdict, Death.

It lay, the lowest thing there, lulled
    Sweet-sleep-like in corruption's truce;
The form whose purpose was annulled,
    While all the other shapes meant use.
It lay, the *he* become now *it*,
    Unconscious of the deep disgrace,
Unanxious how its parts might flit
    Through what new forms in time and space.

It lay and preached, as dumb things do,
    More powerfully than tongues can prate;
Though life be torture through and through,
    Man is but weak to plain of fate:
The drear path crawls on drearier still
    To wounded feet and hopeless breast?
Well, he can lie down when he will,
    And straight all ends in endless rest.

And while the black night nothing saw,
    And till the cold morn came at last,
That old bed held the room in awe
    With tales of its experience vast.
It thrilled the gloom; it told such tales
    Of human sorrows and delights,
Of fever moans and infant wails,
    Of births and deaths and bridal nights.

A SONG OF SIGHING

Would some little joy to-day
   Visit us, heart!
Could it but a moment stay,
   Then depart,
With the flutter of its wings
Stirring sense of brighter things.

Like a butterfly astray
   In a dark room;
Telling:—Outside there is day,
   Sweet flowers bloom,
Birds are singing, trees are green,
Runnels ripple silver sheen.

Heart! we now have been so long
   Sad without change,
Shut in deep from shine and song,
   Nor can range;
It would do us good to know
That the world is not all woe.

Would some little joy to-day
   Visit us, heart!
Could it but a moment stay,
   Then depart,
With the lustre of its wings
Lighting dreams of happy things,
   Oh sad my heart!

WEDDAH AND OM-EL-BONAIN

NOTE. I found this story, and that of the short piece following,[1] which merit far better English versions than I have been able to accomplish, in the *De l'Amour* of De Stendhal (Henri Beyle), chap. 53, where they are given among 'Fragments Extracted and Translated from an Arabic Collection, entitled *The Divan of Love*, compiled by Ebn-Abi-Hadglat.' From another of these fragments I quote a few lines by way of introduction: 'The Benou-Azra are a tribe famous for love among all the tribes of Arabia. So that the manner in which they love has passed into a proverb, and God has not made any other creatures so tender in loving as are they. Sahid, son of Agba, one day asked an Arab, Of what people art thou? I am of the people who die when they love, answered the Arab. Thou art then of the tribe of Azra? said Sahid. Yes, by the master of the Caaba! replied the Arab. Whence comes it, then, that you thus love? asked Sahid. Our women are beautiful and our young men are chaste, answered the Arab.'
   On this theme HEINE has a poem of four unrhymed quatrains, *Der Azra*, of which the sense without the melody may be given in English:—

[1] [i.e. *Two Lovers*, printed on an earlier page in this selection, p. 142.]

Daily went the wondrous-lovely
Sultan's daughter to and fro there
In the evening by the fountain,
Where the waters white were plashing.

Daily stood the youthful captive
In the evening by the fountain,
Where the waters white were plashing;
Daily grew he pale and paler.

And one evening the princess
Stepped to him with sudden question:
'I would know your name, young captive,
And your country and your kindred.'

Then the slave replied: 'My name is
Mohammed, I come from Yemen,
And my kindred are the Azra,
They who perish when they love.'

Part I

Weddah and Om-el-Bonain, scarcely grown
To boy and girlhood from their swaddling bands,
Were known where'er the Azra tribe was known,
Through Araby and all the neighbouring lands;
Were chanted in the songs of sweetest tone   5
Which sprang like fountains 'mid the desert sands:
  They were so beautiful that none who saw
  But felt a rapture trembling into awe.

Once on a dewy evetide when the balm
Of herb and flower made all the air rich wine,   10
And still the sunless shadow of the palm
Sought out the birthplace of the day divine,
These two were playing in the happy calm.
A young chief said: In these be sure a sign
  Great God vouchsafes; a living talisman   15
  Of glory and rich weal to bless our clan.

Proud hearts applauded; but a senior chief
Said: Perfect beauty is its own sole end;
It is ripe flower and fruit, not bud and leaf;
The promise and the blessing meet and blend,   20
Fulfilled at once: then malice, wrath, and grief,
Lust of the foe and passion of the friend,
  Assail the marvel; for all Hell is moved
  Against the work of Allah most approved.

Thus beauty is that pearl a poor man found;   25
Which could not be surrendered, changed, or sold,
Which he might never bury in the ground,
Or hide away within his girdle-fold;

But had to wear upon his brow uncrowned,
A star of storm and terrors; for, behold,
   The richest kings raged jealous for its light,
   And just men's hearts turned robbers at the sight.

But if the soul be royal as the gem,
That star of danger may flash victory too,
The younger urged, and bring the diadem
To set itself in. And the other: True;
If all Life's golden apples crown one stem,
Fate touches none; but single they are few:
   And whether to defeat or triumph, this
   One star lights war and woe, not peaceful bliss.

But nothing recked the children in that hour,
And little recked through fifteen happy years,
Of any doom in their surpassing dower:
Rich with the present, free from hopes and fears,
They dwelt in time as in a heavenly bower:
Their life was strange to laughter as to tears,
   Serenely glad; their partings were too brief
   For pain; and side by side, what thing was grief?

Amidst their clan they dwelt in solitude,
Not haughtily but by instinctive love;
As lion mates with lion in the wood,
And eagle pairs with eagle not with dove;
The lowlier creatures finding their own good
In their own race, nor seeking it above:
   These dreamt as little of divided life
   As that first pair created man and wife.

The calm years flowed thus till the youth and maid
Were almost man and woman, and the spell
Of passion wrought, and each was self-dismayed;
The hearts their simple childhood knew so well
Were now such riddles to them, in the shade
And trouble of the mists that seethe and swell
   When the large dawn is kindling, which shall grow
   Through crimson fires to steadfast azure glow.

That year a tribe-feud, which some years had slept
Through faintness, woke up stronger than before;
And with its stir young hearts on all sides leapt
For battle, swoln with peace and plenteous store;
Swift couriers to and fro the loud land swept
Weaving thin spites to one vast woof of war:
   And Weddah sallied forth elate, ranked man,
   A warrior of the warriors of his clan.

Ere long flushed foes turned haggard at his name;
The beautiful, the terrible: for fire
Burns most intensely in the clearest flame; 75
The comeliest steed is ever last to tire
And swiftest footed; and in war's fierce game
The noblest sword is deadliest in its gyre:
   His gentle gravity grew keen and gay
   In hottest fight as for a festal day. 80

And while he fought far distant with his band,
Walid the Syrian, Abd-el-Malek's son;
Renowned already for a scheme long planned
With silent patience, and a sharp deed done
When its ripe fruit leaned ready for his hand, 85
And liberal sharing of the fruit well won;
   Came south to greet the tribe, and knit anew
   Old bonds of friendship and alliance true.

He had full often from the poets heard
Of these two children the divinely fair; 90
But was not one to kindle at a word,
And languish on faint echoes of an air;
By what he saw and touched his heart was stirred,
Nor knew sick longings and the vague despair
   Of those who turn from every nearest boon 95
   To catch like infants at the reachless moon.

But when one sunset flaming crimson-barred
He saw a damsel like a shape of sleep,
Who moved as moves in indolence the pard;
Above whose veil burned large eyes black and deep, 100
The lairs of an intense and slow regard
Which made all splendours of the broad world cheap,
   And death and life thin dreams; fate-smitten there
   He rested shuddering past the hour of prayer.

Be heaven all stars, we feel the one moon's rise: 105
Who else could move with that imperial grace?
Who else could bear about those fateful eyes,
Too overwhelming for a mortal face?
Beyond all heed of questions and surprise
He stood a termless hour in that same place, 110
   Convulsed in silent wrestling with his doom;
   Haggard as one brought living from the tomb.

And she had shuddered also passing by,
A moment; for her spirit though intent
Was chilled as conscious of an evil eye; 115

But forthwith turned and o'er its one dream bent;
A woman lilting as she came anigh:
But to destroy on earth was Weddah sent;
  There where he is brave warriors fall before him,
  Where he is not pine damsels who adore him.

And thus with purpose like a trenchant blade
Forged in that fierce hour's fire, the Syrian chief
Began new life. When next the Council weighed
The heavy future charged with wrath and grief,
He spoke his will: I ask to wed the maid,
The child of Abd-el-Aziz: and, in brief,
  I bring for dowry all our wealth and might,
  Unto our last heart's blood, to fight your fight.

All mute with marvelling sat. Her sire then said:
From infancy unto my brother's son
She has been held betrothed: our Lord can wed
Full many a lovelier, many a richer one.
But quite in vain they reasoned, flattered, pled;
This was his proffer, other he had none:
  A boy and girl outweighed the Azra tribe?
  'Twas strange! His vow was fixed to that sole bribe.

And as their couriers came in day by day
Pregnant with portents of yet blacker ill;
And all their urgence broke in fuming spray
Against the rock of his firm-planted will;
The baffled current took a tortuous way,
And drowned a happy garden green and still,
  O'erwhelming Abd-el-Aziz with that gibe,
  A boy and girl outvalue all our tribe?

He loved his daughter, and he loved yet more
His brother's son; and now the whole tribe prest
The scale against them: there was raging war,
Too sure of hapless issue in his breast;
Sea-tossed where rocks on all sides fanged the shore.
She heard him moaning: Would I were at rest,
  Ere this should come upon me, in the grave!
  Her poor heart bled to hear him weep and rave.

She flung herself all yearning at his feet;
The long white malehair dashed her brow with tears;
But her tears scalded him; her kisses sweet
Were crueller than iron barbs of spears;
He had no eyes her tender eyes to meet;
Her soft caressing words scarce touched his ears

But they were fire and madness in his brain:
Yet while she clasped he mutely clasped again.

At length he answered her: A heavy doom
Is laid upon me; now, when I am old,
And weak, and bending toward the quiet tomb . . .
Can it then be, as we are sometimes told,
That women, nay, that young girls in their bloom,
Lovely, beloved, and loving, have been bold
   To give their lives, when blenched the bravest man,
   For safety of their city or their clan?

She trembled in cold shadow of a rock
Leaning to crush her where she knelt fast bound;
She grew all ear to catch the coming shock,
And felt already quakings of the ground;
Yet firmly said: Your anguish would not mock
Your daughter, O my Father: pray expound
   The woeful riddle; and whate'er my part,
   It is your very blood which feeds this heart.

He told her all: the perils great and near;
The might of Walid; and the friendship long
Which bound them to his house, and year by year
With mutual kindnesses had grown more strong;
His offer, his demand, which would not hear
A word in mitigation right or wrong.
   Her young blood curdled: bring him to our tent,
   That I may plead; perchance he will relent.

He came; and found her sitting double-veiled,
For grief was round her like a funeral stole.
She pleaded, she o'erwhelmed him, and she failed;
For still the more her passion moved his soul,
The more he loved her; when his heart most quailed,
His purpose stretched most eager for the goal:
   I stake myself, house, friends, all, for the tribe
   Which gives me you; but for no meaner bribe.

So her face set into a stony mask,
And heavy silence crushed them for an hour
Ere she could learn the words to say her task:
Let only mutes appeal to Fate's deaf power!
Behold I pledge myself to what you ask,
My sire here sells me for the settled dower:
   The sheikhs can know we are at one; I pray
   That none else know it ere the wedding-day.

Which shall be when next moon is on the wane
As this to-night: my heart is now the bier
Of that which we have sacrificed and slain;
My own poor Past, still beautiful and dear,
Cut off from life, wants burial; and though vain   205
Is woman's weeping, I must weep I fear
   A little on the well-beloved's tomb
   Ere marriage smiles and blushes can outbloom.

He left them, sire and daughter, to their woe;
Himself then sick at heart as they could be: 210
But set to work at once, and spurred the slow
Sad hours till they were fiery-swift as he:
With messengers on all sides to and fro,
With ravelled webs of subtle policy,
   He gave the sheikhs good earnest of what aid   215
   They had so cheaply bought with one fair maid.

Thus he took Araby's one peerless prize,
And homeward went ungrudging all the cost;
Though she was marble; with blank arid eyes,
Weary and hopeless as the waste they crossed   220
When neither moon nor star is in the skies,
And water faileth, and the track is lost.
   He took such statue triumphing for wife,
   Assured his love would kindle it to life.

She had indeed wept, wept and wailed that moon,   225
But had not buried yet her shrouded Past;
Which ever lay in a most deathlike swoon,
Pallid and pulseless, motionless and ghast,
While Fate withheld from it death's perfect boon:
She kept this doleful mystery locked up fast;   230
   Her form was as its sepulchre of stone,
   Her heart its purple couch and hidden throne.

She went; and sweeter voiced than cooing dove
Hassan the bard his farewell ode must render:
We had a Night, the dream of heaven above,   235
Wherein one moon and countless stars of splendour;
We had a Moon, the face of perfect love,
Wherein two nights with stars more pure and tender:
   Our Night with its one moon we still have here;
   Where is our Moon with its twin nights more dear?   240

Part II

As Weddah and his troop were coming back
From their first foray, which success made brief,

Scouts met him and in sharp haste turned his track
On special mission to a powerful chief,
Who wavered still between the white and black,   5
And lurked for mere self-profit like a thief.
  This errand well fulfilled, at last he came
  To flush her tear-pearls with the ruby fame.

Into the camp full joyously he rode,
Leading his weary escort; as for him,   10
The love and trust that in his bosom glowed
Had laughed away all weariness of limb.
The sheikhs, his full report heard, all bestowed
Well-measured praises, brief and somewhat grim;
  As veterans scanning the enormous night   15
  In which this one star shone so bravely bright.

Then Abd-el-Aziz rose and left the tent,
And he accompanied with eager pace;
And marked not how his frank smiles as he went
Were unreflected in each well-known face;   20
How joyous greetings he on all sides sent
Brought hollow echoes as from caverned space:
  His heart drank sweet wine 'mid the roses singing,
  And thought the whole world with like revels ringing.

He entered with his uncle, and his glance   25
Sank disappointed. But the old man wept
With passion o'er him, eyeing him askance;
And made him eat and drink; and ever kept
Questioning, questioning, as to every chance
Throughout his absence; keen to intercept   30
  The fatal, But my cousin? ready strung
  Upon the tense lips by the eager tongue.

At length it flew, the lover's wingèd dart;
He sped it wreathed with flowers of hope and joy,
It pierced with iron point the old man's heart,   35
Who quivering cried: You are, then, still a boy!
Love, love, the sweet to meet, the smart to part,
Make all your world of pleasure and annoy!
  Is this a time for dalliance in rose bowers?
  The vultures gather; do they scent sweet flowers?   40

It is a time of woe and shame, of strife
Whose victory must be dolorous as defeat:
The sons of Ishmael clutch the stranger's knife
To stab each other; every corpse you meet
Has held a Moslem soul, an Arab life: 45

The town-serfs prisoned in stark fort and street
  Exult while countless tents that freely roam
  Perish like proud ships clashing in the foam.

We might learn wisdom from our foes and thralls!
The mongrels of a hundred barbarous races,   50
Who know not their own sires, appease their brawls,
Leave night and sunward set their impure faces,
To bay in concert round old Syrian walls,
And thrust their three gods on our holy places:
  We have one Sire, one Prophet, and one Lord,   55
  And yet against each other turn the sword.

Thus long he groaned with fevered bitterness,
Till, Say at least my Father she is well!
Stung prudence out of patience: Surely yes!
The children of the faith whom Azrael   60
Hath gathered, do they suffer our distress?—
But smitten by that word the lover fell,
  As if at such rash mention of his name
  That bird of God with wings of midnight came.

Deep in the shadow of those awful plumes   65
A night and day and night he senseless lay;
And Abd-el-Aziz cowered 'mid deeper glooms,
Silent in vast despair, both night and day:
It seemed two forms belonging to the tombs
Had been abandoned in that tent; for they   70
  Were stark and still and mute alike, although
  The one was conscious of their double woe.

At last death left the balance, and the scale
Of wretched life jarred earth: and in the morn
The lover woke, confused as if a veil   75
Of heavy dreams involved him; weak and worn
And cold at heart, and wondering what bale
Had wounded him and left him thus forlorn:
  So still half-stunned with anguish he lay long,
  Fretful to rend the shroud that wrapt his wrong. 80

He turned; and on the pillow, near his head,
He saw a toy, a trifle, that gave tongue
To mute disaster: forthwith on his bed
The coiled-snake Memory hissed and sprang and stung:
Then all the fury of the storm was shed   85
From the black swollen clouds that overhung;
  The hot rain poured, the fierce gusts shook his soul,
  Wild flashes lit waste gloom from pole to pole.

He hardly dared to touch the petty thing,
The talisman of this tremendous spell: 90
A purse of dark blue silk; a golden ring,
A letter in the hand he knew so well.
Still as he sought to read new gusts would fling
Wet blindness in his vision, and a knell
   Of rushing thunder trample through his brain 95
   And tread him down into the swoon again.

He read: Farewell! In one sad word I weave
More thoughts than pen could write or tongue declare.
No other word can Om-el-Bonain leave
To Weddah, save her blessing; and her prayer 100
That he will quail not, though his heart must grieve,
That all his strength and valour, skill and care,
   Shall be devoted loyally to serve
   The sacred Tribe, and never self-ward swerve.

For verily the Tribe is all, and we 105
Are nothing singly save as parts of it:
The one great Nile flows ever to the sea,
The waterdrops for ever change and flit;
And some the first ooze snares, and some may be
The King's sweet draught, proud Cairo's mirror; fit 110
   For all each service of the stream whose fame
   They share, by which alone they have a name.

And since I know that you cannot forget,
And am too sure your love will never change,
I leave my image to your soul: but yet 115
Keep it as shrined and shrouded till the strange
Sad dream of life, illusion and regret,
Is ended; short must be its longest range.
   Farewell! Hope gleams the wan lamp in a tomb
   Above a corpse that waits the final doom. 120

This writing was a dear but cruel friend
That dragged him from the deep, and held him fast
Upon life's shore, who would have found an end,
Peace and oblivion. Turn from such a past
To such a future, and unquailing wend 125
Its infinite hopeless hours! he shrank aghast:
   Yet in this utmost weakness swore to make
   The dreadful sacrifice for her dear sake.

But when he stood as one about to fall,
And would go weep upon her tomb alone, 130
And Abd-el-Aziz had to tell him all,

The cry of anguish took a harsher tone:
Rich harem coverlets for funeral pall,
For grave a Syrian marriage couch and throne!
   A human rival, breathing mortal breath,   135
   And not the star-cold sanctity of Death!

This truth was as a potent poison-draught,
Fire in the entrails, wild fire in the brain,
Which kindled savage strength in him who quaffed
And did not die of its first maddening pain.   140
It struck him like the mere malignant shaft
Which stings a warrior into sense again,
   Who lay benumbed with wounds, and would have died
   Unroused: the fresh wound makes him crawl and hide.

A month he wandered in wild solitude;   145
And in that month grew old, and yet grew strong:
Now lying prone and still as death would brood
The whole long day through and the whole night long;
Now demon-driven day and night pursued
Stark weariness amidst the clamorous throng   150
   Of thoughts that raged with memory and desire,
   And parched, his bruised feet burning, could not tire.

When he came back, o'ermastered by his vow
To serve the Tribe through which he was unblest,
None gazed without remorse upon his brow,   155
None felt his glance without an aching breast:
Magnificent in beauty even now,
Ravaged by grief and fury and unrest,
   He moved among them swift and stern of deed,
   And always silent save in action's need.   160

And thus went forth, and unrejoicingly
Drank deep of war's hot wine: as one who drinks
And only grows more sullen, while yet he
Never the challenge of the full cup shrinks;
And rises pale with horror when the glee   165
Of careless revellers into slumber sinks,
   Because the feast which could not give him joy
   At least kept phantoms from their worst annoy.

The Lion of the Azra is come back
A meagre wolf! foes mocked, who mocked no more   170
When midnight scared them with his fresh attack
After the long day's fighting, and the war
Found him for ever wolf-like on their track,
As if consumed with slakeless thirst of gore:

Since he was cursed from slumber and repose, 175
He wreaked his restlessness on friends and foes.

The lightnings of his keen sword ever flashed
Without a ray of lightning in his glance;
His blade where blades were thickest clove or clashed
Without a war-cry: ever in advance 180
He sought out death; but death as if abashed
Adopted for its own his sword and lance,
    And rode his steed, and swayed aside or blunted
    The eager hostile weapons he affronted.

Once in the thick of battle as he raged 185
Thus cold and dumb amidst the furious cries,
Hassan the bard was near to him engaged,
And read a weird in those forlorn fixed eyes;
And singing of that combat they had waged
Gave voice to what surpassed his own surmise: 190
    For our young Lion of the mateless doom
    Shall never go a cold corpse to the tomb!

Awe silenced him who sang, and deep awe fell
On those who heard it round the campfire's blaze:
But when they questioned he had naught to tell; 195
The vision had departed from his gaze.
The verse took wing and was a mighty spell;
Upon the foe new terror and amaze,
    To friends redoubled force; to one alone,
    The hero's self, it long remained unknown. 200

While Weddah in the South with fiery will
Bore conquest wheresoe'er his banner flew,
Walid with royal heart and patient skill
Upon the Syrian confines triumphed too.
They never met: each felt a savage thrill 205
Which jarred his inmost being through and through
    As still fresh fame the other's fame enlarged:
    Each wished his rival in the ranks he charged.

And when the foemen sued at length for peace
To victors surfeited with war's alarms, 210
Save him who knew all rest in rest must cease,
They said: O warriors, not by your own arms,
Though they are mighty! may their might increase!
But more by Om-el-Bonain's fatal charms,
    Possessing both who lost her and who won, 215
    Have we been baffled, vanquished, and undone.

Whence Hassan sang his sudden daring ode
Of Beauty revelling in the storm of fight:
For if the warriors into battle rode,
Their hearts were kindled by her living light; 220
Either as sun that in pure azure glowed,
Or baleful star in deep despair's black night:
  And whether by despair or joy she lit
  Intenser fires perplexed the poet's wit.

And would you know why empires break asunder, 225
Why peoples perish and proud cities fall;
Seek not the captains where the steedclouds thunder,
Seek not the elders in the council hall;
But seek the chamber where some shining wonder
Of delicate beauty nestles, far from all 230
  The turmoil, toying with adornments queenly,
  And murmuring songs of tender love serenely.

The clashing cymbals and the trumpet's clangour
Are peacefuller than her soft trembling lute;
The armies raging with hot fire of anger 235
Are gentler than her gentle glances mute;
The restless rushings of her dainty languor
Outveer the wind, outspeed the barb's pursuit:
  Well Hassan knows; who sings high laud and blessing
  To this dear fatal riddle past all guessing. 240

Part III

The war was over for the time; and men
Returned to heal its wounds, repair its waste,
And thus grow strong and rich to fight again.
And Weddah, cold in victory's sun, embraced
The uncle whom his glory warmed; and then, 5
Gathering his spoil of gems and gold in haste,
  Rode forth: the clansmen wondered much to find
  His famous favourite steed was left behind.

He set out in the night: none knew his goal,
Though some might fix it in their secret thought. 10
He could no longer stifle or control,
In calm by battle's fever undistraught,
The piteous yearning of his famished soul
Which unappeasably its food besought;
  Fretting his life out like an infant's cry, 15
  Let us but see her once before we die!

When he returned not, soon the rumour spread,
That he had vanished now his work was done;

The prophecy had been fulfilled; not dead,
But in the body borne beyond the sun,   20
He lived eternal life. He heard this said
Himself in Walid's city, where as one
   Who sojourns but for traffic's sake he dwelt;
   And hearing it, more surely shrouded felt.

Courteous and humble as beseemeth trade,   25
While ever on the watch, some gems he sold:
Men said, this young man is discreet and staid,
Yet fair in dealing, nor too fond of gold.
He smiled to hear his virtues thus arrayed,
A smile that gloomed to frowning; but controlled   30
   The haughty spirit surging in his breast;
   The end in view, what mattered all the rest?

The end in reach: for now the favourite slave
Of Om-el-Bonain, as he knew full well;
A frank-eyed girl, whose bosom was a wave   35
Whereon love's lotus lightly rose and fell;
Drew near to him, attracted by his grave
Unsceptred majesty, and by the spell
   Of his intense and fathomless regard,
   Splendid in gloom as midnight myriad-starred.   40

She haggled for a trinket with her tongue
To veil the eager commerce of her eyes;
Those daring smugglers when the heart is young,
For contraband of passion. His disguise
In talk with her but loosely round him hung;   45
She glimpsed a secret and an enterprise;
   Love's flower, unsunned by hope, soon fades; she grieves,
   Yet still returns to scent the rich dead leaves.

Till sick at heart and desperate with delay
He ventured all, abruptly flinging down   50
The weary mask: if death must end the play,
Better at once: I learn that in your town
Dwells Om-el-Bonain, whom you know men say,
Upon her eye-flash dropped a decent frown:
   She is my mistress, and great Walid's wife—   55
   The word his heart sought, stabbed in with a knife.

Your mistress is my cousin; and will be
The friend of who shall tell her I am here.
But if I may not trust your secrecy,
Tell Walid, tell not her: and have no fear   60
That I will harm you for harm done to me,

Unaimed at her. The life I hold not dear
  Might dower you well. But with a passionate oath
  The eager girl swore loyalty to both.

Then hurried from him to her lady sweet,
And thrilled her frozen heart with burning pang:
For life resigned and torpid in defeat
To new contention with its fate upsprang,
This sword of hope found lying at her feet
While love's impetuous clarion summons rang:
  Weddah alive! alive and here! Beware!
  If you now mock, Hell mock your dying prayer!

I saw a merchant: never chief or king
Of form so noble visited our land;
He wore a little ring, a lady's ring,
On the last finger of a feared right hand;
Some woe enormous overshadowing
Made beauty terrible that had been bland;
  He was convulsed when he would speak your name,
  From such abysses of his heart it came.

Now whether this be Weddah's self or not,
My Lady in her wisdom must decide.
The lady's questions ploughed the self-same spot
Over and over lest some grains should hide
Of this vast treasure fallen to her lot:
Swear by the Prophet's tomb I may confide
  In you as in myself until the end;
  And Om-el-Bonain lives and dies your friend.

Brave Amine swore, and bravely held the vow.
Her mistress kept her babbling all that eve,
A pleasant rill. And on the morrow: Now
Go bid him tell all friends that he must leave
In seven days; so much we must allow,
So many starving hours of bliss bereave!
  His travels urge him in his own despite;
  He gives a farewell feast on such a night:

And in the meanwhile he shall fully learn
What is to follow. When this message came,
The thick dark in him 'gan to seethe and burn
Till soul and body fused in one clear flame.
His guests all blinked with wonder to discern
This glowing heart of joy; and flushed with shame
  Unmerited for having thought him cold,
  Who made their old feel young, their young feel old.

The long week passed; the morning came to crown 105
Or kill the lovers' hope. It was a day
Well chosen, for some guests of high renown
Left Walid, who would speed them on their way;
And festal tumult filled the sunny town.
The merchant in departure strolled astray 110
   Amongst the groups about the palace heaving
   To glimpse the rich procession form for leaving.

And when it left, absorbing every eye;
A stream of splendours rolling with the din
Of horn and tabor under that blue sky; 115
Came Amine carelessly and led him in,
With chat of certain anklets she would buy;
And led him lounging onwards till they win
   A storeroom where her mistress daily spent
   Some matin hours on household cares intent. 120

Large chests were ranged around it, one of which
They had made ready with most loving care;
Lurked apertures among the carvings rich,
Above its deep soft couch, for light and air:
Behold your prison cell, your palace niche, 125
The jewel casket of my Lady fair!
   I lock you in; from her must come your key:
   Love's captives pay sweet ransom to get free!

She found her mistress fever-flushed, and told
Their full success: Our prisoner is secure; 130
A lion meek as lambkin of the fold,
Prepared your harshest torments to endure!
But, dearest Lady, as you have been bold,
Be prudent, prudent, prudent, and assure
   Long life to bliss. Now with your leave I go 135
   To be well seen of all the house below.

She took another stairway for descent,
And sauntered round to the front courtyard gate,
Chatting and laughing lightly as she went
With various groups, all busy in debate 140
On those departed guests: and some were shent
For meanness maugre retinue and state,
   And some extolled for bounteous disposition,
   And all summed up with judgement-day precision.

Of all her fellow-slaves it seemed but one, 145
Whose breast was tinder for love's flame would she
Vouchsafe a spark, had spied the venture run:

Soho, my flirting madam, where is he
You brought in here an hour since with your fun?
A happy rogue, whoever he may be! 150
   Have you already tired of this new dandy,
   Or hid him somewhere to be always handy?

The stupid jealous creature that you are!
Where were your eyes, then, not to know his face?
For weeks back he has dealt in our bazaar, 155
And now is on the road to some new place.
He had an emerald and diamond star
I thought might win my poor dear Lady's grace;
   She would not even look at it, alack!
   I packed him off for ever with his pack. 160

Thus these long-hapless lovers for awhile,
Enringed with dreadful fire, safe ambush found,
Screened by its very glare; a magic isle
By roaring billows guarded well till drowned;
A refuge spot of green and liquid smile 165
Whose rampart was the simoom gathering round:
   If darkness hid them, it was thunder gloom
   Whose light must come in lightnings to consume.

And even as Iskander's self, for whom
The whole broad earth sufficed not, found at last 170
Full scope vouchsafed him in the narrow tomb;
So he long pining in the desert vast
As in a dungeon, found now ample room,
Found perfect freedom and content, shut fast
   Alive within that coffer-coffin lonely, 175
   Which gave him issue to that chamber only.

They knew what peril compassed them about,
But could not feel the dread it would inspire;
Imperious love shut other passions out,
Or made them fuel for his altar fire. 180
At first one sole thought harassed them with doubt;
To kill her lord and flee? Then tribe and sire
   Would justly curse them; for in every act
   He had been loyal to the evil pact.

He had indeed wronged them; for well he knew 185
Their love from infancy, their plighted troth,
When merciless in mastery he drew
From her repugnant lips the fatal oath:
That love avenged the wrong of love was due;
But still his blood was sacred to them both; 190

    The tender husband and the proved ally
    They dare not harm; must death come, they could die.

Die! Often he would dream for hours supine
Upon his lidded couch, Life's dream is over;
I wait the resurrection in this shrine: 195
Anon an angel cometh to uncover
The inmost glories of the realm divine,
Because though dead I still am faithful lover;
    My spirit drinks its fill of bliss, and then
    Sinks back into this twilight trance again.   200

Like bird above its young one in the nest
Which cannot fly, he often heard her singing;
The thrill and swell of rapture from her breast
In fountains of delightful music springing:
It seemed he had been borne among the blest,   205
Whose quires around his darksome couch were ringing;
    Long after that celestial voice sank mute
    His heartstrings kept sweet tremble like a lute.

She heard his breathing like a muffled chime,
She heard his tranquil heart-beats through the flow   210
Of busy menials in the morning time;
Far-couched at night she felt a sudden glow,
And straight her breathing answered rhyme for rhyme
His softest furtive footsteps to and fro:
    And none else heard? She marvelled how the sense   215
    Of living souls could be so dull and dense.

Once early, early, ere the dawn grew loud,
She stole to watch his slumber by its gleam;
And blushing with a soft laugh-gurgle bowed
And sank as in the bosom of a stream,   220
An ardent angel in a rosy cloud
Resolving the enchantment of his dream:
    Where there is room for thee, is room for us;
    So may I share thy death-sarcophagus!

She grew so lovely, ravishing, and sweet,   225
Her brow so radiant and her lips so warm;
Such rich heart-music stirred her buoyant feet,
And swayed the gestures of her lithe young form,
And revelled in her voice to bliss complete;
That Walid whirled with his great passion's storm,   230
    Befooled with joy, went doting down his hell:
    Oh, tame and meek, my skittish wild gazelle!

Thus these, sings Hassan, of their love's full measure
Drank swiftly in that circle of swift fire;
A veil of light and ardour to their pleasure 235
Till it revealed their ashes on one pyre:
Some never win, some spend in youth this treasure,
And crawl down sad age starvelings of desire:
　These lavished royal wealth in one brief season,
　But Death found both so rich he gave them reason. 240

Part IV

The tender almond-blossom flushed and white
Sank floating in warm flakes through lucid air;
The rose flung forth into the sea of light
Her heart of fire and incense burning bare;
The nightingale thrilled all the breathless night 5
With passion so intense it seemed despair:
　And still these lovers drank love's perfect wine
　From that gold urn of secrecy divine.

Then Fate prepared the end. A grey old man,
Bowed down with grief who had not bent with time, 10
Made way to Walid in the full divan:
His son, great-hearted and in youth's hot prime,
Was now a fugitive and under ban
For an indignant deed of sinless crime;
　A noble heirloom pearl the suppliant brought 15
　To clear the clouded face ere he besought.

This pearl in Walid's mood of golden joy
Shone fair as morning star in rosy dawn;
He called his minion, Motar: Take this toy
Unto your Lady where she sits withdrawn, 20
With my love-greeting, and this message, boy:
Were this a string of such, a monarch's pawn,
　A pearl for every note, it would not pay
　That song I heard you singing yesterday.

They had been leaning for an hour perchance, 25
Motionless, gazing in each other's eyes;
Floating in deep pure joy, whose still expanse
Rippled but rarely with long satiate sighs;
Their souls so intermingled in the trance,
So far away dissolved through fervent skies, 30
　That it was marvel how each fair mute form
　Without its pulse and breath remained life-warm.

When rapid footsteps almost at the door
Stung her to vigilance, and her fierce start

Shook Weddah, and that lion of proud war 35
Must flee to covert like a timid hart:
But drunken with the message he now bore
The saucy youth flew in, Fate's servile dart,
   Without announcement; and espied, what he,
   Still subtle though amazed, feigned not to see. 40

The message with the goodly pearl he gave:
She could for wrath have ground it into dust
Between her richer teeth, and stabbed the slave
Who brought it; but most bitterly she must
Put on sweet smiles of pleasure, and the knave 45
With tender answer full of thanks entrust.
   He lingered: Our kind lady will bestow
   Some little mark of bounty ere I go?

Her anger cried: Only the message dear
Has saved the messenger from punishment; 50
If evermore as now you enter here
You shall be scourged and starved and prison-pent.
He cowered away from her in sullen fear,
And darted from the room; and as he went
   The sting of her rebuke was curdling all 55
   His blood of vanity to poison gall.

He hissed in Walid's ear the seething spite:
My Lord's pearl by my Lady's was surpassed;
In that rich cedar coffer to the right
I saw the treasure being hidden fast; 60
A gallant, young and beautiful and bright.
Unmothered slave, be that foul lie your last!
   And clove the scandal with his instant sword
   Strong Walid: Motar had his full reward.

When Weddah, plunged from glory into gloom, 65
Heard that last speech of Om-el-Bonain there,
A sudden ominous sense of icy doom
Assailed his glowing heart with bleak despair.
The moment that false slave had left the room
She sprang to seize her lover in his lair: 70
   She bowed all quivering like a storm-swept palm;
   He rose to meet her solemn, pale and calm.

He clasped her with strong passion to his breast,
He kissed her with a very tender kiss:
Soul of my soul! what lives men call most blest 75
Can be compared to our brief lives in bliss?
But one wild year of anguish and unrest;

Three moons of perfect secret love! Were this
  My dying hour, I thankfully attest
  Of all earth's dooms I have enjoyed the best.   80

What, weeping, thou, such kiss-unworthy tears!
The glory of the Azra must not weep,
Whom mighty Weddah worships, for cold fears;
But only for strong love, in stillness deep,
Secluded from all alien eyes and ears.   85
And now to vigil, and perchance to sleep,
  Enshrined once more: be proud and calm and strong;
  Your second visitor will come ere long.

And scarcely was all said when Walid came,
Full gently stealing for a tiger-spring;   90
His love and fury, hope and fear and shame,
All made with venom from that serpent's sting,
Like wild beasts huddled in a den of flame
Within the cool white palace of a king:
  She rose to greet; he deigned no glance of quest,   95
  But went and lolled upon that cedar chest.

I come like any haggler of the mart,
Who having sent a bauble seeks its price:
Will you forgive the meanness of my part,
And one of these fair coffers sacrifice?   100
A clutch of iron fingers gript her heart
Till it seemed bursting in the cruel vice:
  And yet she quivered not, nor breathed a moan:
  Are not myself and all things here your own?

I thank you for the bountiful award;   105
And choose, say this whereon I now sit here?
Take any, take them all; but that, my Lord,
Is full of household stuff and woman's gear.
I want the coffer, not what it may hoard,
However rich and beautiful and dear.   110
  And it is thine, she said; and this the key:
  Her royal hand outheld it steadfastly.

Swift as a double flash from thunder-skies
The angel and the devil of his doubt
Flamed from the sombre windows of his eyes: 115
He went and took the key she thus held out,
And turned as if he would unlock his prize.
She breathed not; all the air ran blood about
  A swirl of terrors and wild hopes of guilt;
  Calm Weddah seized, then loosed, his dagger-hilt.   120

But Walid had restrained himself, and thought:
Shall I unlock the secret of my soul,
The mystery of my Fate, that has been brought
So perfectly within my own control?
That were indeed a work by folly wrought: 125
For Time, in this my vassal, must unroll
   To me, and none but me, what I would learn;
   I hold the vantage, undiscerned discern.

He summoned certain slaves, and bade them bear
The coffer he had sealed with his own seal   130
Into a room below with strictest care;
And followed thoughtful at the last one's heel.
At noontide Amine found her mistress there,
Benumbed with horror, deaf to her appeal;
   The sightless eyes fixed glaring on that door   135
   By which her soul had vanished evermore.

Beneath the cedar whose noonshadow large,
Level from massive trunk, outspread halfway
Adown a swardslope to the river marge,
Where rosebowers shone between the willows grey,   140
The wondering bearers bore their heavy charge;
And where the central shadow thickest lay
   He bade them delve a pit, and delve it deep
   Till watersprings against their strokes should leap.

Then waved them to a distance, while he bowed   145
Upon the coffer, hearkening for a space:
If truth bought that poor wretch his bloody shroud,
I bury thus her guilt and my disgrace;
And you, as by the whole earth disavowed,
Sink into nothingness and leave no trace: 150
   If not, it is a harmless whim enough
   To sepulchre a chest of household stuff.

With face encircled by his hands, which leaned
Upon the wood, he challenged clear and slow:
The hollow sound, his full hot breath thus screened   155
Suffused his visage with a tingling glow;
His pulse, his vesture's rustling intervened
And marred the silence: he drew back, and so
   Knelt listening yet awhile with bated breath:
   The secret lay as mute and still as death.   160

Above there in her chamber Weddah might
Have leapt forth suddenly their foe to kill.
Ev'n here with hazard of swift fight and flight

Escaped or perished as a warrior still;
But thus through him her name had suffered blight: 165
He locked his breath and nerves with rigid will.
  So Walid first let sink his key unused,
  Then signed the slaves back: they wrought on, he mused.

Against the dark bulk swelled the waters thin;
The stones and earth were trampled to a mound. 170
He then broke silence, stern and sad: Within
That coffer ye have buried, sealed and bound,
Lies one of the most potent evil djinn,
Whose hate on me and mine hath darkly frowned;
  He sought to kill your mistress: Hell and Doom 175
  And Allah's curse all guard this dungeon-tomb!

And Walid never spoke of this again,
And none dared ask him; for his brow grew black
His eye flamed evil and appalling when
Some careless word but strayed upon a track 180
That might from far lead to it: therefore men
Spoke only of the thing behind his back.
  The cedar shadow centred by that mound
  Was sacredly eschewed as haunted ground.

But one pale phantom, noon and night and morn, 185
Was ever seen there; quiet as a stone,
Huddled and shapeless, weeping tears forlorn
As silent as the dews; her heart alone
And not her lips, whose seal was never torn,
Upbraiding sluggish death with constant moan. 190
  Hushed whispers circled, piteous eyes were wet;
  The captive djinnee holds her captive yet.

Thus Walid learned too well the bitter truth,
His home dissolved, its marvellous joy a cheat;
Yet gave no sign to her: for there was ruth 195
Of memories gall itself left subtly sweet;
And consciousness of wrong against her youth,
And surfeit of a vengeance so complete:
  He could not stab her bleeding heart; her name
  With his own honour he kept pure from shame. 200

She thought Death dead, or prisoned in deep Hell
As sole assuager of the human lot:
But when the evening of the seventh day fell
Walid alone dared tread the fatal spot:
She crouched as who would plunge into a well, 205
Livid and writhed into a desperate knot;

Her fingers clutched like talons in the mould:
Thus the last time his arms about her fold.

As if to glut the demon with her doom,
And break the spell, there where her corse was found   210
He had it buried; and a simple tomb
Of black-domed marble sealed the dolorous mound;
And there was set to guard the cedar gloom
A triple cirque of cypress-trees around:
    Thus Love wrought Destiny to join his slaves   215
    Weddah and Om-el-Bonain in their graves.

True Amine, freed and richly dowered, no less
Had served until the end her lady dear;
And shrouded for the grave that loveliness
Whose noon-eclipse left life without its peer: 220
Then sought the Azra in her lone distress,
And tended Abd-el-Aziz through the sere
    Forlorn last days; and married in the clan,
    And bore brave children to a valiant man.

Great Walid lived long years beyond this woe,   225
And still increased in wealth and power and glory;
A loyal friend, a formidable foe;
Each Azra was his mother's child, saith story;
And he saw goodly children round him grow
To keep his name green when Death took him hoary: 230
    So prosperous, was he happy too? the sage
    Cites this one counsel of his reverend age:

Have brood-mares in your stables, my young friend,
And women in your harem, but no wife:
A common dagger-blade may pierce or rend,   235
A month bring healing; this, the choicest knife
In Fate's whole armoury, wounds beyond amend,
And with a scratch can poison all your life;
    And it lies naked in your naked breast
    When you are drunk with joy and sleep's rich rest.   240

As surely as a very precious stone
Finds out that jeweller who doth excel,
So surely to the bard becometh known
The tale which only he can fitly tell:
A few years thence, and Walid's heart alone   245
Had thrilled not to a talisman's great spell,
    His deathstone set in Hassan's golden verse;
    Here poorly copied in cheap bronze or worse.

He ends: We know not which to most admire;
The lover who went silent to his doom; 250
The spouse obedient to her lord's just ire,
The mistress faithful to her lover's tomb;
The husband calm in jealousy's fierce fire,
Who strode unswerving through the doubtful gloom
  To vengeance instant, secret and complete, 255
And did not strike one blow more than was meet.

With stringent cords of circumstance dark Fate
Doth certain lives here so entoil and mesh
That some or all must strangle if they wait,
And knife to cut the knots must cut quick flesh: 260
The first strong arm free severs ere too late;
Fresh writhings would but tangle it afresh:
  To die with valiant fortitude, to kill
As priest not butcher; so much scope has Will.

These perished, and he slew them, in such wise 265
That all may meet as friends and free from shame,
Whether they meet in Hell or Paradise.
If he has won long life and power and fame,
Our darlings too have won their own set prize,
Conjoined for evermore in true love's name: 270
  The Azra die when they do love, of old
Was graven with the iron pen, on gold.

May Allah grant eternal joy and youth
In fateless Heaven to one and all of these.
And for himself a little grain of ruth 275
The bard will beg, this once, while on his knees;
Who cannot always see the very truth,
And does not always sing the truth he sees,
  But something pleasanter to foolish ears
That should be tickled not with straws but spears. 280

L'ENVOY

[To Hypatia Bradlaugh, with a copy of the *Magic Ring*, by La Motte Fouqué]

When the sixties are outrun,
And the seventies nearly done,
Or the eighties just begun;
May some young and happy man,
Wiser, kinder, nobler than 5
He who tenders this one, bring
You the real Magic Ring.

This one may have pleasant powers;
Charming idle girlish hours
With its tales from faerie bowers;   10
Tinting hopeful maiden dreams
With its soft romantic gleams;
Breathing love of love and truth,
Valour, innocence and ruth.

But may that one bless the life   15
Of the woman and the wife
Through our dull world's care and strife;
Year by year with rich increase,
Give you love, and joy, and peace;
And at last the good death bring,   20
Sweet as sleep: your Magic Ring.

Sunday { LILAH / ALICE / HYPATIA } 14/2/69

[To Alice and Hypatia Bradlaugh, with a copy of *Undine* which had 'Lilah' inscribed on the flyleaf]

Who was Lilah? I am sure
She was young and sweet and pure;
With the forehead wise men love,—
Here a lucid dawn above
Broad curved brows, and twilight there,   5
Under the deep dusk of hair.

And her eyes? I cannot say
Whether brown, or blue, or grey:
I have seen them brown, and blue,
And a soft green grey—the hue   10
Shakespeare loved (and he was wise);
'Grey as glass' were Silvia's eyes.

So to Lilah's name above
I will add two names I love,
Linking with the bracket curls
Three sweet names of three sweet girls:—   15
Sunday of Saint Valentine,
Eighteen hundred sixty-nine.

IN A CHRISTIAN CHURCHYARD

This field of stones, he said,
May well call forth a sigh;
Beneath them lie the dead,
On them the living lie.

THE CITY OF DREADFUL NIGHT

> Per me si va nella città dolente.
> DANTE.
>
> Poi di tanto adoprar, di tanti moti
> D'ogni celeste, ogni terrena cosa,
> Girando senza posa,
> Per tornar sempre là donde son mosse;
> Uso alcuno, alcun frutto
> Indovinar non so.
>
> Sola nel mondo eterna, a cui si volve
> Ogni creata cosa,
> In te, morte, si posa
> Nostra ignuda natura;
> Lieta no, ma sicura
> Dell' antico dolor. . .
> Però ch' esser beato
> Nega ai mortali e nega a' morti il fato.
> LEOPARDI.

PROEM

Lo, thus, as prostrate, 'In the dust I write
  My heart's deep languor and my soul's sad tears.'
Yet why evoke the spectres of black night
  To blot the sunshine of exultant years?
Why disinter dead faith from mouldering hidden?   5
Why break the seals of mute despair unbidden,
  And wail life's discords into careless ears?

Because a cold rage seizes one at whiles
  To show the bitter old and wrinkled truth
Stripped naked of all vesture that beguiles,   10
  False dreams, false hopes, false masks and modes of youth;
Because it gives some sense of power and passion
In helpless impotence to try to fashion
  Our woe in living words howe'er uncouth.

Surely I write not for the hopeful young,   15
  Or those who deem their happiness of worth,
Or such as pasture and grow fat among
  The shows of life and feel nor doubt nor dearth,
Or pious spirits with a God above them
To sanctify and glorify and love them,   20
  Or sages who foresee a heaven on earth.

For none of these I write, and none of these
  Could read the writing if they deigned to try:
So may they flourish, in their due degrees,
  On our sweet earth and in their unplaced sky.   25
If any cares for the weak words here written,
It must be some one desolate, Fate-smitten,
  Whose faith and hope are dead, and who would die.

Yes, here and there some weary wanderer
   In that same city of tremendous night,   30
Will understand the speech, and feel a stir
   Of fellowship in all-disastrous fight;
'I suffer mute and lonely, yet another
Uplifts his voice to let me know a brother
   Travels the same wild paths though out of sight.'   35

O sad Fraternity, do I unfold
   Your dolorous mysteries shrouded from of yore?
Nay, be assured; no secret can be told
   To any who divined it not before:
None uninitiate by many a presage   40
Will comprehend the language of the message,
   Although proclaimed aloud for evermore.

I

The City is of Night; perchance of Death,
   But certainly of Night; for never there
Can come the lucid morning's fragrant breath
   After the dewy dawning's cold grey air;
The moon and stars may shine with scorn or pity;   5
The sun has never visited that city,
   For it dissolveth in the daylight fair.

Dissolveth like a dream of night away;
   Though present in distempered gloom of thought
And deadly weariness of heart all day.   10
   But when a dream night after night is brought
Throughout a week, and such weeks few or many
Recur each year for several years, can any
   Discern that dream from real life in aught?

For life is but a dream whose shapes return,   15
   Some frequently, some seldom, some by night
And some by day, some night and day: we learn,
   The while all change and many vanish quite,
In their recurrence with recurrent changes
A certain seeming order; where this ranges   20
   We count things real; such is memory's might.

A river girds the city west and south,
   The main north channel of a broad lagoon,
Regurging with the salt tides from the mouth;
   Waste marshes shine and glister to the moon   25
For leagues, then moorland black, then stony ridges;
Great piers and causeways, many noble bridges,
   Connect the town and islet suburbs strewn.

- 4 -

A river girds the city west and south,
The main north channel of a broad lagoon,
Receives partly ~~At length of~~ the salt tides from the mouth;
Waste marshes shine & glister to the moon
    For leagues, then moorland black, then stony ridge
~~Great~~ Some piers & causeways, many, noble bridges
Connect the town ~~with~~ and islet suburbs strewn.

- 5 -   Monday
                11.7.70

Upon an easy slope it lies at large,
And scarcely overlaps the long curved crest
  Which swells but two
~~Some two or three~~ leagues from the river marge.
A trackless wilderness rolls north & west,
Savannahs, savage woods, enormous mountains
Bleak uplands, black prairies with torrent founts,
And eastward ~~means~~ the shipless sea's unrest.

- 6 -

The city is not ruinous, although
Great ruins of an unremembered past,
With others of a few short years ago
More sad, are found within its precincts vast.
The streetlamps always burn; but scarce a casement
In house or mansion front from roof to basement
Doth glow or gleam athwart the mirk air cast.

A page of the Pierpont Morgan MS (see p. 270).

Upon an easy slope it lies at large,
  And scarcely overlaps the long curved crest
Which swells out two leagues from the river marge.
  A trackless wilderness rolls north and west,
Savannahs, savage woods, enormous mountains,
Bleak uplands, black ravines with torrent fountains;
  And eastward rolls the shipless sea's unrest.

The city is not ruinous, although
  Great ruins of an unremembered past,
With others of a few short years ago
  More sad, are found within its precincts vast.
The street-lamps always burn; but scarce a casement
In house or palace front from roof to basement
  Doth glow or gleam athwart the mirk air cast.

The street-lamps burn amidst the baleful glooms,
  Amidst the soundless solitudes immense
Of rangèd mansions dark and still as tombs.
  The silence which benumbs or strains the sense
Fulfils with awe the soul's despair unweeping:
Myriads of habitants are ever sleeping,
  Or dead, or fled from nameless pestilence!

Yet as in some necropolis you find
  Perchance one mourner to a thousand dead,
So there; worn faces that look deaf and blind
  Like tragic masks of stone. With weary tread,
Each wrapt in his own doom, they wander, wander,
Or sit foredone and desolately ponder
  Through sleepless hours with heavy drooping head.

Mature men chiefly, few in age or youth,
  A woman rarely, now and then a child:
A child! If here the heart turns sick with ruth
  To see a little one from birth defiled,
Or lame or blind, as preordained to languish
Through youthless life, think how it bleeds with anguish
  To meet one erring in that homeless wild.

They often murmur to themselves, they speak
  To one another seldom, for their woe
Broods maddening inwardly and scorns to wreak
  Itself abroad; and if at whiles it grow
To frenzy which must rave, none heeds the clamour,
Unless there waits some victim of like glamour,
  To rave in turn, who lends attentive show.

The City is of Night, but not of Sleep;
   There sweet sleep is not for the weary brain;
The pitiless hours like years and ages creep,
   A night seems termless hell. This dreadful strain
Of thought and consciousness which never ceases,   75
Or which some moments' stupor but increases,
   This, worse than woe, makes wretches there insane.

They leave all hope behind who enter there:
   One certitude while sane they cannot leave,
One anodyne for torture and despair;   80
   The certitude of Death, which no reprieve
Can put off long; and which, divinely tender,
But waits the outstretched hand to promptly render
   That draught whose slumber nothing can bereave.[1]

II

Because he seemed to walk with an intent
   I followed him; who, shadowlike and frail,
Unswervingly though slowly onward went,
   Regardless, wrapt in thought as in a veil:
Thus step for step with lonely sounding feet   5
We travelled many a long dim silent street.

At length he paused: a black mass in the gloom,
   A tower that merged into the heavy sky;
Around, the huddled stones of grave and tomb:
   Some old God's-acre now corruption's sty: 10
He murmured to himself with dull despair,
Here Faith died, poisoned by this charnel air.

Then turning to the right went on once more,
   And travelled weary roads without suspense;
And reached at last a low wall's open door,   15
   Whose villa gleamed beyond the foliage dense:
He gazed, and muttered with a hard despair,
Here Love died, stabbed by its own worshipped pair.

Then turning to the right resumed his march,
   And travelled streets and lanes with wondrous strength,   20
Until on stooping through a narrow arch
   We stood before a squalid house at length:
He gazed, and whispered with a cold despair,
Here Hope died, starved out in its utmost lair.

---

[1] Though the Garden of thy Life be wholly waste, the sweet flowers withered, the fruit-trees barren, over its wall hang ever the rich dark clusters of the Vine of Death, within easy reach of thy hand, which may pluck of them when it will.

When he had spoken thus, before he stirred, 25
   I spoke, perplexed by something in the signs
Of desolation I had seen and heard
   In this drear pilgrimage to ruined shrines:
When Faith and Love and Hope are dead indeed,
Can Life still live? By what doth it proceed? 30

As whom his one intense thought overpowers,
   He answered coldly, Take a watch, erase
The signs and figures of the circling hours,
   Detach the hands, remove the dial-face;
The works proceed until run down; although 35
Bereft of purpose, void of use, still go.

Then turning to the right paced on again,
   And traversed squares and travelled streets whose glooms
Seemed more and more familiar to my ken;
   And reached that sullen temple of the tombs; 40
And paused to murmur with the old despair,
Here Faith died, poisoned by this charnel air.

I ceased to follow, for the knot of doubt
   Was severed sharply with a cruel knife:
He circled thus for ever tracing out 45
   The series of the fraction left of Life;
Perpetual recurrence in the scope
Of but three terms, dead Faith, dead Love, dead Hope.[1]

III

Although lamps burn along the silent streets,
   Even when moonlight silvers empty squares
The dark holds countless lanes and close retreats;
   But when the night its sphereless mantle wears
The open spaces yawn with gloom abysmal, 5
The sombre mansions loom immense and dismal,
   The lanes are black as subterranean lairs.

And soon the eye a strange new vision learns:
   The night remains for it as dark and dense,
Yet clearly in this darkness it discerns 10
   As in the daylight with its natural sense;
Perceives a shade in shadow not obscurely,
Pursues a stir of black in blackness surely,
   Sees spectres also in the gloom intense.

---

[1] Life divided by that persistent three $= \dfrac{L\dot{X}\dot{X}}{333} = .2\dot{1}\dot{0}.$

The ear, too, with the silence vast and deep
   Becomes familiar though unreconciled;
Hears breathings as of hidden life asleep,
   And muffled throbs as of pent passions wild,
Far murmurs, speech of pity or derision;
But all more dubious than the things of vision,
   So that it knows not when it is beguiled.

No time abates the first despair and awe,
   But wonder ceases soon; the weirdest thing
Is felt least strange beneath the lawless law
   Where Death-in-Life is the eternal king;
Crushed impotent beneath this reign of terror,
Dazed with such mysteries of woe and error,
   The soul is too outworn for wondering.

IV

He stood alone within the spacious square
   Declaiming from the central grassy mound,
With head uncovered and with streaming hair,
   As if large multitudes were gathered round:
A stalwart shape, the gestures full of might,
The glances burning with unnatural light:—

As I came through the desert thus it was,
As I came through the desert: All was black,
In heaven no single star, on earth no track;
A brooding hush without a stir or note,
The air so thick it clotted in my throat;
And thus for hours; then some enormous things
Swooped past with savage cries and clanking wings:
   But I strode on austere;
   No hope could have no fear.

As I came through the desert thus it was,
As I came through the desert: Eyes of fire
Glared at me throbbing with a starved desire;
The hoarse and heavy and carnivorous breath
Was hot upon me from deep jaws of death;
Sharp claws, swift talons, fleshless fingers cold
Plucked at me from the bushes, tried to hold:
   But I strode on austere;
   No hope could have no fear.

As I came through the desert thus it was,
As I came through the desert: Lo you, there,
That hillock burning with a brazen glare;
Those myriad dusky flames with points a-glow

Which writhed and hissed and darted to and fro;
A Sabbath of the Serpents, heaped pell-mell   30
For Devil's roll-call and some *fête* of Hell:
    Yet I strode on austere;
    No hope could have no fear.

As I came through the desert thus it was,
As I came through the desert: Meteors ran   35
And crossed their javelins on the black sky-span;
The zenith opened to a gulf of flame,
The dreadful thunderbolts jarred earth's fixed frame;
The ground all heaved in waves of fire that surged
And weltered round me sole there unsubmerged: 40
    Yet I strode on austere;
    No hope could have no fear.

As I came through the desert thus it was,
As I came through the desert: Air once more,
And I was close upon a wild sea-shore;   45
Enormous cliffs arose on either hand,
The deep tide thundered up a league-broad strand;
White foambelts seethed there, wan spray swept and flew;
The sky broke, moon and stars and clouds and blue:
    And I strode on austere;   50
    No hope could have no fear.

As I came through the desert thus it was,
As I came through the desert: On the left
The sun arose and crowned a broad crag-cleft;
There stopped and burned out black, except a rim,   55
A bleeding eyeless socket, red and dim;
Whereon the moon fell suddenly south-west,
And stood above the right-hand cliffs at rest:
    Still I strode on austere;
    No hope could have no fear.   60

As I came through the desert thus it was,
As I came through the desert: From the right
A shape came slowly with a ruddy light;
A woman with a red lamp in her hand,
Bareheaded and barefooted on that strand;   65
O desolation moving with such grace!
O anguish with such beauty in thy face!
    I fell as on my bier,
    Hope travailed with such fear.

As I came through the desert thus it was,   70
As I came through the desert: I was twain,

Two selves distinct that cannot join again;
One stood apart and knew but could not stir,
And watched the other stark in swoon and her;
And she came on, and never turned aside, 75
Between such sun and moon and roaring tide:
    And as she came more near
    My soul grew mad with fear.

As I came through the desert thus it was,
As I came through the desert: Hell is mild 80
And piteous matched with that accursèd wild;
A large black sign was on her breast that bowed,
A broad black band ran down her snow-white shroud;
That lamp she held was her own burning heart,
Whose blood-drops trickled step by step apart: 85
    The mystery was clear;
    Mad rage had swallowed fear.

As I came through the desert thus it was,
As I came through the desert: By the sea
She knelt and bent above that senseless me; 90
Those lamp-drops fell upon my white brow there,
She tried to cleanse them with her tears and hair;
She murmured words of pity, love, and woe,
She heeded not the level rushing flow:
    And mad with rage and fear, 95
    I stood stonebound so near.

As I came through the desert thus it was,
As I came through the desert: When the tide
Swept up to her there kneeling by my side,
She clasped that corpse-like me, and they were borne 100
Away, and this vile me was left forlorn;
I know the whole sea cannot quench that heart,
Or cleanse that brow, or wash those two apart:
    They love; their doom is drear,
    Yet they nor hope nor fear; 105
    But I, what do I here?

V

How he arrives there none can clearly know;
    Athwart the mountains and immense wild tracts,
Or flung a waif upon that vast sea-flow,
    Or down the river's boiling cataracts:
To reach it is as dying fever-stricken; 5
To leave it, slow faint birth intense pangs quicken;
    And memory swoons in both the tragic acts.

But being there one feels a citizen;
  Escape seems hopeless to the heart forlorn:
Can Death-in-Life be brought to life again?
  And yet release does come; there comes a morn
When he awakes from slumbering so sweetly
That all the world is changed for him completely,
  And he is verily as if new-born.

He scarcely can believe the blissful change,
  He weeps perchance who wept not while accurst;
Never again will he approach the range
  Infected by that evil spell now burst:
Poor wretch! who once hath paced that dolent city
Shall pace it often, doomed beyond all pity,
  With horror ever deepening from the first.

Though he possess sweet babes and loving wife,
  A home of peace by loyal friendships cheered,
And love them more than death or happy life,
  They shall avail not; he must dree his weird;
Renounce all blessings for that imprecation,
Steal forth and haunt that builded desolation,
  Of woe and terrors and thick darkness reared.

VI

I sat forlornly by the river-side,
  And watched the bridge-lamps glow like golden stars
Above the blackness of the swelling tide,
  Down which they struck rough gold in ruddier bars;
And heard the heave and plashing of the flow
Against the wall a dozen feet below.

Large elm-trees stood along that river-walk;
  And under one, a few steps from my seat,
I heard strange voices join in stranger talk,
  Although I had not heard approaching feet:
These bodiless voices in my waking dream
Flowed dark words blending with the sombre stream:—

And you have after all come back; come back.
I was about to follow on your track.
And you have failed: our spark of hope is black.

That I have failed is proved by my return:
The spark is quenched, nor ever more will burn,
But listen; and the story you shall learn.

I reached the portal common spirits fear,
And read the words above it, dark yet clear, 20
'Leave hope behind, all ye who enter here:'

And would have passed in, gratified to gain
That positive eternity of pain,
Instead of this insufferable inane.

A demon warder clutched me, Not so fast; 25
First leave your hopes behind!—But years have passed
Since I left all behind me, to the last:

You cannot count for hope, with all your wit,
This bleak despair that drives me to the Pit:
How could I seek to enter void of it? 30

He snarled, What thing is this which apes a soul,
And would find entrance to our gulf of dole
Without the payment of the settled toll?

Outside the gate he showed an open chest:
Here pay their entrance fees the souls unblest; 35
Cast in some hope, you enter with the rest.

This is Pandora's box; whose lid shall shut,
And Hell-gate too, when hopes have filled it; but
They are so thin that it will never glut.

I stood a few steps backwards, desolate; 40
And watched the spirits pass me to their fate,
And fling off hope, and enter at the gate.

When one casts off a load he springs upright,
Squares back his shoulders, breathes with all his might,
And briskly paces forward strong and light: 45

But these, as if they took some burden, bowed;
The whole frame sank; however strong and proud
Before, they crept in quite infirm and cowed.

And as they passed me, earnestly from each
A morsel of his hope I did beseech, 50
To pay my entrance; but all mocked my speech.

Not one would cede a tittle of his store,
Though knowing that in instants three or four
He must resign the whole for evermore.

So I returned. Our destiny is fell;
For in this Limbo we must ever dwell,
Shut out alike from Heaven and Earth and Hell.

The other sighed back, Yea; but if we grope
With care through all this Limbo's dreary scope,
We yet may pick up some minute lost hope;

And, sharing it between us, entrance win,
In spite of fiends so jealous for gross sin:
Let us without delay our search begin.

VII

Some say that phantoms haunt those shadowy streets,
    And mingle freely there with sparse mankind;
And tell of ancient woes and black defeats,
    And murmur mysteries in the grave enshrined:
But others think them visions of illusion,
Or even men gone far in self-confusion;
    No man there being wholly sane in mind.

And yet a man who raves, however mad,
    Who bares his heart and tells of his own fall,
Reserves some inmost secret good or bad:
    The phantoms have no reticence at all:
The nudity of flesh will blush though tameless,
The extreme nudity of bone grins shameless,
    The unsexed skeleton mocks shroud and pall.

I have seen phantoms there that were as men
    And men that were as phantoms flit and roam;
Marked shapes that were not living to my ken,
    Caught breathings acrid as with Dead Sea foam:
The City rests for man so weird and awful,
That his intrusion there might seem unlawful,
    And phantoms there may have their proper home.

VIII

While I still lingered on that river-walk,
    And watched the tide as black as our black doom,
I heard another couple join in talk,
    And saw them to the left hand in the gloom
Seated against an elm bole on the ground,
Their eyes intent upon the stream profound.

'I never knew another man on earth
    But had some joy and solace in his life,
    Some chance of triumph in the dreadful strife:
My doom has been unmitigated dearth.'

'We gaze upon the river, and we note
The various vessels large and small that float,
Ignoring every wrecked and sunken boat.'

'And yet I asked no splendid dower, no spoil
　Of sway or fame or rank or even wealth;　　　　　15
　But homely love with common food and health,
And nightly sleep to balance daily toil.'

'This all-too humble soul would arrogate
Unto itself some signalising hate
From the supreme indifference of Fate!'　　　　　20

'Who is most wretched in this dolorous place?
　I think myself; yet I would rather be
　My miserable self than He, than He
Who formed such creatures to His own disgrace.

'The vilest thing must be less vile than Thou　　25
　From whom it had its being, God and Lord!
　Creator of all woe and sin! abhorred,
Malignant and implacable! I vow

'That not for all Thy power furled and unfurled,
　For all the temples to Thy glory built,　　　　30
　Would I assume the ignominious guilt
Of having made such men in such a world.'

'As if a Being, God or Fiend, could reign,
At once so wicked, foolish, and insane,
As to produce men when He might refrain!　　　　35

'The world rolls round for ever like a mill;
It grinds out death and life and good and ill;
It has no purpose, heart or mind or will.

'While air of Space and Time's full river flow
The mill must blindly whirl unresting so:　　　　40
It may be wearing out, but who can know?

'Man might know one thing were his sight less dim;
That it whirls not to suit his petty whim,
That it is quite indifferent to him.

'Nay, does it treat him harshly as he saith?　　　45
It grinds him some slow years of bitter breath,
Then grinds him back into eternal death.'

IX

It is full strange to him who hears and feels,
  When wandering there in some deserted street,
The booming and the jar of ponderous wheels,
  The trampling clash of heavy ironshod feet:
Who in this Venice of the Black Sea rideth?   5
Who in this city of the stars abideth
  To buy or sell as those in daylight sweet?

The rolling thunder seems to fill the sky
  As it comes on; the horses snort and strain,
The harness jingles, as it passes by;   10
  The hugeness of an overburthened wain:
A man sits nodding on the shaft or trudges
Three parts asleep beside his fellow-drudges:
  And so it rolls into the night again.

What merchandise? whence, whither, and for whom? 15
  Perchance it is a Fate-appointed hearse,
Bearing away to some mysterious tomb
  Or Limbo of the scornful universe
The joy, the peace, the life-hope, the abortions
Of all things good which should have been our portions,   20
  But have been strangled by that City's curse.

X

The mansion stood apart in its own ground;
  In front thereof a fragrant garden-lawn,
High trees about it, and the whole walled round:
  The massy iron gates were both withdrawn;
And every window of its front shed light,   5
Portentous in that City of the Night.

But though thus lighted it was deadly still
  As all the countless bulks of solid gloom;
Perchance a congregation to fulfil
  Solemnities of silence in this doom,   10
Mysterious rites of dolour and despair
Permitting not a breath of chant or prayer?

Broad steps ascended to a terrace broad
  Whereon lay still light from the open door;
The hall was noble, and its aspect awed,   15
  Hung round with heavy black from dome to floor;
And ample stairways rose to left and right
Whose balustrades were also draped with night.

I paced from room to room, from hall to hall,
   Nor any life throughout the maze discerned;
But each was hung with its funereal pall,
   And held a shrine, around which tapers burned,
With picture or with statue or with bust,
All copied from the same fair form of dust:

A woman very young and very fair;
   Beloved by bounteous life and joy and youth,
And loving these sweet lovers, so that care
   And age and death seemed not for her in sooth:
Alike as stars, all beautiful and bright,
These shapes lit up that mausoléan night.

At length I heard a murmur as of lips,
   And reached an open oratory hung
With heaviest blackness of the whole eclipse;
   Beneath the dome a fuming censer swung;
And one lay there upon a low white bed,
With tapers burning at the foot and head:

The Lady of the images: supine,
   Deathstill, lifesweet, with folded palms she lay:
And kneeling there as at a sacred shrine
   A young man wan and worn who seemed to pray:
A crucifix of dim and ghostly white
Surmounted the large altar left in night:—

The chambers of the mansion of my heart,
In every one whereof thine image dwells,
Are black with grief eternal for thy sake.

The inmost oratory of my soul,
Wherein thou ever dwellest quick or dead,
Is black with grief eternal for thy sake.

I kneel beside thee and I clasp the cross,
With eyes for ever fixed upon that face,
So beautiful and dreadful in its calm.

I kneel here patient as thou liest there;
As patient as a statue carved in stone,
Of adoration and eternal grief.

While thou dost not awake I cannot move;
And something tells me thou wilt never wake,
And I alive feel turning into stone.

Most beautiful were Death to end my grief,
Most hateful to destroy the sight of thee,
Dear vision better than all death or life.

But I renounce all choice of life or death,
For either shall be ever at thy side,
And thus in bliss or woe be ever well.—

He murmured thus and thus in monotone,
   Intent upon that uncorrupted face,
Entranced except his moving lips alone:
   I glided with hushed footsteps from the place.
This was the festival that filled with light
That palace in the City of the Night.

XI

What men are they who haunt these fatal glooms,
   And fill their living mouths with dust of death,
And make their habitations in the tombs,
   And breathe eternal sighs with mortal breath,
And pierce life's pleasant veil of various error
To reach that void of darkness and old terror
   Wherein expire the lamps of hope and faith?

They have much wisdom yet they are not wise,
   They have much goodness yet they do not well,
(The fools we know have their own Paradise,
   The wicked also have their proper Hell);
They have much strength but still their doom is stronger,
Much patience but their time endureth longer,
   Much valour but life mocks it with some spell.

They are most rational and yet insane:
   An outward madness not to be controlled;
A perfect reason in the central brain,
   Which has no power, but sitteth wan and cold,
And sees the madness, and foresees as plainly
The ruin in its path, and trieth vainly
   To cheat itself refusing to behold.

And some are great in rank and wealth and power,
   And some renowned for genius and for worth;
And some are poor and mean, who brood and cower
   And shrink from notice, and accept all dearth
Of body, heart and soul, and leave to others
All boons of life: yet these and those are brothers,
   The saddest and the weariest men on earth.

XII

Our isolated units could be brought
 To act together for some common end?
For one by one, each silent with his thought,
 I marked a long loose line approach and wend
Athwart the great cathedral's cloistered square,
And slowly vanish from the moonlit air.

Then I would follow in among the last:
 And in the porch a shrouded figure stood,
Who challenged each one pausing ere he passed,
 With deep eyes burning through a blank white hood:
Whence come you in the world of life and light
To this our City of Tremendous Night?—

From pleading in a senate of rich lords
For some scant justice to our countless hordes
Who toil half-starved with scarce a human right:
I wake from daydreams to this real night.

From wandering through many a solemn scene
Of opium visions, with a heart serene
And intellect miraculously bright:
I wake from daydreams to this real night.

From making hundreds laugh and roar with glee
By my transcendent feats of mimicry,
And humour wanton as an elfish sprite:
I wake from daydreams to this real night.

From prayer and fasting in a lonely cell,
Which brought an ecstasy ineffable
Of love and adoration and delight:
I wake from daydreams to this real night.

From ruling on a splendid kingly throne
A nation which beneath my rule has grown
Year after year in wealth and arts and might:
I wake from daydreams to this real night.

From preaching to an audience fired with faith
The Lamb who died to save our souls from death,
Whose blood hath washed our scarlet sins wool-white:
I wake from daydreams to this real night.

From drinking fiery poison in a den
Crowded with tawdry girls and squalid men,
Who hoarsely laugh and curse and brawl and fight:
I wake from daydreams to this real night.

From picturing with all beauty and all grace
First Eden and the parents of our race,
A luminous rapture unto all men's sight:
I wake from daydreams to this real night.

From writing a great work with patient plan
To justify the ways of God to man,
And show how ill must fade and perish quite:
I wake from daydreams to this real night.

From desperate fighting with a little band
Against the powerful tyrants of our land,
To free our brethren in their own despite:
I wake from daydreams to this real night.

Thus, challenged by that warder sad and stern,
    Each one responded with his countersign,
Then entered the cathedral; and in turn
    I entered also, having given mine;
But lingered near until I heard no more,
And marked the closing of the masive door.

XIII

Of all things human which are strange and wild
    This is perchance the wildest and most strange,
And showeth man most utterly beguiled,
    To those who haunt that sunless City's range;
That he bemoans himself for aye, repeating
How Time is deadly swift, how life is fleeting,
    How naught is constant on the earth but change.

The hours are heavy on him and the days;
    The burden of the months he scarce can bear;
And often in his secret soul he prays
    To sleep through barren periods unaware,
Arousing at some longed-for date of pleasure;
Which having passed and yielded him small treasure,
    He would outsleep another term of care.

Yet in his marvellous fancy he must make
    Quick wings for Time, and see it fly from us;
This Time which crawleth like a monstrous snake,
    Wounded and slow and very venomous;
Which creeps blindwormlike round the earth and ocean,
Distilling poison at each painful motion,
    And seems condemned to circle ever thus.

    And since he cannot spend and use aright
        The little time here given him in trust,
    But wasteth it in weary undelight
        Of foolish toil and trouble, strife and lust,   25
    He naturally claimeth to inherit
    The everlasting Future, that his merit
        May have full scope; as surely is most just.

    O length of the intolerable hours,
        O nights that are as æons of slow pain,   30
    O Time, too ample for our vital powers,
        O Life, whose woeful vanities remain
    Immutable for all of all our legions
    Through all the centuries and in all the regions,
        Not of your speed and variance *we* complain.   35

    We do not ask a longer term of strife,
        Weakness and weariness and nameless woes;
    We do not claim renewed and endless life
        When this which is our torment here shall close,
    An everlasting conscious inanition!   40
    We yearn for speedy death in full fruition,
        Dateless oblivion and divine repose.

XIV

    Large glooms were gathered in the mighty fane,
        With tinted moongleams slanting here and there;
    And all was hush: no swelling organ-strain,
        No chant, no voice or murmuring of prayer;
    No priests came forth, no tinkling censers fumed,   5
    And the high altar space was unillumed.

    Around the pillars and against the walls
        Leaned men and shadows; others seemed to brood
    Bent or recumbent in secluded stalls.
        Perchance they were not a great multitude   10
    Save in that city of so lonely streets
    Where one may count up every face he meets.

    All patiently awaited the event
        Without a stir or sound, as if no less
    Self-occupied, doomstricken while attent.   15
        And then we heard a voice of solemn stress
    From the dark pulpit, and our gaze there met
    Two eyes which burned as never eyes burned yet:

    Two steadfast and intolerable eyes
        Burning beneath a broad and rugged brow;   20

The head behind it of enormous size.
  And as black fir-groves in a large wind bow,
  Our rooted congregation, gloom-arrayed,
  By that great sad voice deep and full were swayed:—

O melancholy Brothers, dark, dark, dark!
O battling in black floods without an ark!
  O spectral wanderers of unholy Night!
My soul hath bled for you these sunless years,
With bitter blood-drops running down like tears:
  Oh, dark, dark, dark, withdrawn from joy and light!

My heart is sick with anguish for your bale;
Your woe hath been my anguish; yea, I quail
  And perish in your perishing unblest.
And I have searched the highths and depths, the scope
Of all our universe, with desperate hope
  To find some solace for your wild unrest.

And now at last authentic word I bring,
Witnessed by every dead and living thing;
  Good tidings of great joy for you, for all:
There is no God; no Fiend with names divine
Made us and tortures us; if we must pine,
  It is to satiate no Being's gall.

It was the dark delusion of a dream,
That living Person conscious and supreme,
  Whom we must curse for cursing us with life;
Whom we must curse because the life He gave
Could not be buried in the quiet grave,
  Could not be killed by poison or by knife.

This little life is all we must endure,
The grave's most holy peace is ever sure,
  We fall asleep and never wake again;
Nothing is of us but the mouldering flesh,
Whose elements dissolve and merge afresh
  In earth, air, water, plants, and other men.

We finish thus; and all our wretched race
Shall finish with its cycle, and give place
  To other beings, with their own time-doom:
Infinite æons ere our kind began;
Infinite æons after the last man
  Has joined the mammoth in earth's tomb and womb.

We bow down to the universal laws,
Which never had for man a special clause

Of cruelty or kindness, love or hate:
If toads and vultures are obscene to sight,
If tigers burn with beauty and with might, 65
   Is it by favour or by wrath of Fate?

All substance lives and struggles evermore
Through countless shapes continually at war,
   By countless interactions interknit:
If one is born a certain day on earth, 70
All times and forces tended to that birth,
   Not all the world could change or hinder it.

I find no hint throughout the Universe
Of good or ill, of blessing or of curse;
   I find alone Necessity Supreme; 75
With infinite Mystery, abysmal, dark,
Unlighted ever by the faintest spark
   For us the flitting shadows of a dream.

O Brothers of sad lives! they are so brief;
A few short years must bring us all relief: 80
   Can we not bear these years of labouring breath?
But if you would not this poor life fulfil,
Lo, you are free to end it when you will,
   Without the fear of waking after death.—

The organ-like vibrations of his voice 85
   Thrilled through the vaulted aisles and died away;
The yearning of the tones which bade rejoice
   Was sad and tender as a requiem lay:
Our shadowy congregation rested still
As brooding on that 'End it when you will.' 90

XV

Wherever men are gathered, all the air
   Is charged with human feeling, human thought;
Each shout and cry and laugh, each curse and prayer,
   Are into its vibrations surely wrought;
Unspoken passion, wordless meditation, 5
Are breathed into it with our respiration;
   It is with our life fraught and overfraught.

So that no man there breathes earth's simple breath,
   As if alone on mountains or wide seas;
But nourishes warm life or hastens death 10
   With joys and sorrows, health and foul disease,
Wisdom and folly, good and evil labours,
Incessant of his multitudinous neighbours;
   He in his turn affecting all of these.

That City's atmosphere is dark and dense,
    Although not many exiles wander there,
With many a potent evil influence,
    Each adding poison to the poisoned air;
Infections of unutterable sadness,
Infections of incalculable madness,
    Infections of incurable despair.

XVI

Our shadowy congregation rested still,
    As musing on that message we had heard
And brooding on that 'End it when you will;'
    Perchance awaiting yet some other word;
When keen as lightning through a muffled sky
Sprang forth a shrill and lamentable cry:—

The man speaks sooth, alas! the man speaks sooth:
    We have no personal life beyond the grave;
There is no God; Fate knows nor wrath nor ruth:
    Can I find here the comfort which I crave?

In all eternity I had one chance,
    One few years' term of gracious human life:
The splendours of the intellect's advance,
    The sweetness of the home with babes and wife;

The social pleasures with their genial wit;
    The fascination of the worlds of art,
The glories of the worlds of nature, lit
    By large imagination's glowing heart;

The rapture of mere being, full of health;
    The careless childhood and the ardent youth,
The strenuous manhood winning various wealth,
    The reverend age serene with life's long truth:

All the sublime prerogatives of Man;
    The storied memories of the times of old,
The patient tracking of the world's great plan
    Through sequences and changes myriadfold.

This chance was never offered me before;
    For me the infinite Past is blank and dumb:
This chance recurreth never, nevermore;
    Blank, blank for me the infinite To-come.

And this sole chance was frustrate from my birth,
    A mockery, a delusion; and my breath

Of noble human life upon this earth
So racks me that I sigh for senseless death.

My wine of life is poison mixed with gall, 35
  My noonday passes in a nightmare dream,
I worse than lose the years which are my all:
  What can console me for the loss supreme?

Speak not of comfort where no comfort is,
  Speak not at all: can words make foul things fair? 40
Our life's a cheat, our death a black abyss:
  Hush and be mute envisaging despair.—

This vehement voice came from the northern aisle
  Rapid and shrill to its abrupt harsh close;
And none gave answer for a certain while, 45
  For words must shrink from these most wordless woes;
At last the pulpit speaker simply said,
  With humid eyes and thoughtful drooping head:—

My Brother, my poor Brothers, it is thus;
This life itself holds nothing good for us, 50
  But it ends soon and nevermore can be;
And we knew nothing of it ere our birth,
And shall know nothing when consigned to earth:
  I ponder these thoughts and they comfort me.

XVII

How the moon triumphs through the endless nights!
  How the stars throb and glitter as they wheel
Their thick processions of supernal lights
  Around the blue vault obdurate as steel!
And men regard with passionate awe and yearning 5
The mighty marching and the golden burning,
  And think the heavens respond to what they feel.

Boats gliding like dark shadows of a dream,
  Are glorified from vision as they pass
The quivering moonbridge on the deep black stream; 10
  Cold windows kindle their dead glooms of glass
To restless crystals; cornice, dome, and column
Emerge from chaos in the splendour solemn;
  Like faëry lakes gleam lawns of dewy grass.

With such a living light these dead eyes shine, 15
  These eyes of sightless heaven, that as we gaze
We read a pity, tremulous, divine,
  Or cold majestic scorn in their pure rays:

Fond man! they are not haughty, are not tender;
There is no heart or mind in all their splendour,   20
   They thread mere puppets all their marvellous maze.

If we could near them with the flight unflown,
   We should but find them worlds as sad as this,
Or suns all self-consuming like our own
   Enringed by planet worlds as much amiss: 25
They wax and wane through fusion and confusion;
The spheres eternal are a grand illusion,
   The empyréan is a void abyss.

XVIII

I wandered in a suburb of the north,
   And reached a spot whence three close lanes led down,
Beneath thick trees and hedgerows winding forth
   Like deep brook channels, deep and dark and lown:
The air above was wan with misty light,   5
The dull grey south showed one vague blur of white.

I took the left-hand lane and slowly trod
   Its earthen footpath, brushing as I went
The humid leafage; and my feet were shod
   With heavy languor, and my frame downbent,   10
With infinite sleepless weariness outworn,
So many nights I thus had paced forlorn.

After a hundred steps I grew aware
   Of something crawling in the lane below;
It seemed a wounded creature prostrate there   15
   That sobbed with pangs in making progress slow,
The hind limbs stretched to push, the fore limbs then
To drag; for it would die in its own den.

But coming level with it I discerned
   That it had been a man; for at my tread   20
It stopped in its sore travail and half-turned,
   Leaning upon its right, and raised its head,
And with the left hand twitched back as in ire
Long grey unreverend locks befouled with mire.

A haggard filthy face with bloodshot eyes,   25
   An infamy for manhood to behold.
He gasped all trembling, What, you want my prize?
   You leave, to rob me, wine and lust and gold
And all that men go mad upon, since you
Have traced my sacred secret of the clue?   30

You think that I am weak and must submit;
   Yet I but scratch you with this poisoned blade,
And you are dead as if I clove with it
   That false fierce greedy heart. Betrayed! betrayed!
I fling this phial if you seek to pass, 35
And you are forthwith shrivelled up like grass.

And then with sudden change, Take thought! take thought!
   Have pity on me! it is mine alone.
If you could find, it would avail you naught;
   Seek elsewhere on the pathway of your own: 40
For who of mortal or immortal race
The lifetrack of another can retrace?

Did you but know my agony and toil!
   Two lanes diverge up yonder from this lane;
My thin blood marks the long length of their soil; 45
   Such clue I left, who sought my clue in vain:
My hands and knees are worn both flesh and bone;
I cannot move but with continual moan.

But I am in the very way at last
   To find the long-lost broken golden thread 50
Which reunites my present with my past,
   If you but go your own way. And I said,
I will retire as soon as you have told
Whereunto leadeth this lost thread of gold.

And so you know it not! he hissed with scorn; 55
   I feared you, imbecile! It leads me back
From this accursed night without a morn,
   And through the deserts which have else no track,
And through vast wastes of horror-haunted time,
To Eden innocence in Eden's clime: 60

And I become a nursling soft and pure,
   An infant cradled on its mother's knee,
Without a past, love-cherished and secure;
   Which if it saw this loathsome present Me,
Would plunge its face into the pillowing breast, 65
And scream abhorrence hard to lull to rest.

He turned to grope; and I retiring brushed
   Thin shreds of gossamer from off my face,
And mused, His life would grow, the germ uncrushed;
   He should to antenatal night retrace, 70
And hide his elements in that large womb
Beyond the reach of man-evolving Doom.

And even thus, what weary way were planned,
  To seek oblivion through the far-off gate
Of birth, when that of death is close at hand!
  For this is law, if law there be in Fate:
What never has been, yet may have its when;
The thing which has been, never is again.

XIX

The mighty river flowing dark and deep,
  With ebb and flood from the remote sea-tides
Vague-sounding through the City's sleepless sleep,
  Is named the River of the Suicides;
For night by night some lorn wretch overweary,
And shuddering from the future yet more dreary,
  Within its cold secure oblivion hides.

One plunges from a bridge's parapet,
  As by some blind and sudden frenzy hurled;
Another wades in slow with purpose set
  Until the waters are above him furled;
Another in a boat with dreamlike motion
Glides drifting down into the desert ocean,
  To starve or sink from out the desert world.

They perish from their suffering surely thus,
  For none beholding them attempts to save,
The while each thinks how soon, solicitous,
  He may seek refuge in the self-same wave;
Some hour when tired of ever-vain endurance
Impatience will forerun the sweet assurance
  Of perfect peace eventual in the grave.

When this poor tragic-farce has palled us long,
  Why actors and spectators do we stay?—
To fill our so-short *rôles* out right or wrong;
  To see what shifts are yet in the dull play
For our illusion; to refrain from grieving
Dear foolish friends by our untimely leaving:
  But those asleep at home, how blest are they!

Yet it is but for one night after all:
  What matters one brief night of dreary pain?
When after it the weary eyelids fall
  Upon the weary eyes and wasted brain;
And all sad scenes and thoughts and feelings vanish
In that sweet sleep no power can ever banish,
  That one best sleep which never wakes again.

XX

I sat me weary on a pillar's base,
  And leaned against the shaft; for broad moonlight
O'erflowed the peacefulness of cloistered space,
  A shore of shadow slanting from the right:
The great cathedral's western front stood there,
A wave-worn rock in that calm sea of air.

Before it, opposite my place of rest,
  Two figures faced each other, large, austere;
A couchant sphinx in shadow to the breast,
  An angel standing in the moonlight clear;
So mighty by magnificence of form,
They were not dwarfed beneath that mass enorm.

Upon the cross-hilt of a naked sword
  The angel's hands, as prompt to smite, were held;
His vigilant intense regard was poured
  Upon the creature placidly unquelled,
Whose front was set at level gaze which took
No heed of aught, a solemn trance-like look.

And as I pondered these opposèd shapes
  My eyelids sank in stupor, that dull swoon
Which drugs and with a leaden mantle drapes
  The outworn to worse weariness. But soon
A sharp and clashing noise the stillness broke,
And from the evil lethargy I woke.

The angel's wings had fallen, stone on stone,
  And lay there shattered; hence the sudden sound:
A warrior leaning on his sword alone
  Now watched the sphinx with that regard profound;
The sphinx unchanged looked forthright, as aware
Of nothing in the vast abyss of air.

Again I sank in that repose unsweet,
  Again a clashing noise my slumber rent;
The warrior's sword lay broken at his feet:
  An unarmed man with raised hands impotent
Now stood before the sphinx, which ever kept
Such mien as if with open eyes it slept.

My eyelids sank in spite of wonder grown;
  A louder crash upstartled me in dread:
The man had fallen forward, stone on stone,
  And lay there shattered, with his trunkless head
Between the monster's large quiescent paws,
Beneath its grand front changeless as life's laws.

The moon had circled westward full and bright,
  And made the temple-front a mystic dream,
And bathed the whole enclosure with its light,
  The sworded angel's wrecks, the sphinx supreme:
I pondered long that cold majestic face
Whose vision seemed of infinite void space.

XXI

Anear the centre of that northern crest
  Stands out a level upland bleak and bare,
From which the city east and south and west
  Sinks gently in long waves; and thronèd there
An Image sits, stupendous, superhuman,
The bronze colossus of a wingèd Woman,
  Upon a graded granite base foursquare.

Low-seated she leans forward massively,
  With cheek on clenched left hand, the forearm's might
Erect, its elbow on her rounded knee;
  Across a clasped book in her lap the right
Upholds a pair of compasses; she gazes
With full set eyes, but wandering in thick mazes
  Of sombre thought beholds no outward sight.

Words cannot picture her; but all men know
  That solemn sketch the pure sad artist wrought
Three centuries and threescore years ago,
  With phantasies of his peculiar thought:
The instruments of carpentry and science
Scattered about her feet, in strange alliance
  With the keen wolf-hound sleeping undistraught;

Scales, hour-glass, bell, and magic-square above;
  The grave and solid infant perched beside,
With open winglets that might bear a dove,
  Intent upon its tablets, heavy-eyed;
Her folded wings as of a mighty eagle,
But all too impotent to lift the regal
  Robustness of her earth-born strength and pride;

And with those wings, and that light wreath which seems
  To mock her grand head and the knotted frown
Of forehead charged with baleful thoughts and dreams,
  The household bunch of keys, the housewife's gown
Voluminous, indented, and yet rigid
As if a shell of burnished metal frigid,
  The feet thick-shod to tread all weakness down;

The comet hanging o'er the waste dark seas,
   The massy rainbow curved in front of it
Beyond the village with the masts and trees;
   The snaky imp, dog-headed, from the Pit,
Bearing upon its batlike leathern pinions   40
Her name unfolded in the sun's dominions,
   The 'MELENCOLIA' that transcends all wit.

Thus has the artist copied her, and thus
   Surrounded to expound her form sublime,
Her fate heroic and calamitous;   45
   Fronting the dreadful mysteries of Time,
Unvanquished in defeat and desolation,
Undaunted in the hopeless conflagration
   Of the day setting on her baffled prime.

Baffled and beaten back she works on still,   50
   Weary and sick of soul she works the more,
Sustained by her indomitable will:
   The hands shall fashion and the brain shall pore,
And all her sorrow shall be turned to labour,
Till Death the friend-foe piercing with his sabre   55
   That mighty heart of hearts ends bitter war.

But as if blacker night could dawn on night,
   With tenfold gloom on moonless night unstarred,
A sense more tragic than defeat and blight,
   More desperate than strife with hope debarred,   60
More fatal than the adamantine Never
Encompassing her passionate endeavour,
   Dawns glooming in her tenebrous regard:

The sense that every struggle brings defeat
   Because Fate holds no prize to crown success;   65
That all the oracles are dumb or cheat
   Because they have no secret to express;
That none can pierce the vast black veil uncertain
Because there is no light beyond the curtain;
   That all is vanity and nothingness.   70

Titanic from her high throne in the north,
   That City's sombre Patroness and Queen,
In bronze sublimity she gazes forth
   Over her Capital of teen and threne,
Over the river with its isles and bridges,   75
The marsh and moorland, to the stern rock-ridges,
   Confronting them with a coëval mien.

The moving moon and stars from east to west
  Circle before her in the sea of air;
Shadows and gleams glide round her solemn rest.   80
  Her subjects often gaze up to her there:
The strong to drink new strength of iron endurance,
The weak new terrors; all, renewed assurance
  And confirmation of the old despair.

LINES, 1878

I HAD a Love; it was so long ago,
    So many long sad years:
She died; and then a waste of arid woe,
    Never refreshed by tears:
She died so young, so tender, pure and fair;   5
I wandered in the Desert of Despair.

What kept me then from following my Love?
    I ask in drear amaze;
What held me wingless from my flying Dove,
    To tread Life's barren ways?   10
What drugged my keen intent, for bale or bliss,
To sink or soar in Death's most dark abyss?

How have I lived in this tremendous waste,
    So long, so lone, so lorn?
No well-springs for my soul, no food to taste   15
    For my poor heart forlorn;
No Love, no Faith, no Hope to pass the Sands
And sojourn in the friendly fruitful lands.

My heart hath fed upon itself, reply,
    The bitter, poisoned meat!   20
My soul hath drunk its own scant sources dry,
    Bitter as blood; my feet
Have trodden their old footsteps year by year,
Circling for ever in the desert drear.

Upon the burning sands and bruising stones   25
    I plod the pathless ways;
Of all my fellow-creatures dry bleached bones
    Are all that meet my gaze,
Or men and camels dying or just dead
With eager vultures hanging overhead.   30

Whereon my weary feet and famished heart
    Whereon my wasted brain

Would of that carrion banquet make a part,
  Would perish there full fain;
But we are goaded by some goad unblest 35
From such long-wished-for everlasting rest.

Songs in the Desert! Songs of husky breath,
  And undivine Despair;
Songs that are dirges, but for Life not Death,
  Songs that infect the air 40
Have sweetened bitterly my food and wine,
The heart corroded and the Dead Sea brine.

How strange! we can confront the direst grief
  Erect, and scarcely quail,
If we can only have the poor relief 45
  Of uttering our bale,
In music, sculpture, painting, verse or prose,
Who else were crushed beneath the heavy woes.

So potent is the Word, the Lord of Life,
  And so tenacious Art, 50
Whose instinct urges to perpetual strife
  With Death, Life's counterpart:
The magic of their music, might and light
Can keep one living in his own despite.

Their splendours cleave the deep sepulchral glooms, 55
  Revive the ancient dead;
They build high palaces of lowly tombs
  Wherein high lives are led;
Funereal black to royal purple glows,
And corpses stand up Kings from long repose. 60

And yet, my Love, I do not know a night
  Since first you left me here,
I had not welcomed with serene delight
  A Voice authentic, clear:
Go sleep, go sleep, thy long day's travail done; 65
Thou shalt not wake to see another sun.

Ah Love, my Love, with what perpetual moan,
  While yet I half believed
That you were radiant by the Heavenly Throne,
  From all Earth's pains retrieved, 70
My weak and selfish desolate heart did pine
To have you back here from the realm divine.

You would have kept me from the Desert sands
  Bestrewn with bleaching bones,

And led me through the friendly fertile lands,
    And changed my weary moans
To hymns of triumph and enraptured love,
And made our earth as rich as Heaven above.

But now, my only Love, when I must see
    You are no more, no more;
As I and every living thing shall be
    When pushed off from the shore
Of narrow Life into the Dead Sea waves,
Those never-satiate unsurrendering graves:

Now, when I see that we are all resolved
    Into the Universe
Whence so mysteriously we were evolved;
    That all our parts disperse
Never to build our very selves agen,
Though roses spring from roses, men from men:

Now, when I see that all our little race
    Must have its death as birth;
Motes in infinities of Time and Space,
    Less lasting than our Earth,
This many-insect-peopled drop of dew
Exhaling in a moment from the view:

Yea, now that I have learnt by grievous thought
    Something of Life and Death;
And how the one is like the other, naught,
    Except for painful breath;
And now that I have learnt with infinite toil
To know myself, involved in such a coil:

Why, if there were a living God indeed,
    And I should hear His Voice:
'Her death shall be abolished for thy need,
    That ye may both rejoice;
She shall come back as young as when she died
To thee as young, fit bridegroom for such bride:

And ye shall live together man and wife
    Unto a reverend age;
And love shall be your balm in grief and strife
    Whatever wars may rage;
And young ones fill your home with tender cheer
And keep your name green when yourselves are sere.'

I would reply: 'Lord of the Universe!
    Pity and pardon now!

I shudder from this blessing as a curse;
  Down to the dust I bow,
And from my inmost spirit supplicate
Thou wilt be pleased to alter not our fate. 120

For she has perfect and eternal rest,
  She is not evermore,
Save as an image graven in my breast;
  And I am near the shore
Of that Dead Sea where we find end of woes 125
Unconsciousness, oblivion, full repose.

I would not tear her from her resting place
  For any human bliss;
I would not one of my past years retrace
  Who seek the black abyss; 130
I would not have the burden on my soul
Of bringing babes into this world of dole.'

Yes Love, my Love, dissolved so long ago,
  Alive but in my heart,
It gives me solace now instead of woe, 135
  Sweet joy instead of smart,
To brood and murmur in my desert bare:
She died so young, so tender, pure and fair.

And I have comfort that my own good time
  Must now at length be near: 140
How Life is piteous, and how Death sublime!
  O World of doubt and fear,
Of mystery, grief and yearning that appal,
Why were we ever brought to life at all?

What profit from all life that lives on Earth, 145
  What good, what use, what aim?
What compensation for the throes of birth
  And death in all its frame?
What conscious life has ever paid its cost?
From Nothingness to Nothingness—all lost! 150

A VOICE FROM THE NILE

I come from mountains under other stars
Than those reflected in my waters here;
Athwart broad realms, beneath large skies, I flow,
Between the Libyan and Arabian hills,
And merge at last into the great Mid-Sea; 5
And make this land of Egypt. All is mine:

The palm-trees and the doves among the palms,
The corn-fields and the flowers among the corn,
The patient oxen and the crocodiles,
The ibis and the heron and the hawk,
The lotus and the thick papyrus reeds,
The slant-sailed boats that flit before the wind
Or up my rapids ropes hale heavily;
Yea, even all the massive temple-fronts
With all their columns and huge effigies,
The pyramids and Memnon and the Sphinx,
This Cairo and the City of the Greek
As Memphis and the hundred-gated Thebes,
Sais and Denderah of Isis queen;
Have grown because I fed them with full life,
And flourish only while I feed them still.
For if I stint my fertilising flood,
Gaunt famine reaps among the sons of men
Who have not corn to reap for all they sowed,
And blight and languishment are everywhere;
And when I have withdrawn or turned aside
To other realms my ever-flowing streams,
The old realms withered from their old renown,
The sands came over them, the desert-sands
Incessantly encroaching, numberless
Beyond my water-drops, and buried them,
And all is silence, solitude, and death,
Exanimate silence while the waste winds howl
Over the sad immeasurable waste.

    Dusk memories haunt me of an infinite past,
Ages and cycles brood above my springs,
Though I remember not my primal birth.
So ancient is my being and august,
I know not anything more venerable;
Unless, perchance, the vaulting skies that hold
The sun and moon and stars that shine on me;
The air that breathes upon me with delight;
And Earth, All-Mother, all-beneficent,
Who held her mountains forth like opulent breasts
To cradle me and feed me with their snows,
And hollowed out the great sea to receive
My overplus of flowing energy:
Blessèd for ever be our Mother Earth.

    Only, the mountains that must feed my springs
Year after year and every year with snows
As they have fed innumerable years,
These mountains they are evermore the same,

Rooted and motionless; the solemn heavens
Are evermore the same in stable rest;
The sun and moon and stars that shine on me 55
Are evermore the same although they move:
I solely, moving ever without pause,
Am evermore the same and not the same;
Pouring myself away into the sea,
And self-renewing from the farthest heights; 60
Ever-fresh waters streaming down and down,
The one old Nilus constant through their change.

The creatures also whom I breed and feed
Perpetually perish and dissolve,
And other creatures like them take their place, 65
To perish in their turn and be no more:
My profluent waters perish not from life,
Absorbed into the ever-living sea
Whose life is in their full replenishment.

Of all these creatures whom I breed and feed, 70
One only with his works is strange to me,
Is strange and admirable and pitiable,
As homeless where all others are at home.
My crocodiles are happy in my slime,
And bask and seize their prey, each for itself, 75
And leave their eggs to hatch in the hot sun,
And die, their lives fulfilled, and are no more,
And others bask and prey and leave their eggs.
My doves they build their nests, each pair its own,
And feed their callow young, each pair its own, 80
None serves another, each one serves itself;
All glean alike about my fields of grain,
And all the nests they build them are alike,
And are the self-same nests they built of old
Before the rearing of the pryamids, 85
Before great Hekatompylos was reared;
Their cooing is the cooing soft and sweet
That murmured plaintively at evening-tide
In pillared Karnak as its pillars rose;
And they are happy floating through my palms. 90

But Man, the admirable, the pitiable,
These sad-eyed peoples of the sons of men,
Are as the children of an alien race
Planted among my children, not at home,
Changelings aloof from all my family. 95
The one is servant and the other lord,
And many myriads serve a single lord:

So was it when the pyramids were reared,
And sphinxes and huge columns and wrought stones
Were haled long lengthening leagues adown my banks   100
By hundreds groaning with the stress of toil
And groaning under the taskmaster's scourge,
With many falling foredone by the way,
Half-starved on lentils, onions, and scant bread;
So is it now with these poor fellaheen   105
To whom my annual bounty brings fierce toil
With scarce enough of food to keep-in life.
They build mud huts and spacious palaces;
And in the huts the moiling millions dwell,
And in the palaces their sumptuous lords   110
Pampered with all the choicest things I yield:
Most admirable, most pitiable Man.

Also their peoples ever are at war,
Slaying and slain, burning and ravaging,
And one yields to another and they pass,   115
While I flow evermore the same great Nile,
The ever-young and ever-ancient Nile:
The swarthy is succeeded by the dusk,
The dusky by the pale, the pale again
By sunburned turbaned tribes long-linen-robed: 120
And with these changes all things change and pass,
All things but Me and this old Land of mine,
Their dwellings, habitudes, and garbs, and tongues:
I hear strange voices;[1] never more the voice
Austere priests chanted to the boat of death   125
Gliding across the Acherusian lake,
Or satraps parleyed in the Pharaoh's halls;
Never the voice of mad Cambyses' hosts,
Never the voice of Alexander's Greece,
Never the voice of Cæsar's haughty Rome: 130
And with the peoples and the languages,
With the great Empires still the great Creeds change;
They shift, they change, they vanish like thin dreams,
As unsubstantial as the mists that rise
After my overflow from out my fields,   135
In silver fleeces, golden volumes, rise,
And melt away before the mounting sun;
While I flow onward solely permanent
Amidst their swiftly-passing pageantry.

Poor men, most admirable, most pitiable,   140
With all their changes all their great Creeds change:

[1] 'and Nilus heareth strange voices.' *Sir Thomas Browne.*

For Man, this alien in my family,
Is alien most in this, to cherish dreams
And brood on visions of eternity,
And build religions in this brooding brain 145
And in the dark depths awe-full of his soul.
My other children live their little lives,
Are born and reach their prime and slowly fail,
And all their little lives are self-fulfilled;
They die and are no more, content with age 150
And weary with infirmity. But Man
Has fear and hope and phantasy and awe,
And wistful yearnings and unsated loves,
That strain beyond the limits of his life,
And therefore Gods and Demons, Heaven and Hell: 155
This Man, the admirable, the pitiable.

Lo, I look backward some few thousand years,
And see men hewing temples in my rocks
With seated forms gigantic fronting them,
And solemn labyrinthine catacombs 160
With tombs all pictured with fair scenes of life
And scenes and symbols of mysterious death;
And planting avenues of sphinxes forth,
Sphinxes couched calm, whose passionless regard
Sets timeless riddles to bewildered time, 165
Forth from my sacred banks to other fanes
Islanded in the boundless sea of air,
Upon whose walls and colonnades are carved
Tremendous hieroglyphs of secret things;
I see embalming of the bodies dead 170
And judging of the disembodied souls;
I see the sacred animals alive,
And statues of the various-headed gods,
Among them throned a woman and a babe,
The goddess crescent-horned, the babe divine. 175
Then I flow forward some few thousand years,
And see new temples shining with all grace,
Whose sculptured gods are beautiful human forms.
Then I flow forward not a thousand years,
And see again a woman and a babe, 180
The woman haloed and the babe divine;
And everywhere that symbol of the cross
I knew aforetime in the ancient days,
The emblem then of life but now of death.
Then I flow forward some few hundred years, 185
And see again the crescent, now supreme
On lofty cupolas and minarets
Whence voices sweet and solemn call to prayer.

So the men change along my changeless stream,
And change their Faiths; but I yield all alike   190
Sweet water for their drinking, sweet as wine,
And pure sweet water for their lustral rites:
For thirty generations of my corn
Outlast a generation of my men,
And thirty generations of my men   195
Outlast a generation of their gods:
O admirable, pitiable Man,
My child, yet alien in my family.

And I through all these generations flow
Of corn and men and gods, all-bountiful,   200
Perennial through their transientness, still fed
By earth with waters in abundancy;
And as I flowed here long before they were,
So may I flow when they no longer are,
Most like the serpent of eternity: 205
Blessèd for ever be our Mother Earth.

TO H. A. B.
ON MY FORTY-SEVENTH BIRTHDAY
Wednesday November 23 1881

WHEN one is forty years and seven,
  Is seven and forty sad years old,
He looks not onward for his Heaven,
  The future is too blank and cold,
    Its pale flowers smell of graveyard mould;   5
He looks back to his lifeful past;
  If age is silver, youth is gold:—
Could youth but last, could youth but last!

He turns back toward his youthful past
  A-throb with life and love and hope,   10
Whose long-dead joys in memory last,
  Whose shining days had ample scope;
    He turns and lingers on the slope
Whose dusk leads down to sightless death:—
  The sun once crowned that darkening cope,   15
And song once thrilled this weary breath.

Ah, he plods wearily to death,
  Adown the gloaming into night,
But other lives breathe joyous breath
  In morning's boundless golden light;   20
    Their feet are swift, their eyes are bright,

Their hearts beat rhythms of hope and love,
  Their being is a pure delight
In earth below and heaven above.

And *you* have hope and joy and love, 25
  And you have youth's abounding life,
Whose crystal currents flow above
  The stones and sands of care and strife.
May all your years with joys be rife,
May you grow calmly to your prime, 30
  A maiden sweet, a cherished wife,
A happy mother in due time.

All good you wish me, past my prime,
  I wish with better hope to you,
And richer blessings than old Time 35
  And Fate or Fortune found my due:
For you are kind and good and true,
And so when *you* are forty-seven
  May spouse and children in your view
Make Home the happiest life-long Heaven. 40

THE SLEEPER

THE fire is in a steadfast glow,
  The curtains drawn against the night;
Upon the red couch soft and low
  Between the fire and lamp alight
She rests half-sitting, half-reclining, 5
Encompassed by the cosy shining,
  Her ruby dress with lace trimmed white.

Her left hand shades her drooping eyes
  Against the fervour of the fire,
The right upon her cincture lies 10
  In languid grace beyond desire,
A lily fallen among roses;
So placidly her form reposes,
  It scarcely seemeth to respire.

She is not surely all awake, 15
  As yet she is not all asleep;
The eyes with lids half-open take
  A startled deprecating peep
Of quivering drowsiness, then slowly
The lids sink back, before she wholly 20
  Resigns herself to slumber deep.

The side-neck gleams so pure beneath
    The underfringe of gossamer,
The tendrils of whose faery wreath
    The softest sigh suppressed would stir.   25
The little pink-shell ear-rim flushes
With her young blood's translucent blushes,
    Nestling in tresses warm as fur.

The contour of her cheek and chin
    Is curved in one delicious line,   30
Pure as a vase of porcelain thin
    Through which a tender light may shine;
Her brow and blue-veined temple gleaming
Beneath the dusk of hair back-streaming
    Are as a virgin's marble shrine.   35

The ear is burning crimson fire,
    The flush is brightening on the face,
The lips are parting to suspire,
    The hair grows restless in its place
As if itself new tangles wreathing,   40
The bosom with her deeper breathing
    Swells and subsides with ravishing grace.

The hand slides softly to caress,
    Unconscious, that fine-pencilled curve
'Her lip's contour and downiness,'   45
    Unbending with a sweet reserve;
A tender darkness that abashes
Steals out beneath the long dark lashes,
    Whose sightless eyes make eyesight swerve.

The hand on chin and throat downslips,   50
    Then softly, softly on her breast;
A dream comes fluttering o'er the lips,
    And stirs the eyelids in their rest,
And makes their undershadows quiver,
And like a ripple on a river   55
    Glides through her breathing manifest.

I feel an awe to read this dream
    So clearly written in her smile;
A pleasant not a passionate theme,
    A little love, a little guile;   60
I fear lest she should speak, revealing
The secret of some maiden feeling
    I have no right to hear the while.

The dream has passed without a word
  Of all that hovered finely traced;   65
The hand has slipt down, gently stirred
  To join the other at her waist;
Her breath from that light agitation
Has settled to its slow pulsation;
  She is by deep sleep re-embraced.   70

Deep sleep, so holy in its calm,
  So helpless, yet so awful too;
Whose silence sheds as sweet a balm
  As ever sweetest voice could do;
Whose trancèd eyes, unseen, unseeing,   75
Shadowed by pure love, thrill our being
  With tender yearnings through and through.

Sweet sleep; no hope, no fear, no strife;
  The solemn sanctity of death,
With all the loveliest bloom of life;   80
  Eternal peace in mortal breath:
Pure sleep from which she will awaken
Refreshed as one who hath partaken
  New strength, new hope, new love, new faith.

AT BELVOIR
Sunday July 3 1881
A BALLAD, HISTORICAL AND PROPHETIC
In maiden meditation, fancy free.

My thoughts go back to last July,
  Sweet happy thoughts and tender;—
'The bridal of the earth and sky,'
  A day of noble splendour;
A day to make the saddest heart   5
  In joy a true believer;
When two good friends we roamed apart
  The shady walks of Belvoir.

A maiden like a budding rose,
  Unconscious of the golden   10
And fragrant bliss of love that glows
  Deep in her heart infolden;
A Poet old in years and thought,
  Yet not too old for pleasance,
Made young again and fancy-fraught   15
  By such a sweet friend's presence.

The other two beyond our ken
  Most shamefully deserted,
And far from all the ways of men
  Their stealthy steps averted:
Of course our Jack would go astray;
  Erotic and erratic;
But Mary!—well, I own the day
  Was really too ecstatic.

We roamed with many a merry jest
  And many a ringing laughter;
The slow calm hours too rich in zest
  To heed before and after:
Yet lingering down the lovely walks
  Soft strains anon came stealing,
A finer music through our talks
  Of sweeter, deeper feeling:

Yes, now and then a quiet word
  Of seriousness dissembling
In smiles would touch some hidden chord
  And set it all a-trembling:
I trembled too, and felt it strange;—
  Could I be in possession
Of music richer in its range
  Than yet had found expression?

The cattle standing in the mere,
  The swans upon it gliding,
The sunlight on the waters clear,
  The radiant clouds dividing;
The solemn sapphire sky above,
  The foliage lightly waving,
The soft air's Sabbath peace and love
  To satisfy all craving.

We mapped the whole fair region out
  As Country of the Tender,
From first pursuit in fear and doubt
  To final glad surrender:
Each knoll and arbour got its name,
  Each vista, covert, dingle;—
No young pair now may track the same
  And long continue single!

And in the spot most thrilling-sweet
  Of all this Love-Realm rosy
Our truant pair had found retreat,

Unblushing, calm and cosy: 60
Where seats too wide for one are placed,
   And yet for two but narrow,
It's 'Let my arm steal round your waist,
   And be my winsome marrow!'

Reclining on a pleasant lea 65
   Such tender scenes rehearsing,
A freakish fit seized him and me
   For wildly foolish versing:
We versed of this, we versed of that,
   A pair of mocking sinners, 70
While our lost couple strayed or sat
   Oblivious of their dinners.

But what was strange, our maddest rhymes
   In all their divagations
Were charged and over-charged at times 75
   With deep vaticinations:
I yearn with wonder at the power
   Of Poetry prophetic
Which in my soul made that blithe hour
   With this hour sympathetic. 80

For though we are in winter now,
   My heart is in full summer:
Old Year, old Wish, have made their bow;
   I welcome each new-comer.
'The King is dead, long live the King! 85
   The throne is vacant never!'
Is true, I read, of everything,
   So of my heart for ever!

My thoughts go on to next July,
   More happy thoughts, more tender; 90
'The bridal of the earth and sky,'
   A day of perfect splendour;
A day to make the saddest heart
   In bliss a firm believer;
When two True Loves may roam apart 95
   The shadiest walks of Belvoir.

There may be less of merry jest
   And less of ringing laughter,
Yet life be much more rich in zest
   And richer still thereafter; 100
The love-scenes of that region fair
   Have very real rehearsing,

And tremulous kisses thrill the air
  Far sweetlier than sweet versing;

The bud full blown at length reveal 105
  Its deepest golden burning;
The heart inspired with love unseal
  Its inmost passionate yearning:
The music of the hidden chord
  At length find full expression; 110
The Seraph of the Flaming Sword
  Assume divine possession.

MODERN PENELOPE
(RIDDLE SOLVED)

WHAT did she mean by that crochet work?
  The work that never got done,
Lolling as indolent as a Turk,
  Looking demure as a Nun:
What subtle mystery might lurk 5
  (Of course there must be one)
In that Penelope web of work,
  The work that never got done?

She lolled on the low couch just under the light
  So very serene and staid: 10
We had some other guests that night,
  One sang, another played,
A couple discovered the stars were bright,
  Of course a youth and a maid,
I watched her knitting under the light 15
  So very serene and staid.

I knew that she was a rogue in her heart,
  As roguish as ever could be,
And she knew that I knew, yet would not dart
  A single glance at me, 20
But seemed as it were withdrawn apart
  Amid the companie,
A nun in her face, with a rogue in her heart
  As roguish as ever could be.

I like a riddle when its knot 25
  Involves a pretty girl,
I puzzle about, now cold, now hot,
  Through every loop and twirl,
For the question is 'Who' as well as 'What'?

  And the answer is thus a pearl,   30
And really you cannot study the knot,
  Unless you study the girl.

With a graceful lazy kittypuss air
  She fingered the net and the ball:
At first she started to work on the square,   35
  And then she undid all:
To make it round was next her care,
  But the progress was strangely small,
With a graceful lazy kittypuss air
  Trifling with net and ball.   40

About her lips a quiet smile
  Came hovering, then took rest:
A butterfly in the selfsame style
  Will choose some sweet flower's breast:
Her eyes were drooping all the while,   45
  But the drooping lids expressed
The satisfaction of a smile
  Like a butterfly at rest.

Her hands kept floating to and fro
  Like a pair of soft white doves,   50
In gentle dalliance coy and slow
  Around a nest of Loves:
And against my chair her couch was low,
  And six was the size of her gloves,
They were charming those hands there to and fro   55
  Like a pair of soft white doves.

Her fair face opened like a flower,
  And a sigh thrilled the smile on her lips,
And her eyes shone out with a dazzling power
  From the dream of their half-eclipse   60
As she welcomed the trill of 'A summer shower'
  With plausive finger-tips—
Oh! her eyes so bright, and her face like a flower,
  And the exquisite smile of her lips!

Those hands kept floating soft and white   65
  Our hearts to mesmerise,
Those dark eyes keep half-veiled their light
  To lure and lure our eyes;
That web is but a subtle sleight
  To mesh us by surprise: 70
Do I not read your riddle right,
  Penelope the wise?

O you nun in face with the rogue in your heart
  As roguish as ever can be,
You have played an immensely wiser part 75
  Than the old Penelope:
You have caught twin loves in the toils of your art,
  And neither will ever get free:
You have won the game of a heart for a heart,
  And when shall the settling be? 80

PROEM

O ANTIQUE fables! beautiful and bright,
And joyous with the joyous youth of yore;
O antique fables! for a little light
Of that which shineth in you evermore,
To cleanse the dimness from our weary eyes, 5
And bathe our old world with a new surprise
Of golden dawn entrancing sea and shore.

We stagger under the enormous weight
Of all the heavy ages piled on us,
With all their grievous wrongs inveterate, 10
And all their disenchantments dolorous,
And all the monstrous tasks they have bequeathed;
And we are stifled with the airs they breathed;
And read in theirs our dooms calamitous.

Our world is all stript naked of their dreams; 15
No deities in sky or sun or moon,
No nymphs in woods and hills and seas and streams;
Mere earth and water, air and fire, their boon:
No God in all our universe we trace,
No Heaven in the infinitude of space, 20
No life beyond death—coming not too soon.

Our souls are stript of their illusions sweet,
Our hopes at best in some far future years
For others, not ourselves; whose bleeding feet
Wander this rocky waste where broken spears 25
And bleaching bones lie scattered on the sand;
Who know *we* shall not reach the Promised Land;—
Perhaps a mirage glistening through our tears.

And if there be this Promised Land indeed,
Our children's children's children's heritage, 30
Oh, what a prodigal waste of precious seed,
Of myriad myriad lives from age to age,

Of woes and agonies and blank despairs
Through countless cycles, that some fortunate heirs
May enter, and conclude the pilgrimage! 35

But if it prove a mirage after all!
Our last illusion leaves us wholly bare,
To bruise against Fate's adamantine wall,
Consumed or frozen in the pitiless air;
In all our world, beneath, around, above, 40
One only refuge, solace, triumph,—Love,
Sole star of light in infinite black despair.

O antique fables! beautiful and bright,
And joyous with the joyous youth of yore;
O antique fables! for a little light 45
Of that which shineth in you evermore,
To cleanse the dimness from our weary eyes,
And bathe our old world with a new surprise
Of golden dawn entrancing sea and shore.

THE POET AND HIS MUSE

I sighed unto my Muse, 'O gentle Muse
    Would you but come and kiss my aching brow,
And thus a little life and joy infuse
    Into my brain and heart so weary now;
Into my heart so sad with emptiness 5
    Even when unafflicted by the stress
        Of all our kind's poor life;
Into my brain so feeble and so listless,
    Crushed down by burthens of dark thought resistless
Of all our want and woe and unresulting strife. 10

'Would you but come and kiss me on the brow,
    Would you but kiss me on the pallid lips
That have so many years been songless now,
    And on the eyes involved in drear eclipse;
That thus the barren brain long overwrought 15
    Might yield again some blossoms of glad thought,
        And the long-mute lips sing,
And the long-arid eyes grow moist and tender
    With some new vision of the ancient splendour
Of beauty and delight that lives in everything. 20

'Would you but kiss me on the silent lips
    And teach them thus to sing some new sweet song;
Would you but kiss my eyes from their eclipse
    With some new tale of old-world right and wrong:

Some song of love and joy or tender grief
Whose sweetness is its own divine relief,
    Whose joy is golden bliss;
Some solemn and impassioned antique story
Where love against dark doom burns out in glory,
Where life is freely staked to win one mutual kiss.

'Would you but sing to me some new dear song
    Of love in bliss or bale alike supreme;
Some story of our old-world right and wrong
    With noble passion burning through the theme:
What though the story be of darkest doom,
If loyal spirits shining through its gloom
        Throb to us from afar?
What though the song with heavy sorrows languish,
If loving hearts pulse to us through its anguish?
Is not the whole black night enriched by one pure star?'

And lo She came, the ever-gentle Muse,
    Sad as my heart and languid as my brain;
Too gentle in her loving to refuse,
    Although her steps were weariness and pain;
Although her eyes were blank and lustreless,
Although her form was clothed with heaviness
        And drooped beneath the weight;
Although her lips were blanched from all their blooming,
Her pure face pallid as from long entombing,
Her bright regard and smile sombre and desolate.—

'Sad as thy heart and languid as thy brain
    I come unto thy sighing through the gloom,
I come with mortal weariness and pain,
    I come as one compelled to leave her tomb:
Behold, am I not wrapt as in the cloud
Of death's investiture and sombre shroud?
        Am I not wan as death?
Look at the withered leafage of my garland,
Is it not nightshade from the sad dim far land
Of night and old oblivion and no mortal breath?

'I come unto thy sighing through the gloom,
    My hair dishevelled dank with dews of night,
Reluctantly constrained to leave my tomb;
    With eyes that have for ever lost their light;
My vesture mouldering with deep death's disgrace,
My heart as chill and bloodless as my face,
        My forehead like a stone;
My spirit sightless as my eyes are sightless,

My inmost being nerveless, soulless, lightless,
My joyous singing voice a harsh sepulchral moan. 70

'My hair dishevelled dank with dews of night
   From that far region of dim death I come,
With eyes and soul and spirit void of light,
   With lips more sad in speech than stark and dumb:
Lo, you have ravaged me with dolorous thought 75
Until my brain was wholly overwrought,
     Barren of flowers and fruit;
Until my heart was bloodless for all passion,
Until my trembling lips could no more fashion
Sweet words to fit sweet airs of trembling lyre and lute. 80

'From the sad regions of dim death I come;
   We tell no tales there for our tale is told,
We sing no songs there for our lips are dumb,
   Likewise our hearts and brains are graveyard mould;
No wreaths of laurel, myrtle, ivy or vine, 85
About our pale and pulseless brows entwine,
     And that sad frustrate realm
Nor amaranths nor asphodels can nourish,
But aconite and black-red poppies flourish
On such Lethean dews as fair life overwhelm. 90

'We tell no tales more, we whose tale is told;
   As your brain withered and your heart grew chill
My heart and brain were turned to churchyard mould,
   Wherefore my singing voice sank ever still;
And I, all heart and brain and voice, am dead; 95
It is my phantom here beside your bed
     That speaketh to you now;
Though you exist still, a mere form inurning
The ashes of dead fires of thought and yearning,
Dead faith, dead love, dead hope, in hollow breast and brow.' 100

When It had moaned these words of hopeless doom,
   The Phantom of the Muse once young and fair,
Pallid and dim from its disastrous tomb,
   Of Her so sweet and young and *débonnaire*,
So rich of heart and brain and singing voice, 105
So quick to shed sweet tears and to rejoice
     And smile with ravishing grace;
My soul was stupefied by its own reaping,
Then burst into a flood of passionate weeping,
Tears bitter as black blood streaming adown my face. 110

'O Muse, so young and sweet and glad and fair,
   O Muse of hope and faith and joy and love,

THE POET AND HIS MUSE

O Muse so gracious and so *débonnaire*,
 Darling of earth beneath and heaven above;
If Thou art gone into oblivious death,
Why should I still prolong my painful breath?
 Why still exist, the urn
Holding of once-great fires the long-dead ashes,
No sole spark left of all their glow and flashes,
Fires never to rekindle more and shine and burn?

'O Muse of hope and faith and joy and love,
 Soul of my soul, if Thou in truth art dead,
A mournful alien in our world above,
 A Phantom moaning by my midnight bed;
How can I be alive, a hollow form
With ashes of dead fires once bright and warm?
 What thing is worth my strife?
The Past a great regret, the Present sterile,
The Future hopeless, with the further peril
Of withering down and down to utter death-in-life.

'Soul of my soul, canst Thou indeed be dead?
 What mean for me if I accept their lore
Thy words, O Phantom moaning by my bed,
 "I cannot sing again for evermore"?
I nevermore can think or feel or dream
Or hope or love—the fatal loss supreme!
 I am a soulless clod;
No germ of life within me that surpasses
The little germs of weeds and flowers and grasses
Wherewith our liberal Mother decks the graveyard sod.

'I am half-torpid yet I spurn this lore,
 I am long silent yet cannot avow
My singing voice is lost for evermore;
 For, lo, this beating heart, this burning brow,
This spirit gasping in keen spasms of dread
And fierce revulsion that it is not dead,
 This agony of the sting:
What soulless clod could have these tears and sobbings,
These terrors that are hopes, these passionate throbbings?
Dear Muse, revive! we yet may dream and love and sing!'

INSOMNIA

Sleepless himself to give to others sleep.
He giveth His beloved sleep.

I HEARD the sounding of the midnight hour;
 The others one by one had left the room,
In calm assurance that the gracious power

INSOMNIA

    Of Sleep's fine alchemy would bless the gloom,
Transmuting all its leaden weight to gold,
To treasures of rich virtues manifold,
    New strength, new health, new life;
Just weary enough to nestle softly, sweetly,
Into divine unconsciousness, completely
Delivered from the world of toil and care and strife.

Just weary enough to feel assured of rest,
    Of Sleep's divine oblivion and repose,
Renewing heart and brain for richer zest
    Of waking life when golden morning glows
As young and pure and glad as if the first
That ever on the void of darkness burst
    With ravishing warmth and light;
On dewy grass and flowers and blithe birds singing
And shining waters, all enraptured springing,
Fragrance and shine and song, out of the womb of night.

But I with infinite weariness outworn,
    Haggard with endless nights unblessed by sleep,
Ravaged by thoughts unutterably forlorn,
    Plunged in despairs unfathomably deep,
Went cold and pale and trembling with affright
Into the desert vastitude of Night,
    Arid and wild and black;
Foreboding no oasis of sweet slumber,
Counting beforehand all the countless number
Of sands that are its minutes on my desolate track.

And so I went, the last, to my drear bed,
    Aghast as one who should go down to lie
Among the blissfully unconscious dead,
    Assured that as the endless years flowed by
Over the dreadful silence and deep gloom
And dense oppression of the stifling tomb,
    He only of them all,
Nerveless and impotent to madness, never
Could hope oblivion's perfect trance for ever:
An agony of life eternal in death's pall.

But that would be for ever, without cure!—
    And yet the agony be not more great;
Supreme fatigue and pain, while they endure,
    Into Eternity their time translate;
Be it of hours and days or countless years,
And boundless æons, it alike appears
    To the crushed victim's soul;

Utter despair foresees no termination,
  But feels itself of infinite duration;
The smallest fragment instant comprehends the whole.

  The absolute of torture as of bliss
    Is timeless, each transcending time and space;
  The one an infinite obscure abyss,
    The other an eternal Heaven of grace.—
  Keeping a little lamp of glimmering light
  Companion through the horror of the night,
      I laid me down aghast
  As *he* of all who pass death's quiet portal
  Malignantly reserved alone immortal,
In consciousness of bale that must for ever last.

  I laid me down, and closed my heavy eyes,
    As if sleep's mockery might win true sleep;
  And grew aware, with awe but not surprise,
    Blindly aware through all the silence deep,
  Of some dark Presence watching by my bed,
  The awful image of a nameless dread;
      But I lay still, fordone;
  And felt its Shadow on me dark and solemn
  And steadfast as a monumental column,
And thought drear thoughts of Doom, and heard the bells chime
    One.

  And then I raised my weary eyes and saw,
    By some slant moonlight on the ceiling thrown
  And faint lamp-gleam, that Image of my awe,
    Still as a pillar of basaltic stone,
  But all enveloped in a sombre shroud
  Except the wan face drooping heavy-browed,
      With sad eyes fixed on mine;
  Sad weary yearning eyes, but fixed remorseless
  Upon my eyes yet wearier, that were forceless
To bear the cruel pressure; cruel, unmalign.

  Wherefore I asked for what I knew too well:
    O ominous midnight Presence, What art Thou?
  Whereto in tones that sounded like a knell:
    'I am the Second Hour, appointed now
  To watch beside thy slumberless unrest.'
  Then I: Thus both, unlike, alike unblest;
      For I should sleep, you fly:
  Are not those wings beneath thy mantle moulded?
  O Hour! unfold those wings so straitly folded,
And urge thy natural flight beneath the moonlit sky.

'My wings shall open when your eyes shall close
  In real slumber from this waking drear;
Your wild unrest is my enforced repose;
  Ere I move hence you must not know me here.'
Could not your wings fan slumber through my brain,   95
Soothing away its weariness and pain?
  'Your Sleep must stir my wings:
Sleep, and I bear you gently on my pinions
Athwart my span of hollow night's dominions,
Whence hour on hour shall bear to morning's golden springs.'   100

That which I ask of you, you ask of me,
  O weary Hour, thus standing sentinel
Against your nature, as I feel and see
  Against my own your form immovable:
Could I bring Sleep to set you on the wing,   105
What other thing so gladly would I bring?
  Truly the Poet saith:
If that is best whose absence we deplore most,
Whose presence in our longings is the foremost,
What blessings equal Sleep save only love and death?   110

I let my lids fall, sick of thought and sense,
  But felt that Shadow heavy on my heart;
And saw the night before me an immense
  Black waste of ridge-walls, hour by hour apart,
Dividing deep ravines: from ridge to ridge   115
Sleep's flying hour was an aërial bridge;
  But I, whose hours stood fast,
Must climb down painfully each steep side hither,
And climb more painfully each steep side thither,
And so make one hour's span for years of travail last.   120

Thus I went down into that first ravine,
  Wearily, slowly, blindly, and alone;
Staggering, stumbling, sinking depths unseen,
  Shaken and bruised and gashed by stub and stone;
And at the bottom paven with slipperiness,   125
A torrent-brook rushed headlong with such stress
  Against my feeble limbs,
Such fury of wave and foam and icy bleakness
Buffeting insupportably my weakness
That when I would recall, dazed memory swirls and swims.   130

How I got through I know not, faint as death;
  And then I had to climb the awful scarp,
Creeping with many a pause for panting breath,
  Clinging to tangled root and rock-jut sharp;

Perspiring with faint chills instead of heat, 135
Trembling, and bleeding hands and knees and feet;
    Falling, to rise anew;
Until, with lamentable toil and travel
Upon the ridge of arid sand and gravel
I lay supine half-dead and heard the bells chime Two; 140

And knew a change of Watchers in the room
    Without a stir or sound beside my bed;
Only the tingling silence of the gloom,
    The muffled pulsing of the night's deep dread;
And felt an Image mightier to appal, 145
And looked; the moonlight on the bed-foot wall
    And corniced ceiling white
Was slanting now; and in the midst stood solemn
And hopeless as a black sepulchral column
A steadfast shrouded Form, the Third Hour of the night. 150

The fixed regard implacably austere,
    Yet none the less ineffably forlorn.
Something transcending all my former fear
    Came jarring through my shattered frame outworn:
I knew that crushing rock could not be stirred; 155
I had no heart to say a single word,
    But closed my eyes again;
And set me shuddering to the task stupendous
Of climbing down and up that gulf tremendous
Unto the next hour-ridge beyond hope's farthest ken. 160

Men sigh and plain and wail how life is brief:
    Ah yes, our bright eternities of bliss
Are transient, rare, minute beyond belief,
    Mere star-dust meteors in Time's Night-abyss;
Ah no, our black eternities intense 165
Of bale are lasting, dominant, immense,
    As Time which is their breath;
The memory of the bliss is yearning sorrow,
The memory of the bale clouds every morrow
Darkening through nights and days into the night of Death. 170

No human words could paint my travail sore
    In the thick darkness of the next ravine,
Deeper immeasurably than that before;
    When hideous agonies, unheard, unseen,
In overwhelming floods of torture roll, 175
And horrors of great darkness drown the soul,
    To be is not to be
In memory save as ghastliest impression,

And chaos of demoniacal possession. . . .
I shuddered on the ridge, and heard the bells chime Three.   180

And like a pillar of essential gloom,
   Most terrible in stature and regard,
Black in the moonlight filling all the room
   The Image of the Fourth Hour evil-starred
Stood over me; but there was Something more,   185
Something behind It undiscerned before,
   More dreadful than Its dread,
Which overshadowed It as with a fateful
Inexorable fascination hateful,—
A wan and formless Shade from regions of the dead.   190

I shut my eyes against that spectral Shade,
   Which yet allured them with a deadly charm,
And that black Image of the Hour, dismayed
   By such tremendous menacing of harm;
And so into the gulf as into Hell;   195
Where what immeasurable depths I fell,
   With seizures of the heart
Whose each clutch seemed the end of all pulsation,
And tremors of exanimate prostration,
Are horrors in my soul that never can depart.   200

If I for hope or wish had any force,
   It was that I might rush down sharply hurled
From rock to rock until a mangled corse
   Down with the fury of the torrent whirled,
The fury of black waters and white foam,   205
To where the homeless find their only home,
   In the immense void Sea,
Whose isles are worlds, surrounding, unsurrounded,
Whose depths no mortal plummet ever sounded,
Beneath all surface storms calm in Eternity.   210

Such hope or wish was as a feeble spark,
   A little lamp's pale glimmer in a tomb,
To just reveal the hopeless deadly dark
   And wordless horrors of my soul's fixed doom:
Yet some mysterious instinct obstinate,   215
Blindly unconscious as a law of Fate,
   Still urged me on and bore
My shattered being through the unfeared peril
Of death less hateful than the life as sterile:
I shuddered on the ridge, and heard the bells chime Four.   220

   The Image of that Fifth Hour of the night
     Was blacker in the moonlight now aslant

Upon its left than on its shrouded right;
  And over and behind It, dominant,
The shadow not Its shadow cast its spell,
Most vague and dim and wan and terrible,
  Death's ghastly aureole,
Pregnant with overpowering fascination,
Commanding by repulsive instigation,
Despair's envenomed anodyne to tempt the Soul.

I closed my eyes, but could not longer keep
  Under that Image and most awful Shade,
Supine in mockery of blissful sleep,
  Delirious with such fierce thirst unallayed;
Of all worst agonies the most unblest
Is passive agony of wild unrest:
  Trembling and faint I rose,
And dressed with painful efforts, and descended
With furtive footsteps and with breath suspended,
And left the slumbering house with my unslumbering woes.

Constrained to move through the unmoving hours,
  Accurst from rest because the hours stood still;
Feeling the hands of the Infernal Powers
  Heavy upon me for enormous ill,
Inscrutable intolerable pain,
Against which mortal pleas and prayers are vain,
  Gaspings of dying breath,
And human struggles, dying spasms yet vainer:
Renounce defence when Doom is the Arraigner;
Let impotence of Life subside appeased in Death.

I paced the silent and deserted streets
  In cold dark shade and chillier moonlight grey;
Pondering a dolorous series of defeats
  And black disasters from life's opening day,
Invested with the shadow of a doom
That filled the Spring and Summer with a gloom
  Most wintry bleak and drear;
Gloom from within as from a sulphurous censer
Making the glooms without for ever denser,
To blight the buds and flowers and fruitage of my year.

Against a bridge's stony parapet
  I leaned, and gazed into the waters black;
And marked an angry morning red and wet
  Beneath a livid and enormous rack
Glare out confronting the belated moon,
Huddled and wan and feeble as the swoon
  Of featureless despair:

When some stray workmen half-asleep but lusty
Passed urgent through the rainpour wild and gusty,
I felt a ghost already, planted watching there.   270

  As phantom to its grave, or to its den
    Some wild beast of the night when night is sped,
  I turned unto my homeless home again
    To front a day only less charged with dread
Than that dread night; and after day, to front   275
Another night of—what would be the brunt?
    I put the thought aside,
To be resumed when common life unfolded
In common daylight had my brain remoulded;
Meanwhile the flaws of rain refreshed and fortified.   280

  The day passed, and the night; and other days,
    And other nights; and all of evil doom;
  The sun-hours in a sick bewildering haze,
    The star-hours in a thick enormous gloom
With rending lightnings and with thunder-knells;   285
The ghastly hours of all the timeless Hells:—
    Bury them with their bane!
I look back on the words already written,
And writhe by cold rage stung, by self-scorn smitten,
They are so weak and vain and infinitely inane. . . .   290

  'How from those hideous Malebolges deep
    I ever could win back to upper earth,
  Restored to human nights of blessed sleep
    And healthy waking with the new day's birth?'—
How do men climb back from a swoon whose stress,   295
Crushing far deeper than all consciousness,
    Is deep as deep death seems?
Who can the steps and stages mete and number
By which we re-emerge from nightly slumber?—
Our poor vast petty life is one dark maze of dreams.   300

DESPOTISM TEMPERED BY DYNAMITE

  There is no other title in the world
So proud as mine, who am no law-cramped king,
No mere imperial monarch absolute,
The White Tsar worshipped as a visible God,
As Lord of Heaven no less than Lord of Earth—   5
  I look with terror to my crowning day.

  Through half of Europe my dominions spread,
And then through half of Asia to the shores

Of Earth's great ocean washing the New World;
And nothing bounds them to the Northern Pole,
They merge into the everlasting ice—
    I look with terror to my crowning day.

Full eighty million subjects worship me—
Their father, high priest, monarch, God on earth;
My children who but hold their lives with mine
For our most Holy Russia dear and great,
Whose might is concentrated in my hands—
    I look with terror to my crowning day.

I chain and gag with chains and gags of iron
The impious hands and mouths that dare express
A word against my sacred sovranty;
The half of Asia is my prison-house,
Myriads of convicts lost in its Immense—
    I look with terror to my crowning day.

I cannot chain and gag the evil thoughts
Of men and women poisoned by the West,
Frenzied in soul by the anarchic West;
These thoughts transmute themselves to dynamite;
My sire was borne all shattered to his tomb—
    I look with terror to my crowning day.

My peasants rise to their unvarying toil,
And go to sleep outwearied by their toil,
Without the hope of any better life.
But with no hope they have no deadly fear,
They sleep and eat their scanty food in peace—
    I look with terror to my crowning day.

My palaces are prisons to myself;
I taste no food that may not poison me;
I plant no footstep sure it will not stir
Instant destruction of explosive fire;
I look with terror to each day and night—
    With tenfold terror to my crowning day.

LETTERS

A NOTE TO THE LETTERS

THIS selection of Thomson's letters has been included because they show a side of his nature which did not find expression in his poetry. All were used by Salt in his *Life* (now out of print), and the ones which are addressed to Thomson's sister-in-law and to Agnes Gray are only extant there, so far as I know. I have taken the texts of the others from sources nearer to the originals: those to the Bradlaughs were given by Hypatia in her *Childish Reminiscences of James Thomson* (*Our Corner*, August and September 1886), and there is a copy (not holograph) of the letter to Rossetti in the Bodleian collection, Don d.109/1.

1. Extract from a letter to Agnes Gray.

> Richmond Barracks, Dublin,
> 14 May 1859.

..... I take the liberty of sending you by this post two volumes of verse which fell into my hands some time back. The author, Robert Browning, is about the strongest and manliest of our living poets. His wife (*née* Elizabeth Barrett Barrett, to adopt the style of wedding-cards) is beyond all comparison the greatest of English poetesses—*those whose works are published*, I mean.[1] I happen to have her last book, and will send it to you some day. You will probably not care for these poems at first; but they are worth your study, and you may find, as I did, that they improve much with longer acquaintance. If I might school you a bit, I should order you always to look up in a dictionary what words you don't understand, and always to puzzle over difficult passages until they become either perfectly clear or thoroughly hopeless. No lazy reading will ever master a masterly writer. Should you care enough for Browning to wish thoroughly to comprehend him, I shall of course be happy to render you what little assistance may be in my power towards the clearing up of obscurities. The final poem, you will perceive, is addressed to his wife. To the best of my remembrance he used not to write so large a proportion of love-poetry aforetime; his marriage must do its best to excuse the poor fellow for his present extravagance in that article. My notion was that your poets, though always fluttering about Love like moths about a rushlight, generally took good care not to singe seriously their precious selves. This unfortunate Mr. Browning, however, seems to have flung himself headlong into the flame, determined to get burnt up—wings and all.

2. To Mrs. Bradlaugh.

> 240 Vauxhall Bridge Road, Pimlico, S.W.,
> 16 November 1869.

DEAR MRS. BRADLAUGH,—As Grant[2] tells me you want a copy of last month's *Fraser*, I have great pleasure in forwarding you one. You will find the article, 'Suggestions on Academical Organisation', very interesting, as also Bonamy Price's Reply to the Article on Currency, July, 1869—I would also commend as worthy the most careful study the paper on Professor Tyndall's Theory of Comets.

---

[1] Agnes herself wrote poetry.
[2] John Grant, the army schoolmaster, whose son Kenneth is mentioned in 10 as travelling to Midhurst to stay with the Bradlaughs.

I was surprised to find in the Magazine a lot of verses[1] which I remember being offered to Mr. B. three or four years ago for the *N. R.*, and which he wisely refused. The Editor of *Fraser* must have been very soft when he accepted them. He was having his holiday in Ireland at the time, and perhaps had taken too much punch when he happened to read them.

Having at last had my noble portrait[2] taken, I enclose the least bad copy I can pick out. With love to all, yours faithfully,

JAMES THOMSON.

P.S.—The portrait would have doubtless had a much more benevolent expression but for the fact that I had to wait a full hour while a lady was having her beautiful baby taken. Baby had four expositions (I think they call them), Mamma making wonderful efforts to secure its steadfastness, and the photographic artist making the most comical whistlings and chirpings with the notion that these would conduce to the same great end. I am happy to believe that baby winked or started or spoiled the business somehow through all four expositions. The artist at length, ashamed to keep me waiting any longer, told Mamma that the gentleman below must be done before they had another try at triumphant baby. You will doubtless discover all the amiability of that hour in my expression.

3. To Hypatia Bradlaugh.

240 Vauxhall Bridge Road, London, S.W.

5 July 1871.

My dear Hypatia,

This is exactly how the case stood, to the best of my recollection.

Yourself, Alice, and I, with two or three more who were very vague people and apt to change into other persons, had been roaming about for a long day in a country place something like Jersey. We had dinner at an inn, and were very jolly. Roaming farther, I found myself upon the top of a sandy sort of a cliff looking down upon a sandy beach, and you girls just pulling to land in a boat. You were nearly touching land among a group of boatmen when your boat settled quietly down by the stern, and I saw your heads go quietly under water. I cried out, 'The girls are in the water!'; but saw the boatman pulling you out. I wanted to get to you, but couldn't attempt to run down the cliff. Presently, however, a tall guardsman stepped lightly down on business of his own, and his example gave me courage. I found it as easy to run down a concave slope as a fly finds it to walk on the ceiling.

---

[1] i.e. *Sunday up the River*.   [2] See Frontispiece.

When I reached the shore, you and Alice and another girl were all nestled rosy and cosy in a kind of caboose or bathing machine, muffled or sunk up to your necks in a heap of boatman's guernseys or some such garments. You said that you were none the worse for your ducking save a few bruises. I said that you must have something to restore you. You all agreed to this; and one proposed dinner with ale (although we had just had a dinner before), another tea. It was resolved that you should have a meat tea, and I went off to be your waiter. I went up by an easy path to the inn, and entered a room. I found a pale tall old-fashioned semi-genteel lady there, dressed and with her bonnet on, and I said: 'Can you serve—'. She cut me short in a very mild and cutting manner, saying: 'If you want to be served, the servant is in the next room. *I* am a teetotaller, Sir, and don't serve.' Here she opened the door, and said to the girl in the next room: 'Serve this gentleman, and give him a copy of the *Independent*' (which I understood to be a teetotal publication). 'Well,' said I, 'ma'am, it seems funny to me that you should boast of your teetotalism and yet keep a public-house'; for I was rather nettled by her ways. The girl nudged my elbow from behind as a hint to go on with my scolding; the mistress spit fire at the girl for liking to see her insulted. I then told Mary that I only wanted to be served with tea, a good meat tea for three or four, when I heard a knock at the door and a voice crying out cruelly: 'It is quite eight o'clock, Sir; eight o'clock. Are you sure you are awake?' So I had to leave you there in the caboose or bathing-machine, buried in guernseys waiting for your dinner-tea; and had to be awake and get up myself. Was it not a sad case? I hope you won't starve. I hope all the people at home won't suffer too much from anxiety.

This remarkable adventure of ours this morning put me in mind that I have not written to you for an age. So I resolved to write this very day.

How are you enjoying this delightful summer? Are your chilblains very bad? Do you often slide on the pond? Or is the country all one pond, and do you go to school by boat? I had to get up this morning and throw coats on my bed, being awakened by the cold. It is raining this moment as hard as it can, and has been raining for I don't know how many days. June chilled us to the bone, July is drowning us.

When Mr. Grant last wrote me, he had been foolish enough to get up early to work in his garden, and had just managed to lose his purse with more than £2 in it. That was a nice fat worm for some other early bird. Moral: Never get up early if you can help it, and never have two pounds in your purse.

As I am sure to be interrupted again in a few minutes (for I am really writing this at the office, in spite of the humbugging heading), I may as well finish it up while I can.

I hope you will let me hear from you soon, if only to tell me whether you suffered much from your dip, what sort of a tea you were served with, and how you got out of the caboose and home. Love to all and best wishes.

Yours affectionately,

JAMES THOMSON.

4. To Mrs. Bradlaugh.
240 Vauxhall Bridge Road, London, S.W.,

28 October 1871.

DEAR MRS. BRADLAUGH, This morning I sent by book-post Thalberg's arrangement of 'Home, sweet Home,' as desired by Alice. The price is only one-half what appears marked. I had my sister-in-law[1] in town for three or four days the week before last. She is a quaint little creature, whom I feel inclined to like. Unfortunately I couldn't have any quiet chat with her, as she had come to meet her mother and friends, who had been having a month in the Isle of Wight, and the said friends consisted of one widow, two old maids, and one young maid. Fancy me going to Drury Lane with five of them under my charge! I did it with the utmost coolness and self-possession, I can assure you. Sister-in-law is not very strong, and I think brother is not very strong either.

I spent an evening at Turner Street[2] last week with Hypatia. Mr. B. came in before I left, looking better, I think, than I had ever seen him since I came to London. He appeared as though he could have supped off a creature the size of me, and not have been troubled with indigestion if he had eaten it all.

I saw Austin [Holyoake] last evening. His wife has a regular engagement now at Sadler's Wells, and has been very well spoken of in the London daily papers under the name of Miss Alice Austin. Curiously enough, the manager's wife acts in her maiden name, and this is Emma Austin. I thought this was Mrs. Bayston at first. Yesterday I got a letter from Grant. He says that he has written twice to you without an answer. A pretty creature you are to grumble about people not writing to you, when you never reply if they do. And you have no writing at all to do except in the way of letters, while some persons I know have to write morning, noon, and night, till pen and ink make them feel sea-sick.

Hoping you are all well, with love and best wishes,—Yours truly,

JAMES THOMSON.

[1] Mrs. John Thomson:—see Letters 5, 12 and 14.
[2] Charles Bradlaugh's home, where the girls went on visits to their father. See footnote 2, p. xix.

5. From a letter to Mrs. John Thomson dated 1 January 1872.

... You think I have left Mr. B., and wonder what I am about, and I often wonder myself. Mr. B. gave up city business altogether more than eighteen months ago, in order to devote himself solely to the great business of illuminating the benighted intellect of this nation on social, political, and religious matters. For some time after he left I did nothing, an occupation which would suit me exceedingly well, and for which I have fine natural talents that I have taken care to cultivate to the best of my abilities. That is, would suit me extremely well on a fortune, or in a semi-tropical climate, but here, without money, it is a luxury too ethereal for my taste. Afterwards, I did some work in a printing office, reading proofs, revising, etc.; and as to this I will only say that if ever you have the misfortune to be condemned to penal servitude, and they offer to commute the sentence for such work in a printing office, you had far better stick to the penal servitude. I then became secretary *pro tem.* to one of the thousand companies which came into being last year, and in some very hard commercial campaigning have already had two companies killed under me. I am at present astride a third, which may carry me out safely or may not; it has received three or four shot and sabre wounds already, but seems tough and tenacious of life. By the bye, our slain companies brought no one down but the riders; our friendly foes the shareholding public having received all their money back. As I was nearly thirty when I came to London, I could not go through the regular course in any business, and have had to seize whatever honest chance offered. Perhaps some fine day I shall turn up a trump and win a good stake; it is much more probable that I shan't. In the meantime, having no one to look to but myself, I quietly take things as they come, and quietly let things go as they go, fortifying myself with that saying of the philosopher that it matters not in this vale of tears whether we wipe our eyes with a silk or cotton handkerchief, or blink through tortoiseshell or gold-rimmed eyeglasses. Perhaps the said philosopher had himself the silk handkerchief and gold-rimmed glasses, or perhaps he did not use a handkerchief nor wear eyeglasses, and was thus enabled to be so philosophical on the subject. Not that I need to wipe my eyes in this vale of tears, for I always find the prospect either much too sad or much too comical for weeping.

6. To W. M. Rossetti.

Central City, Colorado, U.S.A.,
5 August 1872.

DEAR SIR, Your letter of the 28th April reached me here about a fortnight since, having been forwarded by a friend. I cannot say anything about the Shelley notes[1] now, as the only books I could find room for in my portmanteau were the Globe Shakespeare and Pickering's diamond Dante (with Cary's version squeezed in for the notes and general assistance). But I hope on my return to resume the attentive reading of your Shelley, and to send you any remarks upon it which may occur to me and seem worth sending. Your liberal reception of the few already sent would encourage me to proceed, even were I not impelled by so strong an interest in the subject.

Mr. Bradlaugh promised to forward you a copy of the *National Reformer* containing a piece of verse called 'In the Room' which I left behind me. I learn that it appeared in the issue for May 19th but don't know whether you received a copy or not.

From the close of your letter I gather that you somewhat misapprehended what I said about my business trip. When I wrote to the effect that I was going in search of the heathen Chinee in the Rocky Mountains, I did not mean to convey that I was about to start for China. I believed that John Chinaman had already swarmed thus far east from California, and was alluding to the popular poem by Bret Harte, a writer who seems to me capable of doing really excellent work, and some of whose poems and sketches I am very fond of. As to the Chinese they have not got here yet, with the exception of four or five who are male laundresses (the proper masculine for this feminine noun I am quite ignorant of), and whom I never see.

I have been out here since the 15th May, having left London on the 27th April, but have seen very little of the country as yet, business confining me to this place. I am hoping to have some trips around shortly. Every village out here is termed a City: this Central with Blackhawk and Nevada, the three virtually forming one straggling town, numbers between four and five thousand people. Of these the great majority are miners, perhaps one thousand being Cornishmen, who earn from $3 to $4 a day wages, and much more when they take leases, or work by contract. The stores are well stocked, but nearly everything is very dear. The working miner can get most of the mere necessaries of life almost as cheap as at home; the comforts and little luxuries are so priced that I find living here twice or three times as expensive. A small glass of English beer costs twenty-five cents, or say a shilling currency. To get your boots blacked (I always clean my own) you pay 25 cents; but then they get a 'Dolly Varden shine', and are wrought upon by a 'Boot Artist'. A 'tonsorialist' very naturally charges 75 cents or three shillings for cutting your hair; etc., etc., etc. We have churches, chapels, schools, and a new large hotel in which a very polite dancing party assembled the other evening. This week we

---

[1] Textual notes made by Thomson on Rossetti's edition of the *Complete Poetical Works*, which had appeared in 1870.

are to have a concert, and also a lecture on the Darwinian Theory, admission one dollar. We have a theatre, in which we now and then have actors. The old rough days with their perils and excitement are quite over; the 'City' is civilized enough to be dull and commonplace while not yet civilized enough to be sociable and pleasant. There are no beggars, and petty larceny is almost unknown; storekeepers extort your money blandly and quietly, and the large larceny of selling mines at preposterous prices makes the people despise all larceny that is petty. You might as well carry a revolver between Euston Square and Somerset House as here. I brought one under persuasion, and have never taken it out of the bag.

This Central City is the headquarters of gold-mining in Colorado Territory, but it has been very dull for some time past, the working of most of the large mines having been suspended, in some cases through want of capital, in others through litigation (mines are wonderful breeders of lawsuits), and in others because the ores are not rich enough to pay the enormous charges for haulage and reduction and smelting out here, though they would be of immense value in an old country. However a railroad connecting with the whole east is now within ten miles of us, and is being pushed on rapidly, so things are likely to improve ere long.

The houses, chiefly of wood, and some of them pretty enough in themselves though spoiled by their surroundings, are huddled and scattered along the bottom and slopes of a winding ravine, intermingled with prospectholes, primitive loghuts, mill-sheds, of which many are idle, fragments of machinery that proved useless from the first, heaps of stones and poor ores, and all sorts of rubbish. No one has ever cleared up anything here; the streets and roads are usually many inches deep in dust, which the rare heavy rains and the more frequent turning on of some foul sluice make mud which is verily abominable unto one who cleaneth his own boots. Men dig a shaft shallow or deep, and leave it gaping for anyone to tumble into. Trees are cut down and the stumps all left to make night-wandering safe and agreeable. The hills surrounding us have been flayed of their grass, and scalped of their timber; and they are scarred and gashed and ulcerated all over from past mining operations; so ferociously does little man scratch at the breasts of his great calm mother when he thinks that jewels are there hidden. The streams running down the ravines, or as they say here, the creeks running down the gulches, are thick with pollution from the washing of dirt and ores. We are 8,300 feet above the level of the sea, and 3,000 feet above Denver, which lies about forty miles eastward. The highest peaks of the Rocky Mountains hereabout are over 14,000 feet; we are among the foothills. To get out of the City in any direction one most climb for a considerable distance. These foothills are distributed remarkably amongst the snowy ranges of the mountains, curtain beyond curtain, fold within fold, twisting and heaving inextricably. Those immediately around the City are of flat tame curves, as if crouching to their abject mercenary doom; but beyond there are keen crests and daring serrated contours, green with firs and cottonwood-aspens or nobly dark with pines; and one massy range ends in a promontory whose scarped precipitous upper flank gleams grand and savage in its stony nakedness, like the gleaming of set white teeth in some swart Titanic barbarian. Some of the loftier hillsides are as smooth meadows; but their grass at this season can scarcely be distinguished through the multitudinous flames and broad blaze of countless species of wild flowers, nearly all of the most positive intense colours—scarlet, crimson, purple, azure, yellow, white. Few of them remind me of English flowers, and the people here (if I may judge by the few I have asked) don't seem to know their names. From these higher hills one gets magnificent views—vast billowy land seas, with dense woods and deep ravines and exquisite emerald dells, whereon and whereover sleep and sweep immense shadows, and of all shades even at noonday from bright green to solid black; beyond, a crescent of the mountains, some with broad fields or deep furrows of snow, some sheathed wholly with this white splendour; eastward toward the plains, what the keenest eye cannot distinguish from a distant sealine, faint or dark blue level to the horizon, with pale streaks like the shadows of clouds and long shoals and the haze of evaporation. The sky is wonderfully pure, azure or deep burning blue; the clouds are large and white; however hot the sun there are cool fresh breezes on these hills. There are few birds, and they scarcely sing. Butterflies abound, some of them almost as brilliant as the flowers. Crickets keep up a continual song like the whistling of the wind through reeds; and one species take long jumps and short rapid flights, making such a rattle with some bodily machinery that one can scarcely believe it comes from so small a creature.

The nights are always cool, and mosquitoes there are none. Snakes or any other vermin I have not heard of. One would have to go some distance now to find any wild animals such as bears and cougars.

I don't think that I have been out a single night, however cool and clear with moon and stars, without seeing frequent lightnings play up from behind the surrounding hills. Almost every day we have a slight shower. On the day of my arrival we had a hailstorm with thunder as we drove up the cañon, the largest stones being quite as big as goodsized walnuts. Our horses were so nervous that we had to unhitch and hold them. A few days after they had snow, thunder and lightning all together among the same hills. Occasional waterspouts sweep away bridges and destroy roads for miles. I have seen from here a terrible storm raging over the plains, dead-silent through remoteness: white lightnings momentarily surging up, veiling the stars, making the lower clouds ghostly, striking pale reflections from clouds at the zenith; and these broad sheets of white light were seamed and riven by intense darting lines of forked lightning, zigzag, vertical, transverse, oblique.

We have no dew here at night; one can lie out in a blanket between earth and sky with perfect safety and comfort.

Six miles from us is Idaho, the pleasantest place I have yet seen in the mountains. Going to it you ascend about a thousand feet in three miles to the divide (and climbing on foot tests your wind in this thin pure air) and then descend about 1,800 feet in three miles, winding down Virginia Cañon, whose hill-walls range from six to twelve hundred feet in height, and are still well-wooded with firs and pines. The roadway is good, wild flowers abound, and a clear rill runs down with you all the way.

Idaho, which its boldly prophetic inhabitants call the Saratoga of the West, and which is just now full of visitors, lies comfortably at large on the level floor of a broad and long valley. The houses are of wood, shingle-roofed, most of them neat, many of them pretty. The hills around rise to the height of a thousand feet, and as little mining has been attempted on them, they are delightfully green, and their timber has not been felled. Between them southwards you see the scalped heads of two mountains (until lately covered with snow) reckoned about 11,000 feet high, with a lower rounded height between; these are the Old Chief, the Squaw and the Pappoose. Westwards also you glimpse snowy mountains. A stream, rapid and broad in summer after the rains and melting of the snows, runs from west to east through the midst of the village the whole length of the valley. Excellent trout have been caught in it. Two creeks join it from the south in this valley. There is a hot water spring impregnated with soda and sulphur, which feeds private and swimming baths. There is a cold spring chemically allied to it, which people drink with faith or hope, and which to me tastes like seltzer-water bewitched. There are beautiful walks and rides in all directions. I reckon that this village of Idaho or Idaho Springs will indeed ere long be one of the fashionable holiday resorts of America. Gray's Peak, over 14,000 feet, is within twenty-four miles of it. A good horse-trail goes right up to the scalped crest of Old Chief, a distance of about eight miles.

I have chatted with the man who first struck Virginia Cañon and found the Idaho Creek (South Clear Creek) through the dense woods which filled the valley, and caught fine trout for himself and fellow-prospectors. This was in '59. Men used to make marvellous sums by mining and gold-washing then, and pay marvellous prices for the necessaries of life. For some years existence was pretty rough, though never perhaps half so wild as in California during the early days of its gold-fever.

I was told in Idaho (by a Justice of the Peace too) of a couple of men who were on terms of shoot at sight, of whom one tried to avoid and the other sought a meeting. At length the latter attained his desire, and in the 'difficulty' which ensued was shot by the other, who was tried but got off clear as the evidence was not considered perfect. The dead man had $64 odd in his pockets, so it was resolved to give him a decent burial. They stopped the funeral procession at a store, drank to his salvation out of his own money, and also took a bottle of whisky with them to the burial place, that they might be not altogether without comfort when they had finally deposited him in the earth. Both deserved shooting, said the Justice of the Peace philosophically; and himself was one of the funeral party.

In a tobacconist's here among specimens of ore is an object labelled 'Burr from the pine tree on which Pennsyltuck was hanged.' Pennsyltuck was so called because Pennsylvania and Kentucky somehow shared the honour of raising him. He was a bad lot, so bad that the citizens at length determined to promptly relieve him and themselves of his noxious existence. Accordingly, without any tedious legal preliminaries, they took him forth and hanged him on a pine tree and there left him. As the night was very cold, someone suggested that it was doubtful whether Pennsyltuck met his death by strangulation or freezing. As the citizens on cool reflection thought it wise to discourage Lynch law, they generally agreed to consider that he had been frozen to death.

As to the drinking, one anecdote (true or not) will suffice. An officer sent out to cater for some division of the army in the West returned with six waggon-loads of whisky and one of provisions. The commanding officer, having overhauled the stock, cried out 'What the hell shall we do with all these provisions?'

I did not intend to inflict all this nonsense upon you, but having begun to write, it seemed queer to send a mere note five or six thousand miles and not say something about this country; so, having leisure, I let my pen run away with me. Fortunately you are not in any way called upon to read what I was not called upon to write.

I may be here for two or three months yet for all I know. I am, dear Sir, yours truly,

JAMES THOMSON.

7. Extract from a letter to an unknown recipient, printed in the *Secular Review* of 15 July 1882.

I think we must forgive the Americans a good deal of vulgarity and arrogance for some generations yet. They are intoxicated with their vast country and its vaster prospects. Besides, we of the old country have sent them for years past, and are still sending them, our half-starved and ignorant millions. The Americans of the War of Independence were really a British race, and related to the old country as a Greek colony to its mother city or state. But the Americans of to-day are only a nation in that they instinctively adore their Union. All the heterogeneous ingredients are seething in the cauldron with plenty of scum and air-bubbles atop. In a century or two they may get stewed down into homogeneity—a really wholesome and dainty dish, not to be set before a king though, I fancy. I resisted the impression of the mere material vastitude as long as possible, but found its influence growing on me week by week; for it implies such vast possibilities of moral and intellectual expansion. They are starting over there with all our experience and culture at their command, without any of the obsolete burdens and impediments which in the course of a thousand years have become inseparable from our institutions, and with a country which will want more labour and more people for many generations to come.

I am quite well again. Though never, perhaps, very strong, and rarely so well as to feel mere existence a delight (as to a really healthy person it must be; no inferior condition, in my opinion, deserves the name of health), I am seldom what we call unwell. When travelling about I always find myself immensely better than when confined to one place. With money, I believe I should never have a home, but be always going to and fro on the earth, and walking up and down in it, like him of whom I am one of the children.

8. To Hypatia and Alice Bradlaugh.[1]

230 Vauxhall Bridge Road,
21 Février 1874.

Mes chères petites filles,

Je vous dois mille remerciments pour vos bonnes lettres, et je vous aurais écrit plus tôt si je n'aurais pas été très affairé depuis l'Election. Je vous remercie pour les fleurs cueillies par Mlle. Fatima et envoyées par Mlle. Lina; la senteur des violettes était charmante. Mais pourquoi donc Lina, n'écrit elle pas en Français? Elle le peut faire assez bien, pourtant. Peut-être parcequ'elle ne se portait pas bien ce jour-là. J'espère que cette méchante migraine ne la tourmente pas encore.

M. Austin [Holyoake] reste chez lui, et je suis occupé tous les jours en lui aidant comme je le puis, à faire ses comptes, etc. Il

---

[1] After the girls had been to school in Paris, Thomson suggested that they should correspond in French. As Alice (the elder) was plump and Hypatia lean, he had nicknamed them Fatima and Lina.

est très faible; mais je ne crois pas que sa santé est pis, quoique elle n'est guère mieux, à cause de son séjour en ville. L'autre jour un médecin éminent est venu le voir et l'a très soigneusement examiné. Vous apprendrez avec regrette qu'il ne donna pas d'espoir de guérison. On ne peut pas faire pour lui, a-t-il dit, que de procurer qu'il meure le plus lentement et avec le moins de souffrance possible. C'est un mot triste pour sa famille et ses amis.

Dimanche dernier j'ai diné chez M. J.[1] Le soir on a fait de la musique et nous avons dansé gaîment, Madame et moi; elle portait les pantoufles de Monsieur, parceque ses bottines la gênaient. Elle n'est point begueule, cette bonne dame là.

Je crains beaucoup que vous ne sortez pas pour fumer tous les soirs, comme vous avez fait jadis, quand j'étais aussi heureux d'être chez vous. Moi, je garde toujours mon brûle-gueule, et je fume avec une régularité religieuse; mais c'est tout autre chose, et infiniment moins gai, que de fumer seul chez soi au lieu de fumer en se promenant avec deux jeunes filles, bonnes, jolies, spirituelles et charmantes.

Comme vous rirez de mon pauvre baragouinage français! détestable, misérable, atroce, honteux, etc.! (Voilà que je fais comme Fatima quand elle écrivait des exercises, en y mettant tous les adjectifs possibles.) Moi, je m'en ris, et sans gêne, moi-même. Ecrivez-moi bientôt, je vous prie.

9. To Hypatia Bradlaugh.

60 Tachbrook Street, S.W.

[May 1874]

Ma chère Lina,

Pourquoi, donc, n'écrivez-vous pas en Français? Que vous êtes oisive! Savez-vous que vous êtes aussi très-impertinente de vous moquer du nom de la rue dans laquelle je demeure? *Brook* est toujours un très joli mot avec nous autres Anglais; et quant à *Tach*, quand quelqu'un jeune et beau vous dira tout bas à l'oreille, 'Tâche de me voir toute seule ce soir dans le petit sentier, ô ma bien aimée!' (soit dans les environs de West Cowes ou de quelqu' autre ville) je parie que vous ne trouverez pas le mot *Tâche* ni baroque ni déplaisant.

Il a fait assez froid ce mois [May] de vous glacer après les jours caniculaires desquels vous vous plaigniez en Avril. Probablement il ne faut point beaucoup de chaleur de rendre toute languissante une petite fillette si paresseuse qu'elle s'abandonne sans effort à oublier notre belle langue française!

Moi, je suis pour le present à cheval sur un *si*, c'est à dire sur une compagnie anonyme; mais je crains beaucoup qu'elle ne sera tuée sous moi, comme toutes les autres, et cela très prochainement.

---

[1] Probably W. E. Jaques, an old friend.

10. To Alice and Hypatia Bradlaugh.¹

My dear Fatima, My dear Lina;
My dear Lina, My dear Fatima;

I don't know which to address. One *did* write me a nice long letter in French; but then she followed it with two telegrams in mere English.—Ah, but the other hasn't written in French at all. That truly is shameful. But do you know, Sir, that you are writing in English yourself? So I am!!! The fact is that the day is too hot for French; I find that the genders are melted into one, and the accents have all evanesced. Now, altho' I may freely 'confound' the genders colloquially, I am not going to do so in writing; therefore, avaunt French!

I am heart-broken that I did not see you before you left. I did mean coming on the Sunday, but it was hot then, too, and so I got lazy.

To console you for not seeing me I send you two gentlemen. A Serious Man and an Attic Philosopher (I mean the *cove under the tiles*).² I don't know which either or both of you prefer, so I send both addressed to both. (I tossed up several times to settle the question, but got tired of the ties.) The Serious Man will remind you of that desperate boarding school life you led in Paris: which of you gained the Vicomte Moréal? Did Hypatia object to him because he was a poet? or did she ignore his verses on the ground that they were quite innocent of poetry?

Speaking of verses, I must thank Fatima for forwarding the letter of 'M. E. Lewes'. She didn't tell me whether it was in one enclosed to Papa or simply addressed to the care of that wicked individual. You know of course that 'M. E. Lewes' means George Eliot, who means Adam Bede (or A damn Beed as Hypatia profanely calls it—I'm sure I don't know why) etc. etc.

Do you know I was half a mind to see the end of the prizefight between Iconoclast, C.B.³, (it's liberal of the Queen to give him this title) and Brewin' (Mischief) Grant? Luckily I didn't and so was at home to see Mr. Grant (not Brewin or Bruin) but the stern parient of Kenneth (the Kenneth who with precocious wisdom terms all girls 'duffers'—he means 'dufferinissimas'). He told me how one of you knocked off Kennie's hat in the train, *i.e.*, out of the train—and showed no compunction for it. He also told me how the said Ken, still in the dignity of a new hat, sank nobly into his illustrated paper opposite an old gentleman who momentarily expected the experienced Ken to ask him whether he objected to a smoke. These and other things have I heard.

---

¹ Hypatia dates this letter as June 1874.
² *L'Homme Sérieux* by Charles de Bernard (pseud.), 1805-50, and *Le Philosophe sous les Toits* by Emil Souvestre, 1806-54.
³ Iconoclast was Charles Bradlaugh's pseudonym.

I don't think I shall take the trouble to read a note in English from either of you any more. So write in French, my good little children. Does Dora still remember your second grandfather.

Yours, (3 p.m.) deliquescent.

JAMES THOMSON.

P.S.—I hope really you will like the two books I send, else I would not send them. I enjoyed them much myself a few centuries ago, in the days when I was young.

I find that the writing is very bad; but then I have bad ink and a bad pen. I could get better ink and pen with exertion, but exertion is strictly forbidden in the 'Castle of Indolence' of James Thomson on the afternoon of 5th June, 1874—Oaks Day.

11. To Alice and Hypatia Bradlaugh.

60 Tachbrook Street, S.W.

2 July 1874.

Ma chère Fatima, Ma chère Lina,

Je vous remercie beaucoup, chacune pour sa bonne lettre. Je n'ai pas écrit plus tôt, seulement parceque, comme vous-même quand vous étiez dernièrement ici à Londres, j'ai été très-occupé.

Les traits de Kenneth, le petit badaud, ont donné beaucoup de plaisir à M. et Mme. Grant. Pauvre garçon! Quand il sera de retour, il va sans dire que ses compagnons d'école, sans doute tous badauds aussi, le trouveraient tout à fait rustique.

J'ai regretté beaucoup d'entendre que Lina ne se porta pas bien. J'espère qu'elle va mieux maintenant.

Hier soir j'ai recontré Papa, au bureau de la rédaction du grand journal le *National Reformer*. Il écrit encore cette semaine dans le dit journal, qu'il n'est pas assez riche de retenir un sécretaire à lui; et voilà que souvent il retient deux![1] Il se porte trés-bien.

Mlle. Lina aime beaucoup Prosper Chevassu:[2] pourquoi? Parce qu'il est tapageur, entêté, emporté? Moi, j'aime le vieux Marquis— Qu'il est admirable, quand il conspire avec Henriette sous prétexte de lire les journaux, et quand il commente sur les poèmes lugubres de M. Moréal, et dans le duel décisif avec sa femme. Mais, à mon avis, la grande scène du livre se passe dans le pensionnat, quand la Marquise donne à Henriette l'anneau d'alliance, croyant que c'est renvoyé par Moréal; et donc, voyant par la joie franche d'Henriette que c'est lui-même qui a été dupée, veut l'arracher de

---

[1] i.e. his two daughters.
[2] Hypatia's note on this: 'Moved by a spirit of mischief, I had written him that of all the characters in "L'Homme Sérieux" I liked best Prosper Chevassu.'

ses mains. Ca sera une scène splendide de comédie au théâtre.

Mille amitiés à tous et à toutes. Je vous embrasse, mes chères petites enfants.

Votre ami sincère,

JACQUES THOMSON.

12. To Mrs. John Thomson: extracts from two letters.

60 Tachbrook Street, S.W.

April 18, 1874.—Please note that I have changed my address, moving, however, but a very short distance, as this neighbourhood suits me. I do not yet know whether I shall stay here long; but the house is nice and clean, and the landlady seems a very decent body. As inscrutable destiny decides that I am to lodge with married women and old maids alternately, I am with a family woman this time, though I have really not yet learnt whether the husband is dead or living.

Friendly regards to your parents; much love to their lazy little daughter and their son-in-law who is so assiduous, being of the race of the Thomsons. I guess that *we* are all lineally descended from my namesake, the childless architect of the Castle of Indolence. As for *you*, your ancestor must have been a Bruce, who, having watched the spider make a couple of attempts, yawned and thought the animal very stupid to exert itself so much, and fell fast asleep before it could make a third, and never awoke until all the wars were over, and Bannockburn was an ancient tradition.

July 27, 1874.—You cruel little women, to call longing for holidays 'insane'! As for me, I am always 'insanely' longing for holidays in hot weather. As soon as the glass reaches 70° in the shade, my pure conscience finds work of any kind very sinful, and thorough *idlesse* the only way to sanctification and beatification. And yet I have to work; this is a wicked world, and also 'a mad world, my masters,' as the old playwright has it.

As to Lilian in Bulwer Lytton's 'Strange Story,' I know nothing at all of that lay-figure. When I was even younger than you are still, I read some of that book-wright's romances, and became enduringly convinced that he was one of the most thorough and hollow humbugs of the age; false and flashy in everything; with pinchbeck poetry, pinchbeck philosophy, pinchbeck learning, pinchbeck sentiment; stealing whatever good thing he could lay his hands on, and making it a bad thing as he uttered it. So you won't persuade me to think of you in connection with his Lilian of 'A Strange Story.' No; but if you keep very very good, and write me many many nice letters, I may think of you in connection with the lady of Shelley's 'Sensitive Plant,' or her to whom he sent 'Lines with a Guitar.' Read these poems (if you haven't them, may I send them to you?), and then you will see how you are thought of by—Your lazy brother,

JAMES THOMSON.

13. To Mrs. Bradlaugh.

60 Tachbrook Street, S.W.,
29 November 1874.

MY DEAR MRS. BRADLAUGH,—I have rather less than more news to send you than you have to send me. Grant and I go to the concerts on Monday evenings, and that is my only dissipation just now, except that I have had a couple of suburban strolls with young Foote.[1] Grant, as you say, does not look well, and I fear that he is not so. The redoubtable Kenneth I haven't yet seen, not having called at the barracks since that tall grenadier returned to town.

I am sorry indeed for poor Hypatia with her teeth and headaches. She must be very careful in pronouncing the most Germanic of the Germanic words, else they will certainly twist and tug out what sound teeth she has left. As for the German round-about sentences, as they give people who are well the headache, they ought, on the homœopathic system, to cure those who have it. We shall see how they affect her. By the bye, it seems that I frightened *les chères petites enfants* by saying that the grammar would do for the first year or two of their studies. I meant to speak, not of the grammar, but of the dictionary: when they get on a certain way in the language, they will want one with more idioms in it. If they want full directions for acquiring German, they had better refer to Hans Breitmann (whose book, I believe, their papa gave them), who has an excellent poem on the subject:—

> 'Whilst dou learn die Deutsche Sprache?
> Denn set it on your card,
> Dat all the nouns have shenders,
> Und de shenders all are hard.'

There is to be an amateur performance for the benefit of the Secular or some such club at the King's Cross Theatre on the 15th December, Tuesday. Mr. and Mrs. Watts, Othello and Desdemona; Mr. Foote and Mrs. Holyoake, Iago and Emilia. I saw a sort of first rehearsal the other evening, but only a few persons were there, and they had different acting editions of the drama; so I soon came away.

I should be very glad to come to see you all at Christmas, but I fear that I must put off my visit until after B.'s return from America.

[1] G. W. Foote, Secularist writer: see Introduction p. xv and elsewhere.

Besides the writing, there is a good deal to do at the office. The responsibility of the acting editorship weigheth heavily on Watts' shoulders as yet; Atlas with the world on his back was nothing to him.

With love to all, and hoping you are well,—

Yours truly,

JAMES THOMSON.

14. To Mrs. John Thomson.

Salt quotes this as written in the last year of T.'s life, and the Bodleian MSS. (Don c.73) include a copy of a letter to him from his sister-in-law, Julia Thomson, which must have been the occasion of these reminiscences. It is dated 23 January, and she says she is sending it to him at Leicester: she has evidently separated from her husband and is living with her parents (entries in T.'s diary for 1878 indicate that his brother and sister-in-law had quarrelled, and that Julia had come to him for help). 'Aunt Mary', who is staying with 'your brother', has 'swooped down' upon Julia and is trying to act as peacemaker in a way that Julia dislikes: she is evidently trying to discredit the Thomson mother (and presumably to ascribe the weaknesses of the family to the maternal side), and Julia asks whether T. can help her to get at the truth of the relationship between his parents.

I was just past eight years old and at the school when mother died, so I can only give you very early impressions. These are, that father and mother were very happy together when he was at home, until, when I was about six, he returned from his last voyage paralyzed in the right side, the result, as I understand, of a week of terrible storm, during which time he was never able to change his drenched clothes. Before then I think he was a good husband and a kind father; her I always remember as a loving mother and wife. He may have been a bit gay, in the sense of liking a social song and glass, being, I believe, much better looking and more attractive in company than either of his sons. She was more serious, and pious too, following Irving from the Kirk when he was driven out. I remember well Irving's portrait under yellow gauze, and some books of his on the interpretation of prophecy, which I used to read for the imagery. The paralysis at first unhinged father's mind, and he had some fits of violence; more generally his temper was strange, disagreeable, not to be depended upon. I remember him taunting her with being his elder. Mother must have had a sad time of it for a year or so. His mental perturbations settled down into a permanent weakness of mind, not amounting to imbecility, but very, very different, I should say, from his former brightness and decision. Before I went to the school he used to take me to chapels where the members of the congregation ejaculated groaning responses to the minister's prayer, and to small meetings in a private room where the members detailed their spiritual experiences of the week. Good, bad, or indifferent, these were not the sort of things with which he had anything to do in his days of soundness. The right hand remained useless, but the leg had gradually grown strong enough to walk well, though with an awkward dragging pace.

I think mother, who was mystically inclined with Edward Irving, had also a cloud of melancholy overhanging her; first, perhaps, from the death of her favourite brother, John Parker Kennedy, drowned on the Goodwin Sands; then probably deepened by the death of my little sister, of whom I remember being devotedly fond, when she was about three and myself five, of measles caught from me. Had she or someone else lived, I might have been worth something; but, on the whole, I sincerely judge that it was well for both to die when they did, and I would not, for my own selfish comfort, call them back if I could. At first I would doubtless have done so, but not for many years past.

We had also good friends, mother and daughter, named Smith, whom I knew still some years on in my schooldays, and then lost sight of. Speaking generally, you know far more of my family than I do, who have been Ishmael in the desert from my childhood.

INTRODUCTORY NOTE

THE collection of Thomson's manuscripts in the Bodleian Library, Oxford, was made by Bertram Dobell, and acquired by the Library from his son in 1952. Many of the poems were copied by their author into small notebooks (approximately 7" x 4½"), and there are some rough pencil drafts in a smaller notebook, Don f.8. The poems which were on separate leaves have been pasted into larger bindings, and the most important of these (Don d.108) includes a collection which Thomson made for his friend John Grant. I have indicated these several MSS. by their Bodleian Catalogue numbers. There is also a notebook of transcripts made by Dobell of poems which he did not use in his editions.

The British Museum collection (Add. MSS. 38532-5) was bought from J. W. Barrs in 1912. It contains drafts for two-thirds of the *City of Dreadful Night*, and three other notebooks, besides corrected proofs of 'Sunday Up the River'. These MSS. I have indicated by *B.M.*

Where a poem was printed in book form in Thomson's lifetime, and therefore shows his final choice of words, I have only indicated the MS. variants, without distinguishing deletions from alternatives, or an early MS. from a later. In other cases I have been more explicit. I have treated Dobell's *Poetical Works of James Thomson* as the basis of this edition, and have indicated where my text differs from his. After giving the MS. sources—where they exist—for each poem, and a reference to any journal publication, I give the edition in which it first appeared (see list of abbreviations).

It is always a difficult matter to decide how many variants to put into the Notes. I have tried to choose those which show some significant change in the author's intention, or are of interest because they illustrate his method of working. Thomson's MSS. are less heavily punctuated than the two books of poems which he published in his lifetime, and this is true even of the MSS. (contained in Don d.108) of poems which he prepared for those editions but did not finally include. This suggests that his printers added a good many punctuation marks, in which his editor must acquiesce because he himself did. But there is no such obligation with the poems which Dobell edited after Thomson's death, and I have therefore followed the MS. punctuation (which is nearer to modern practice than Dobell's) wherever it was reasonable to do so. For Thomson was a careful copyist and corrector of his own poems: though a number of mistakes crept into the 1880 and 1881 volumes, he had errata slips printed after publication, and when there were misprints in the *National Reformer* versions, he generally printed a correction in the succeeding number.

Besides the handful of poems in this selection which had not hitherto been published (or were published only in part), there remain among the notebooks half a dozen or more which seemed to me better left in obscurity. (Two were published posthumously in *Progress*, without Thomson's name, but were deliberately excluded from Dobell's edition.) There are also translations of Novalis's *Hymns to Night*: the Heine translations were collected together and published in 1909.

ABBREVIATIONS

N.R.   National Reformer.

1880   *The City of Dreadful Night and Other Poems*. London: Reeves and Turner, 1880.

1881   *Vane's Story, Weddah and Om-El-Bonain, and Other Poems*. London: Reeves and Turner. This actually appeared in October 1880, but as it has 1881 on the title-page, I have named it thus to distinguish it from the other book.

1884   *A Voice from the Nile and Other Poems*. London: Reeves and Turner, 1884. Bertram Dobell's collection of the poems which Thomson had written in 1881 and 1882 and had intended to publish; and Dobell's own selection of the early poems.

1892   *Poems, Essays and Fragments*, edited by J. M. Robertson. London, A. and H. B. Bonner (that is, Hypatia Bradlaugh and her husband), 1892. This contained hitherto unpublished poems, all written before 1870, and taken from the *National Reformer*, from MSS. supplied by Dobell, and from a magazine article by Hypatia Bradlaugh.

1895   *The Poetical Works of James Thomson*, in two volumes. London: Reeves and Turner and Bertram Dobell, 1895. Edited with a long introductory memoir by Bertram Dobell.

Salt   *The Life of James Thomson* by Henry S. Salt. Revised Edition. London: Watts & Co., 1914.

C.D.N.   *The City of Dreadful Night*.

alt.   alternative—i.e. the author has left a choice of words; and when there is more than one, the sign / is used to separate the alternatives.

canc.   cancelled by the author.

Dob.   Bertram Dobell's text of 1895.

Grant   The MS. copies in Don d.108 made for John Grant, to distinguish them from other copies under the same catalogue number.

NOTES TO THE POEMS

FOUR POINTS IN A LIFE
(p. 1)

Two MS. versions are in Don d.108, the first on blue paper evidently torn from a notebook, the second prepared for the 1881 volume by T. but not used. T. has corrected MS. I to conform with MS. II in many places, even in punctuation, which is lighter than is the rule in his printed collections. As I do not know the authority for Dobell's 1895 text (which contains one obvious misprint), I have preferred MS. II, prepared for press by the author, except in one place where he has written *much* for *must* in error; I have also left five helpful commas which are to be found in MS. I and not in II.

Other printed versions are in *Tait's Edinburgh Magazine*, October 1858, and (Part I only) in *1892*, which agrees with MS. II except in one place.

The title in *Tait* is 'Four Stages in a Life', and the signature is 'Crepusculus'. In MS. II the poems are not grouped under one title, are dated only with the year, and are separately numbered 25-28; MS. I has the main title as printed by Dobell. The variants given below are from *Tait* only, unless otherwise described.

I MSS. dated 1852, when T. would have been seventeen or eighteen
4 not] now *Dob.*
15 agony] anguish
18 depths] depth *Dob.*
21 cynic] bitterest
24 must] wilt *Dob.*, *Tait* and *1892*
25-26 Converting, lifting, purifying me,
    A holy love—a reverend awe for thee.
II MS. I dated 10.1.57
5 Fighting with] struggling in
9 failing] falling
19 could] would *Dob.*
25 Ah] But *Dob.* and *Tait*

III MS. I dated June 1854
1 Dearest] lady
3 bitter] deadly *Dob.*, *MS. I* and *Tait*
20 can burn] will make
IV MS. I dated 6.6.58
3 give] weave
9 glimpse] catch *Dob.* and *Tait*
13 the green] all the *Dob.* and *Tait*; swell] seem *Dob.*/ grows *Tait*
26 I think] It seems *Dob.* and *Tait*
30 burning] golden *Tait*; lives] shines *Dob.* and *Tait*. The word in both MSS. is probably *lives* but could possibly be *lines*.
32 laggard] lingering *Dob.* and *Tait*
35 every] any *Dob.*
38 bear] bare
47 life] might
48 missed] lost *Dob.* and *Tait*

THE APPROACH TO ST. PAUL'S
(p. 4)

MS. Don e.37, dated 1855. Unpublished. Compare 'A Recusant'.

SUGGESTED BY MATTHEW ARNOLD'S GRANDE CHARTREUSE
(p. 5)

MS. Don d.108; *1884*.
MS. dated July 1855. Pages obviously taken from a notebook, into which T. had copied several of his early poems, with table of Contents at end.

II, 57 ever] constant *alt*.
III, 40 captains] leaders *canc*.

THE DOOM OF A CITY
(p. 12)

MSS. Don e.38 and Don d.108, which was a copy made for John Grant. Dobell printed most of the poem for the first time in his 1884 selection, but omitted Part I up to section xvi. Both for this edition and that of 1895 he used the notebook Don e.38, which is evidently the later of the two MSS., though in some places its readings are cancelled in *Grant*. The *e.38* book is dated 11.2.63; the poem dated Nov. 1857. Part III, section ii was printed in the *National Reformer*, 18.8.67. T. used II, 77-83 as an epigraph to Part III of his *Lady of Sorrow* (*Essays and Phantasies*).

Dobell did occasionally follow *Grant*, and since *e.38* was obviously not T.'s definitive version, I have done the same in two or three further instances where *Grant's* readings seemed better, or *e.38* left alternatives to choose from. I have also adopted the punctuation of *Grant* in a few places.

T. added some notes in the copy made for Grant, which are given in quotation marks in their context. As epilogue he says: 'I call it a Fantasia, because (lacking the knowledge and power to deal with the theme in its epical integrity) I have made it but an episode in a human life, instead of a Chapter in the History of Fate. Thus it is throughout alloyed with the feelings and thoughts, the fantasies, of the supposed narrator; and the verse has all the variableness and abrupt transitions of a man's moods, instead of the solemn uniformity of the laws of Fate.

'The City of the Statues is from the tale of Zobeide in the History of the Three Ladies of Bagdad and the Three Calenders. This episode and the account of the Kingdoms of the Sea in "Prince Beder and . . ." impressed my boyhood more powerfully than anything else in the Arabian Nights.

'The Voyage is certainly tiresome, and probably foolish: but a penny steam-boat will not carry one to a City where the people are all petrified,—not simply in soul and mind, but also in flesh and blood and bone.'

In the tale mentioned by T., the inhabitants of the city have been turned into black stones as a punishment for fire-worship, all except the King's son who was faithful to Allah. One may add as a probable source T.'s memory, conscious or unconscious, of some of the apocalyptic writings of Edward Irving which he had read as a boy: see for instance the *Discourse on the Prophecies of Daniel and the Apocalypse*, 1826, with its 'Judgements', and its admonition: 'Be ye a voice, and having warned the people of one city, flee in haste to another, and warn them also.' Compare also the 'stone cut out of the mountain without hands' which breaks the image in pieces, with the strange episode of the shattering of the angel in the *City of Dreadful Night*.

The variants are from *Grant* unless otherwise specified, as are T.'s own notes.
Part I
5 rich] kind
8 such rem. as] fell Remorse which
11 Becomes relief from impotent unrest
17 infinite] pathless
23 whispers] echoes
25 Awful and boundless realms of vague Eternity
31 corpses] Phantoms
135 vision] terrors; powerless] nerveless
157 the sea-giant] that sea-monster
188 wan] cold
211 jaggèd] ragged
216 sorrow] sorrows *Dob.*
227 barren] dismal
238 riven] river *Dob.* (a misreading of *n* in MSS.)
270 gleam] light
273 ponderous *both MSS.*] fiendish *Dob.*
291 wastes *both MSS.*] waste *Dob.*
294 pure] best
343 lucid] lucent
Part II
13 solemn] lustrous
26 magic] waveless
29 Blazoned] Pregnant
56 golden, large and] large and soft and
62 mist of light was] golden light grew
83 more] as . . . as
90 sweet] poor
97 dumb blind] pallid
103 never-darkened light] never-shadowed might
121 carven] moulded
161 thin *Grant*] dim *Dob.* and *e.38*, canc. in *Grant*
184 pain] guilt
242 joy *both MSS.*] wealth *Dob.*
282 wildly] wild and
322 are all things] all objects
324-5 'De Quincey has a like simile in the "Opium-Eater":—"The fierce chemistry of his dreams burns daily objects into insufferable splendour."'
333 regal *MSS.*] royal *Dob.*
334 Olympian forms divine, and ladies fair
335 lily] lotus
350 bay] hills

NOTES

375 'The dedication suggested by that of Bacon's "Advancement of Learning".'
438 omitted in *Grant*
439 'See Shelley's "Misery, a Fragment".'
443 nor after] scarcely in
454 your] Thine
461 dark shadows] sick weakness
505 restful] ordered
509 rife *Dob.* and *Grant*] ripe *e.38*

Part III
21 couches] crouches *N.R.*
41 in one] together *N.R.*
48 course] race
55 But as the Eternal is changeless, all-wise, all-just, all holy *Grant:* and lines 56-57 are omitted

In Don d.108 is a fragment, written in pencil on the back of a £5 Share Certificate form of the Alhambra Palace Company, giving additional lines after 56:
  That of all—the weak, the strong, wise, foolish, wicked, holy,
  Each each day is fed with the food befitting him fully and solely;
  Each sowed and reaped his crop of corn, and none could steal or borrow,
  Each made his bread for the very day, not yestreen or to-morrow,
  Each craves his own befitting loaf, be it bread of joy or sorrow—
followed by 57-58.
113 linger *Dob.*] lingers *MSS.*
125 ashen] dismal
126 Hissed] Roared
136 'This is, I conceive, the true meaning of Aeon, as developed in one of De Quincey's papers, "On the Scriptural expression Eternity".'
140 pealed] flowed
163 vast] quick
203 cloudglooms] gloom-clouds
210 fair and still] fair though scarred
303 divine] sublime
396 sombre] holy
403 The original lines were:
  Wherefrom the free and living tide hath flown
  And left me stranded on it lorn and lone,
T. has corrected it, with pencil note on 'dark waste wide':
  'A makeshift: the remarkable past-participle [ie *flown*] escaped me until now!'
458 Avenging] Eternal
470 crouch] couch
484 the] yon *Dob.* and *e.38*

490 bosom] torpor
542 sleeps on] cowers wan
573-620 'Written in 1855: adopted here because something of the kind was wanted, and its existence hindered me from writing a new Chorus specially for this piece. It does not fit in precisely, and is the only bit of thus adopted work.'
588 called] of *Dob.* and *Grant*, and as alt. in *e.38*
597 doubting] ruling
605 bland] blind, *Grant* and *1884*
Part IV
20 topaz] beryl
43 Before] Beneath; drowsy] tranquil
51 portentous] for warning
57 shapeless] great black; monstrous] great black
71 unexpected] unsuspected
74 Instead of the next 13 lines *Grant* has:
  Lay on me heavier than a weight of years,
  Imperious to get free.
  Straight as an arrow from the mark it sought . . .
  While, wretched and distraught, I lingered impotent
  The Spirit . . etc.
85 Him I watched] I watched him *Dob.* and alt. in *e.38*
101 are palaced] revel as; scorn] contemn
103 world] earth; complacently] triumphantly
112 earth-surrounding] land-involving
126 another] a hundred
127 another] one
134 moth-eaten] worm-eaten
137 *Grant* here has the stanza beg. at 147
rulers] statesmen
139 pencil note in *Grant*: 'Emerson'
144 the *before* ineffable *Grant*
149 other thousands] thousand *Dob.*
155 Dry bones still kept in a whole by cord-sinews . . .
163-4 reversed in order in *Grant*
165 His right was . . .] he fought for freedom, for chastity . . .
184 scarce better] as evil
194 sages] wise men
195 smile] cry
202 justice of God] truth of the Lord; by] as

A CHANT
(p. 54)

MS. Don e.37; *1884*.

Punctuation as in **MS.**, which is dated 1857.

LINES ON HIS TWENTY-THIRD BIRTHDAY
(p. 54)

MSS. Don e.36 and Don d.108 (Grant), both dated Mon. 23 Nov. 1857, the former headed *Dublin*; part printed in Memoir.

Dobell did not include the poem in the text of his edition, because as he says 'the author, shortly before his death, desired that it might not be published, as he had then altogether outgrown the mood in which it was written.' However, he quoted nearly a third of the poem in his introductory Memoir, and for its biographical interest, at any rate, it claims a place in this selection. The variants are from Don e.36.

At the end of Grant's copy is this note: 'I send you the above as a curiosity; I could not write in the same mood nowadays.'

57 brought] bought
103 worn-out] frigid *canc.*
123 squall] gale
124 voyage] sail *Grant*, alt. in *e.36*
151 firm] fine

A RECUSANT
(p. 58)

MSS. Don e.36; Don d.108 (two versions: one the copy prepared for the 1880 vol. by T., the other made by him for Grant); *N.R.* 22.11.62; *Secularist* 1.5.76; *1880*.

MS. Don e.36 dated 5.8.58. 'Composed in Spring Dublin: Arbour Hill Behind Royal Barracks' Title (canc., and uncanc. in *Grant*) *Nonconformity*; printed in *N.R.* as *Heresy*.

5 slender incense] incense vapour
6 Ascending] Upquivering
7 heart feels most] lone heart **feels**
13 Conscience] Reason
14 pure] bare

THE LORD OF THE CASTLE OF INDOLENCE
(p. 58)

One page of MS. only, in Don d.108, on the back of 'A Happy Poet', a longer poem (not included in this collection), which was also, as Dobell points out, connected in T.'s mind with his namesake Thomson's 'Castle of Indolence'. (At the bottom of an early draft of that poem T. has written: 'Wed. 7.10.57 Humiliation day'.) *Tait's Edinburgh Magazine* March 1860, signed 'Crepusculus'; *1880*, where it is dated 1859.

Stanza II is stanza VI in *Tait*

11 sunfire] sunshine
12 flowers] leaves
14 golden] fulgent
17-18 He swayed our realm with steadfast, placid ease,
   As sways the shining moon her ever-restless seas.
29 world] earth
41 wastes] realms
45 drifting] gliding
46 constant heed] weary head
47 The soldier painful battlings hard prolong
50 troubled] 'wildered
53 earth] world
56 imperceptibly] out insensibly
72 carolled round] danced around
83 penetrated] comprehended
90 drunkenness] pleasure half
92 ever ample] inexhaustive
107 divine] as his

A REAL VISION OF SIN
(p. 61)

MS. Don e.39; *Progress* Nov. 1884; *1895*. Dated Fri. 4.3.59.

On the manuscript T. wrote in pencil: 'Written in disgust at Tennyson's, which is very pretty and clever and silly and truthless.' As Dobell points out, T. seems to have had in mind Tennyson's 'Two Voices', though 'The Vision of Sin' is also hinted at. Presumably it was the optimistic ending of 'The Two Voices' which drew forth these verses in the same metre, with their rather too-obvious effort to disgust.

Text from *e.39*: variants from *Progress* and *Dob*.

73 through *omitted*
74 couched] crouched
78 until she moaned
93 drooped] dropped

MATER TENEBRARUM
(p. 65)

MSS. Don e.36 and Don d.108 (Grant); *N.R.* 14.7.67 (5-10 only); *1881*.

Don e.36 is dated 21.11.59. At the bottom of Grant's MS. in this note: 'Written in an access of fierce emotion, one evening while waiting for Waters to go to a dance.' T. used lines 5-10 as an epigraph for his prose *A Lady of Sorrow (Essays and Phantasies)*.

9 thy tenderest] those pure loving
16 dust] sod
25 disease and] and want and

THE 'MELENCOLIA' OF ALBRECHT DÜRER
(p. 66)

MS. Don d.104, undated, and copied by Dobell in Don e.48. Unpublished. This is presumably a first sketch for the portrait which appears in the *C.D.N.*, last section. See p. xxxi for a comparison of this poem with Shelley's 'On the Medusa of Leonardo', and p. xxii for T.'s association of the figure with the 'character and intellectual destiny' of George Eliot.

At the end of his transcript Dobell writes: 'Taken from one of Thomson's MS. books belong[ing] to Mr. J. W. Barrs. It must have been a quite early composition.' The holograph copy is written in a steady hand on two sheets of blue unlined paper torn from a notebook (6½″ x 4⅛″). The conception of 'Fate—God petrified' implies a date later than *The Doom of a City*; the first appearance of the titanic Mother-figure in T.'s published work is in the prose *Our Lady of Sorrow* (1862-64).[1] I have accordingly placed the poem at the beginning of the second group (1860-74), though it is impossible to date it accurately.

Dürer's 'Melencolia' is a copperplate engraving of 1514, and T. possessed a copy of it by Johan Wiricx (see his letter to Rossetti quoted on p. 273). The engraving is one of the favourite documents of Romanticism, and there have been countless interpretations of its symbolism. A useful summary is given on pp. 76-83 of the Phaidon Press *Dürer*, by Wilhelm Waetzoldt, 1955; see also E. Panovsky's *Albrecht Dürer, I*, pp. 156-71, O.U.P. 1945. The archaic spelling Mel*e*ncolia is Dürer's own.

THROUGH FOULEST FOGS . . .
(p. 67)

No manuscript; *1892*. Dobell notes 'Undated. Probably written in the sixties'.

TO OUR LADIES OF DEATH
(p. 68)

MSS. Don e.36, Don e.39; *N.R.* 28.2.63; *1880*.

[1] See *Essays and Phantasies*, p. 21.

Dated 29.5.60 and 8.12.60.

The *N.R.* version was entitled 'To the Youngest of our Ladies of Death', and prefaced by this note addressed to Charles Bradlaugh:—

'My dear Iconoclast,—I transcribed this piece for you, intending to introduce it with a few remarks upon the doctrine of the immortality of the human soul; but I have not been able to catch the few right words, and the rhyme itself is so lengthy, that I must not also inflict upon the patient reader a long preface of reason, or unreason. Suffice it, then, for me to affirm that in my calmest and purest hours of contemplation, my own verdict upon my own life attests this poem (which was written more than a year since) to be genuine as the utterance of my individual self; whether it is true or not for others, themselves must decide. It may be worth while to remark that the Three Ladies were suggested by the sublime sisterhood of 'Our Ladies of Sorrow' in the 'Suspiria de Profundis,' and that the stanza was moulded under the influence of 'The Guardian Angel' in 'Men and Women.' So, if any good reader finds no good in this poem, let me humbly suggest that he or she may most easily and profitably forget it in the study of those noble works of Thomas de Quincey and Robert Browning.—Fraternally yours—B.V.'

In de Quincey's *Suspiria*, which is a sequel to the *Opium Eater*, the three Ladies are of Tears, of Sighs, and of Shadows; their purpose—'to plague his heart until we had unfolded the capacities of his spirit'. For the difference between Thomson's stanza and Browning's, see Introduction, p. xl.

14 jest] taunt; parry] ward off
105 Thou Night essential] Of night compacted
113 The wicked, selfish, foolish, pitiless
121 Demon] Mother
124 riant] joyous
141 Thy] Thine T. wrote 'Thine hair' in both MSS. and the *N.R.*, which perhaps bears out Rossetti's description (*Salt* p. 53), 'his *h*'s were sometimes less aspirated than they should be'.
154 ruined] sleeping, *N.R.*
Or in deep mountain-clefts where sun ne'er shone *e.36*
166 Libyan] desert/secret

189 infinite love and faith] inexhaustive love
211 cosmic] rhythmic
223 And pray to Thee, thou calm oblivious Death

TWO SONNETS
(p. 73)

MS. Don e.36; *1881*.
MS. date: 16.12.60.

I, 14 will] must
II, 14 My Grief thrills harmony from every string

ON GEORGE HERBERT'S POEMS
(p. 74)

MS. Don e.37; *1895*.
Punctuation as in MS., which is dated 15.1.62.

SIX SONNETS TO JOSEPH AND ALICE BARNES
(p. 74)

MS. Don e.36; quoted in full in Dobell's Memoir in *1895*.

Begun 25.3.62 and finished 10.4.62, according to the MS. dates. Punctuation and use of capitals from MS., where the second sonnet has the title 'Women who Bless and are Blessed', added by T. in a shaky hand in 1881, when he apparently copied the sonnet out 'for Mr. Hall's collection' and gave it to Mathilde Blind, as he writes in the notebook. T. lived with Mr. and Mrs. Barnes during his time at Ballincollig—see Introduction p. xii.

III, 2 The reference here and in Sonnet VI is to Matilda Weller: see Introduction p. xii.

THE THREE THAT SHALL BE ONE
(p. 76)

MSS. B.M., Don e.37, Don d.108; *Secularist* 3.6.76; *1880*.
MS. date: 30.11.63.

16 minstrelsy] melody
23 gem] begem
36 red] brown

SUNDAY AT HAMPSTEAD
(p. 78)

MSS. B.M., Don e.37, Don e.40, Don f.8 (Part XI only); *N.R.* 15.7.66 and 22.7.66; *1880*.

In the notebook Don e.37 the parts are interspersed with other poems, and arranged in a slightly different sequence, from which Parts X and XI are missing. B.M. has partly illegible pencil drafts of V-X. Don e.40 (notebook dated 25.11.65) contains the final arrangement. The dates are as follows:
Parts I & II, 2.8.63 (a Sunday)
Part III, 5.8.63
Part XII, originally numbered IV, 10.8.63
Part IV, 6.10.63
Parts V & VI, 12.4.65
Parts VII, VIII, IX, Good Friday 14.4.65
Part X, 23.3.65
Part XI in *f.8* is dated 25.5.65
  7 half] brown
  9 will we] let us
 13 Though] *misprinted* Through, *N.R., Dob.*
 16 patient, stupid] ill-used, stolid
 36 loll] roll
II 8 far] small; living] light and
III 13 a vast machinery] iron wheels whirling
IV 10 Low-wandering far apart
   14 Parade] Stalk through
   38 We can't do nothing at all
   39 Hot-cross-bun] Good Friday
   64 loving] beautiful/charming/lovely
   73 couch] sit
   75 slim] tall/poplar-tops
   76 boys] men
V 6 with stiff clay] thick with mud
VI 10 grey] white
   18 cheese] cream
VII 5 stairlike] steeply
VIII 15 passionate gestures] tears and trembling
   20 awkward] weary
IX 23-25 added later in pencil, *e.40*:
   Thou sage Philosopher! we'll go, we'll go,
   And drink the beers we drank (the world's an O)
   This same night fifty thousand years ago.
e.37 has the lines as printed, also as a pencilled afterthought.

THOMAS COOPER'S ARGUMENT
(p. 86)

MSS. Don e.41, B.M. (part); *N.R.* 13.2.64; *1892*, as 'On a Debate between Mr. Bradlaugh and Mr. Thomas Cooper on the Existence of God'.

In the *National Reformer*, Charles

Bradlaugh quotes the poem as written by his friend B.V., in the course of an account of his own debate with Thomas Cooper. This version is the one here printed, and is the same as Dobell's and *1892*, with the addition of one comma.

Don e.41 has the title: 'Thomas Cooper loqr. (in debate with C.B. at Hall of Science, City Road, Feb. '63 or '64)'

10 Self] Earth
16 Jacob's] David's *canc.*
27 But as I have not been I for ever
43 Without] Unless; was] were
67 round] dark
69 The dot *i* must have
70 But] Though

THE FIRE THAT FILLED
(p. 88)

MSS. B.M. (two drafts), Don e.37, and Don d.107, the sheet prepared for press by T., and given by Dobell to T. B. Mosher, the American publisher of T.'s works; *1881*.

MS. date: 29.2.64. In *B.M.*, the stanzas are reversed in order.

3 grey] dark
7 singer's] poet's *and so throughout*
9 fulgent] glowing/radiant
13 Thus] My; extends] outspreads

FROM THE MIDST OF THE FIRE
(p. 89)

MSS. B.M., Don e.37, Don e.39; *N.R.* 14.7.67; *Essays and Phantasies* (1881).

B.M. date: 21.10.63.

In *e.39* the poem forms the 'Envoy' to the prose fantasy 'Our Lady of Sorrow', and is so printed in the *N.R.* and *Essays and Phantasies*, after an introductory note: 'About three years before his death I received from my friend Vane certain manuscripts with the somewhat fierce Envoy:—'.

VANE'S STORY
(p. 89)

MSS. Don e.36, Don e.42; *N.R.* 13 & 27 May, 3 June, 1866; *1881*.

The Prologue is dated 9.11.64, the rest of the piece between 17.9.64 and 5.8.65. Some almost illegible fragments (between ll.171 & 225) are in B.M., dated Feb. 1864.

Most of the variants are from Don e.36, where a number of lines from the final version have been added in the margins. The *N.R.* true variants agree with those of *e.42* with one exception, which is noted.

Dobell notes: 'This poem was originally called "Gray's Story". The author once told me that he afterwards altered the name to Vane because of its suggesting something vain or unreal.' T. said the same in writing to W. M. Rossetti, 15.12.80.

2 clear verm.] steadfast ruby
17 restless] noisy
71-74 an afterthought
130 fathomless] unexplored
155 puny] little
173 More and Vane
279 Footnote in *e.42*: 'Goethe's Epigrams (Lahme Xenien IV p. 84) "Was lehr' ich dich vor allen Dingen? Möchte über meinen eignen Schatten springen!"'
353 modest little] well-proportioned
412 Some lines follow in the MSS. which were printed in *N.R.* but omitted by T. in *1881* and Dob. in *1895*, with asterisks to mark the omission:
Than when you plagued me here of old
With infinite witchcraft! Was I told
You once demurely begged *I am*
To serve some sauce up with the Lamb,
As without condiment such food
Was apt to pall however good? . . .
456 Shiraz] festal/Sharon's
475 Dobell suggests that possibly the 'Friend' is meant to be Heine; this seems very improbable, especially since Heine is invoked by name later in the poem.
548 aeonian] millenial
593 stolid,] solid *Dob.*
627 By no means] Confound it
727 Bear] take
749-75 an afterthought
833-4 and footnote, an afterthought
881 of yore] before
903 restless wanderer] man called Shelley
904 You call damned] Obscure and
915-20 an afterthought
919-20 missing in *e.36*
920 loved] knew *1881*, corr. in errata slip
943 Auspicious] A charming

266 NOTES

949 the pale and sallow] that was so pallid/and never coloured
953 dull and mournful] sad and homeless
1008 Goddess] Angel
1084 Note in MSS.: 'Faust & Margaret together for the second time'; *e.42* adds: 'also Illusions Perdues—the Sonnet (Balzac)'
1097 fulgent] fragrant
1104-55 an afterthought
1133 Dim] Blue
1134 breezes stirring] wandering airs in
1150-1 Now stars surround us wheeling whirling
And the great steadfast moon is twirling
1154 long] short
1155 holy] long long
1159 king's] saint's
1179-86 an afterthought

The Epilogue is not in *e.36*, but T. has written 'Conclude with Heine's Epilogue'. Lines 9-30 are a translation from Heine ('Epilog' from the *Letzte Gedichte*, and not from the *Lazarus* sequence), and are given in a slightly different version among T.'s other Heine translations in Don e.37.

7 *Our*] In
15 likewise] also
25 Pelides] Achilles *N.R. only*

VERSICLES
(p. 118)

MSS. No. 1: B.M., Don e.37; Nos. 2, 3 and 4: Don f.8. The fourth versicle is written between Nos. 2 and 3 in *f.8* (a small notebook of pencil drafts), with a fragment of translation, but T. did not print it. The others were printed in *N.R.* 25.11.66 under this title, and in *1892*.
No. 1 is dated 11.3.65; No. 2, 5.9.66. The version printed here of 1, 2 and 3 is from *N.R.* Dobell's version is the same as *1892*.

2 may] shall *Dob*.
you let your shaft *B.M.*
5 birth] fate *f.8*
7-9 Every one doth strangely seek
Other spheres in which he's weak;
Whence we find in every man *f.8*
13 Patience my children, you are funny fellows *f.8*
funny] puny *Dob*.
15 snatch] catch *f.8*

LOW LIFE
(p. 119)

MSS. B.M., Don e.41; *Secularist* 19.8.76; *1884*.
MS. dated 2.4.65. (64 in *B.M.* is clearly a slip.)
15 Harley] Harmer
58 run] ran *Dob*.

POLYCRATES ON
WATERLOO BRIDGE
(p. 121)

MSS. B.M., Don e.41, Don d.105; *N.R.* 14.10.66; *1881*.
Dated 7.4.65. Polycrates, ruler of Samos, was advised to avert the nemesis that his great good fortune might bring on him, by throwing into the sea something that he valued.
Order of 13th & 14th stanzas reversed in *N.R.* 7-9 omitted in *B.M.*
43 dearest] choicest

ONCE IN A SAINTLY PASSION
(p. 122)

MSS. Don f.8, Don e.37; *1884* (and quoted in Dobell's Memoir in *1895*).
Punctuation from MSS. *e.37* is dated 28.5.65.

ON THE TERRACE AT RICHMOND
(p. 122)

MSS. Don f.8, Don e.41, Don d.108, the copy prepared for press by T., but omitted from the volumes printed. Unpublished.
MSS. dated 28.5.65. Variants from *f.8*:

I, 11 A man as good as ever breathed
12 'A poet...' T.'s namesake, author of *The Castle of Indolence*
23 much less] decreased
III, 7 He charged his heirs to ever seek
18 For me he dropped] Saw clearly through

From SUNDAY UP THE RIVER
Parts I and II
(p. 125)

MSS. Don e.40, B.M. (pencil draft and corr. proof for *Fraser's*); *Fraser's Magazine*, October 1869; *1880*.
MS. dated 8.3.65. An earlier version of the poem, called *Two up the River*; *A Midsummer Day's Dream*, is in Don d.108: it does not include the two parts here printed.

The fourth stanza is added at the bottom of the MS. as a substitute for the following lines, to which Froude (editor of *Fraser's*) had objected:
   The broad-boughed trees were deluged
     With radiance divine;
   Like prophets grand all still they stand
     Before Heaven's opening shrine.
I, 13 pale] wan
II, 15 beats] throbs
   19 streaming] charming

ART
(p. 126)

MSS. Don f.8, Don e.37, Don e.40; *N.R.* 17.2.67; *1880*.
   Original title canc.: 'Elementary philosophy of Love Poems'. Dated 18.6.65. Order of couplets in Part III varied in MSS.
I, 11 highest] faintest
   16 shrivels] burns through
III, 8 portrait] likeness
   10 pale stone
   15 puff out the] pour the rich
   16 make love with] court/flirt with
   19 Words may be lovely and sweet
        and grand

A POLISH INSURGENT
(p. 128)

MSS. Don f.8, Don e.41; *N.R.* 18.3.66; *1880*.
   For T.'s connexion with the Committee formed to help the Polish insurgents, see Introduction p. xvii.
   MSS. dated 5.2.66, so that the date 1863 given in *1880* presumably refers to the rebellion.
14 Pencil note referring to *like so*: 'Embracing an imaginary big belly; so big, that the tips of his tense fingers of either hand barely touch.'
35 when] while
42 red is our] but it burns
50 Of thine agony of] Moaning in your

MR. MACCALL AT CLEVELAND HALL
(p. 129)

MSS. Don f.8, Don e.41; *1892*.
   Dated 17.4.66. *f.8* has title 'A Casual Report', and the first and last stanzas are missing.
12 British] Queen's *f.8*
   alt.: Can any muff or minion
49 In the lifted profile face *alt.*

LIFE'S HEBE
(p. 131)

MSS. Don. f.8, Don e.41; *N.R.* 13.1.67; *1880*.
   MSS. dated 5.9.66. A prose argument for the poem is on an earlier page of *f.8*, dated 29.5.66, and the title in *f.8* is *Life*.
20 lay faint but never] as if in fever
28 sweet] clear
31 As he went] Striding off
48 Kissed her lips and kissed her face

DAY
(p. 133)

MSS. Don f.8, Don e.41; *N.R.* 25.8.67; *1881*.
   Dated 1.12.66.
14 grain] star/slab

NIGHT
(p. 133)

MSS. B.M., Don e.36 and 37; *N.R.* 25.8.67; *1881*.
   MS. date: 11.2.64, but T. grouped this with 'Day' written in 1866. In *e.36* the poem has the title 'Desolate'.
1 He] I
6 Lonely] Blind, lone
24 again] was/blackly

PHILOSOPHY
(p. 134)

MSS. Don f.8, Don e.41; *N.R.* 20.1.67; *1880*.
   Dated 6.12.66. *f.8* has the following prose note under the heading 'Philosophy', dated 14.7.66:
   My eyes had nothing to look for, they looked through and through—
   Saw the skeleton and the nerves and the veins and the raw flesh under the skin of the beautiful—
   Now they have something to look for; a little hope fluttering soft wings, a fairness related to them, an aspiration not so high as the stars but higher than the clouds—
   Therefore they no more look through and through—
   Happy are the eyes that see only life-surfaces—wretched are the eyes that see only death-entrails.
   The entrails are hidden beneath the bloom of the skin, because they ought not and should not be seen.
   The corpse is encoffined and buried from sight; that the saddest graves may be flowering grass-mounds.

I, 2 glory] action
II, 5 massy] solid
   10 unfurled] outfurled
III, 6 nearest] lowest
    8 masterful] tyrannous
    10 lustre] splendour
IV, 15 solid] stable
f.8 has also the following verse, dated 28.1.67:
   Most of your poetry is now dyspeptic,
   Most of your creeds and dogmas but hepatic;
   As too much bile will make a man a sceptic,
   A little more will make him a fanatic.

THE NAKED GODDESS
(p. 135)

MSS. Don f.8, Don e.41; *N.R.* 23.6.67; *1880*.

The epigraph is from No. VII of Leopardi's *Canti*, 'Alla Primavera, o delle Favole Antiche', l.25-28, a poem which has clearly influenced Thomson's, although he had only begun Italian in earnest some four months before he began to write it.
'Mysterious dances of immortal feet shook the precipitous ridges and impenetrable woods (which are now the remote nest of the winds).'
Titles 'La Diva Ignuda', deleted and 'Civilisation' (*f.8*). Dates: 19.12.66—31.3.67.

8 Flashing] Bearing
45 slanting] level
90 haught] *altered by Dob. to* hot
186 cerement] cerecloth
244 of murrain] by hundreds
288 faint shadow] sole headland
289 modern] ancient
303 statue] image
313 whelming] conquering

TWO LOVERS
(p. 142)

MS. B.M.; *N.R.* 5.1.68; *1881*.
MS. dated 15.12.67. A corrected proof of the *N.R.* version is in Don d.105. The source of the story, as for that of *Weddah*, is Stendhal's *De L'Amour*, chapter 53. There, the story is more improbable in that the friend arrives in time to hear the dying recantation of the Christian girl.

73 travel] distance
81 Shall] Can
93 Fate] faith *1881*, corrected in errata slip

After 116 *B.M.* and *N.R.* have another stanza:
   (And when the giants into battle go,
      Wise dwarfs on both sides take to their good heels:
   That to the pigmy is a fatal blow
      Which the big fellow laughs at if he feels.)

IN THE ROOM
(p. 146)

MSS. Don f.8, B.M., Don e.41, the latter dated Sunday 29.12.67; Sunday 23.2.68; *N.R.* 19 May 1872; *1880*.
N.R. version is the same as *1880*, with slight variants in punctuation, but has the following footnote to the title:
'This room is believed to have been situate in Grub Street, concerning the name of which street the following curious note from Johnson's Contradictionary may come home to here and there a reader:—"Some assert that this renowned street is so named on the well-known ironical principle, because its inhabitants have never much and often nothing to eat. Others because these inhabitants drag out a crawling existence on leaves, differing from most other *larvae* in this, that it is only as by a miracle that any one of the swarm ever develops into the brilliant and winged condition of the *imago* or butterfly; the bulk perishing of atrophy in their grub state, probably through lack of succulence in the leaves on which they desperately try to subsist. But, whatever the etymology of the name, which perhaps no amount of grubbing industry could now settle, it is certain that in our days this Grub Street is the street not of grub but of grubs."'
Don f.8 contains the first draft. *B.M.* shows the progress of composition, with certain stanzas added later in the notebook.

8 mult. lower] lower inarticulate
14 night's uproar] night secure
36 wholesome] spicy
54 looked] glared
84 worn-out] musty/yellow/dull and stupid
89 Lucy] Lizzie/Annie
102 pleasant] rosy/ruddy
104 While nimble as a fly just born
Stanza XV (113-20) is differently arranged in *f.8*, and deleted.
Stanza XVI (121-8) was a later addition.
After the succeeding stanza in *B.M.* T.

wrote: 'Here (10 p.m.) J. G. [i.e. John Grant] came in to tell me that his little girl died half an hour before.'
130 ponderous] solemn
132 As if firm-rooted] Solidly rooted
136 experienced] consummate
138 Not anything] Nothing at all
139 so many] the wane of
145 solemn] mystic
The last four lines of stanza XIX (149-52) and the first four of the succeeding stanza were later additions.
173 with slow] at one
Stanzas XXIII (177-84) and XXV (193-200) were the last to be written, on 23.2.68.
In f.8, the first version of stanza XXIV (185-92) was the final stanza of the poem, as follows:—

He lay, the lowest thing there lulled
  Calm sleeplike in corruption's truce;
A form whose purpose was annulled
  While all the other shapes were use.
And until dawn the bed told tales
  Of human sorrows and delights
Of fever moans and infant wails;
  Of births and deaths and bridal nights.

This was dated Sunday 12.1.68. The next day, Thomson wrote down 185-92 as in the present text, and added the final stanza more or less as printed.

A SONG OF SIGHING
(p. 151)

MSS. Don f.8, B.M.; *N.R.* 28.5.72; *1881*.
MSS. untitled, dated 13.1.68.

23 lustre] flutter
24 Leaving dreams of gladsome things
25 Omitted in f.8

WEDDAH AND OM-EL-BONAIN
(p. 151)

MSS. B.M. has complete first draft, and fair copy to III 112; Don f.9 has the other half of this copy; Don d.105, title-page and preliminary note only; *N.R.* 19 November, 3 & 24 December 1871; 21 & 28 January, 1872; *1881*.
MSS. dated as begun 27.6.68 and ended 4.4.69.
When this poem appeared in the *N.R.*, Thomson sent a copy to William Rossetti, who admired it, and thus began their acquaintance. Froude had rejected it for *Fraser's Magazine*, so Thomson told Rossetti, 'finding the story beautiful, and the treatment excellent in arrangement and conception, but deficient in melody of versification, in smoothness and sweetness'. (*Salt* p. 55)

Der Azra is not given in *N.R.* or *f.9*; B.M. has the German original only. For the final line, I follow *d.105* and *1881*; *Dob.* has when they love must perish.
The MSS. contain many variants, of which I give only a few examples.
Part I, 70 spites] feuds; vast] broad
125 *1881*: asked, *corr. in errata slip*
Part II, 9 tear-] wan
100 *Dob.* and *1881* insert a stop at end of line: I prefer MS. and *N.R.* punctuation
136 impalpable and heartless Death
 impassible and reachless Death
Part III, 89 Amine] Adah *throughout*
102 flushed] twitched
166 Secluded by waste sands encroaching round
After 176 *B.M.* (first draft) has another stanza, which T. crossed through.
199-200 T. has underlined the unwanted rhymes of *drinks* and *sinks*, with his customary tick in the margin to remind himself of a blemish to be removed if possible.
Part IV, 19 Motor] Malech *once*, Merab *thereafter*
138 From sevenfold twisted trunk
170 were trampled to] though hard stamped made
203-4 But Walid as the seventh evening fell
 Since none else dared, must tread the fatal spot
211 simple] ponderous/massy
247 deathstone] ruby
271 The Azra perish when they love
272 Fate's pen of iron
274 fateless] pangless

L'ENVOY
(p. 175)

MSS. B.M. (two drafts); quoted in full by Hypatia Bradlaugh in her articles on T. in *Our Corner*, August and September 1886; *1892*.
Hypatia says that T. bought a copy of the *Magic Ring* by La Motte Fouqué as a Christmas present for her when she was ten years old, and gave it to her with this poem written on the fly-leaf, dated 23.12.68.

20-21 . . . the priceless thing
 Woman's real Magic Ring.

LILAH, ALICE, HYPATIA
(p. 176)

MSS. B.M., Don d.108; *Our Corner* 1 August 1886; *1892*.
B.M. has this note: 'Written in an *Undine* which I picked up in Holywell St. for sixpence. On its flyleaf remained the name "Lilah".' T. gave the book to the Bradlaugh girls, as Hypatia describes in *Our Corner*. The version in *d.108* spells the name *Lillah* and has minor differences.

12 Note in *B.M.*: 'And Chaucer's sweet Prioresse . . . "hire eyen grey as glas" '

IN A CHRISTIAN CHURCHYARD
(p. 176)

MS. B.M.; *N.R.* 7.5.71, with signature X; *1892*.
The MS. title is 'A Graveyard', and the date, 16.1.70, is that on which T. began the *C.D.N.*, writing the two stanzas which bring the Narrator to 'the huddled stones of grave and tomb'.

THE CITY OF DREADFUL NIGHT
(p. 177)

MSS. B.M. (two drafts), Pierpont Morgan Library, New York; *N.R.* 22 March, 12 & 26 April, 17 May 1874; *Secularist* 1.1.76 (1st two stanzas of XV only); *1880*.

Thomson told Dobell that he had destroyed the MS. of this poem, as Dobell records in a letter to the American publisher T. B. Mosher, preserved in the Bodleian Library. But also in the Bodleian is a letter of 10.1.1893 to Mosher from a Secularist friend of Thomson's called G. G. Flaws (alias Oliver H. S. Leigh, also Gegeëf), in the course of which he says: 'I was in fact the only one who was with him during his last sad weeks.[1] For several of them I gave up my whole time to him, and placed him in different lodging houses each night. During these weeks he confided many things to me, including various MSS. and letters, which I of course have here with me, and I have his own volume of "The City", with his notes, and also his carefully revised copy of the poem, as completed for publication.' Flaws, who was in financial difficulties after abandoning his wife and eloping to America, sold this MS. to W. C. Stedman, and it was acquired by the Pierpont Morgan Library in 1911. I located it there through the kindness of the American Council of Learned Societies, and have collated it with the printed text by means of a micro-film which the Library was so good as to make for me.

The poem is 'written on 62 pp. in two 12mo memorandum books' (to quote the Library's description), and was made, with a good deal of fresh correction and rearrangement, from earlier drafts of which two are in the British Museum, acquired from J. W. Barrs in 1912. The earlier is in pencil, and has the title 'The City of Night' with 'Dreadful' added with a query on the line above. It contains fifteen sections, though not the first fifteen of the poem as we know it, beginning with II and ending with the Proem. T. had clearly intended this to be the final piece, as some scribbled memoranda show, and had thought of starting with the 'Melencolia', though it does not appear in either of the B.M. drafts. The other draft is in ink, and contains the same sections as that in pencil, though in a different order. The dates of composition, copied in each notebook, show that these drafts contain the poem as written up to a month before T.'s departure for Spain in July 1873. The Morgan MS. contains the whole poem except for one stanza (lacking also in *N.R.*), written out in the sequence that we know, except that the Proem still appears last, and Parts XIII and XVII have exchanged places. The punctuation (altered in *1880*) is much the same as that of *N.R.* The careful dating given to each part is of such interest that I set out the sequence here, with indications of the stanza-form. These show at a glance that Thomson wrote blocks in the same measure, and later disposed them as his ear and dramatic sense approved. I have used the letter A to indicate the characteristic seven-line stanza (see Introduction p. xl), and B to indicate the ababcc of the Shakespearian sonnet sestet (occasionally varied with aabccb). Where sestets are followed or interrupted by stanzas of three or four lines I have marked them Bx. Part IV alone, with its double refrain, falls into no category.

---

[1] Not strictly true, but its partial truth is attested by W. Stewart Ross in the *Agnostic Review*, 6.5.89, and by Percy Holyoake's letters.

Part	Metre	Date of Composition
II	B	16 & 20 January, 6 March 1870
XVIII	B	22, 23, 24 & 26 May 1870
XX	B	12 June, 7 & 9 July 1870
I	A	10, 11, 15, 16 & 19 July 1870
V	A	26 & 27 August 1870
XI	A	27 & 28 August 1870
VII	A	28 August 1870
IV	A	28 August, 5 October 1870, 13 August 1871
X	Bx	6 & 13 October 1870
VI	Bx	14 & 20 October 1870
III	A	23 October 1870
VIII	Bx	May & 2 June 1873
XIX	A	6 June & 1 October 1873
IX	A	7 June 1873
Proem	A	11 June 1873
XXI	A	13 June 1873 (verse 1 only)
XII	Bx	3 July 1873
XIV	Bx	3, 4 & 5 July 1873 (leaves for Spain, 22 July; returns 23 September)
XVII	A	1 & 2 October 1873
XIII	A	4 & 29 October 1873
XV	A	4 October 1873
XVI	Bx	6 & 11 October 1873
XXI	A	24, 26, 28 & 29 October (continued from verse 1, written four months earlier)

The Morgan MS. is headed by the *Inferno* quotation and three others which T. later discarded:—
'A land of darkness, as darkness itself, and of the shadow of death; without any order, and where the light is as darkness.' [*Job* X.22]
'Can man by no means creep out of himself
And leave the slough of viperous grief behind?' John Marston
[*Antonio and Mellida* Part I, i, 5-6]
'And evermore shall the burthen of the agony of thy present evil wear thee down; for he that shall (can?) deliver thee exists not in nature.'
Aeschylus [*Prometheus Bound*, 26-27]
The B.M. ink copy contains the Job and Dante quotations, the lines from *Titus Andronicus* with which the Proem opens, and, from Shelley's *Triumph of Life*:
'And others mournfully within the gloom
Of their own shadows walked and called it death.'
The three quotations which T. finally used are derived as follows:

1. *Inferno*, Canto III, i
2. Leopardi, Canto XXIII: 'Canto Notturno di un Pastore errante dell'Asia', 93-98. 'In so much using then, so much movement of every celestial and earthly thing, circling without rest to return whence they were moved, I can see neither use nor profit.'
3. Leopardi, 'Coro di Morti': 'Chorus of Mummies in the Laboratory of Frederick Ruysch'; the first 5½ and last two lines. (See *Poems of Leopardi* ed. G. L. Bickersteth, p. 504. Cambridge 1923)
'In thee O death, who in the universe art alone eternal, to whom all created things turn, our naked nature reposes. Not happy, but safe from the old suffering. For Fate denies blessedness both to the living and the dead.'
I give a larger proportion of the MS. variants in this poem than in the others, but still not all, and (as said above) since we have T.'s final decisions in his text of 1880, I have not attempted to indicate which variants are deleted in the MSS., and which are given as alternatives alongside words which he finally used. Although most of the text as we know it is in the Morgan MS. it contains a good number of these alternatives.

PROEM
1 as] all Quotation from *Titus Andronicus III*, i, 12-13

3 spectres] terrors
4 exultant] -ing [after which the *y* of *years* would have been lost]
6 mute] dumb
7 discords] dirges
13 helpless] torpid; to try to] if we can
14 Our woe in words as sharp and void of ruth
19 spirits] creatures
25 . . . or in their Heaven on high
27 Fate] Doom
32 fellowship] comradeship/sympathy

I
5 may shine] shine down
24 Regurging with] At limit of
30 long curved] bosomed
35 rolls] moans
41 palace] mansion
44 soundless] silent
45 mansions] houses
67 abroad] in words
73 pitiless] sombre [T. was haunted by this adjective]
74 dreadful] rigid
84 Footnote. This seems to be T.'s own composition, as different versions occur among other jottings in two of the B.M. notebooks.

II
11 He gazed and murmured with a dull . .
15 open] wicket
24 utmost] latest
40 sullen] sombre

III
4 *sphereless* is underlined, T.'s mark of dissatisfaction
14 While dazed with cold awe by such gl. intense
26 beneath] under *N.R.* also

IV
10 stir] cry *N.R.* also
25-33 dated 13.8.71 in *B.M.*
36 javelins] fire-darts
44 Air] Earth/Calm (*N.R.* Calm)
82-83 T. made several attempts at these lines, of which the first was: 'She bore a large black sign upon her breast, A deep black band ran down her snow-white vest'
91 lamp-] blood-
94 level] clamourous/long-ranked
106 But I am lonely here

V
8 one there haunting feels

VI
1 forlornly] in sad dream

VII
1 shadowy] sombre/gloomy/murky

VIII
8 solace] comfort
26 Who broughtst it into being
31 ignominious] inexpiable
43 *petty* underlined
45 harshly] hardly
47 eternal] unconscious

X
In all three drafts, this section is placed at the centre of the poem—'the inmost oratory of my soul'.
1 mansion] palace
6 Portentous] A portent
41 One crucifix all black, another white
45 *eternal* underlined here and in the foll. stanzas, and T. began to write *perpetual* above. *B.M.* has *immortal*
66 Except his moving lips as still as stone

XI
23 Admired and envied and renowned for worth
26 soul] mind

XII [not in *B.M.*]
10 through] in
16 daydreams] day's dream (and throughout)
Versions of 17-20 and 25-29 are added at the top of the MS.
19 miraculously bright] creative as [?pure] light/omnisciently bright
45-46 plan . . man] pen . . men

XIII [Not in *B.M.* This is XVII in MS., though the number XIII is added in brackets]
15 his marvellous] besotted
17 monstrous] endless
22-28 and 36-42 were added some three weeks after the rest, when T. was completing his poem with the 'Melencolia' section. He wrote them in with some variants on the first page of the notebook, and after the date Wed. 29.10.73 wrote 'I hope the end'.
25 Of toil and trouble, strife and sateless lust
Of disappointment, weariness and lust
29 intolerable] immeasurable
35 Men of your changeful swiftness can complain!

XIV [Not in *B.M.*]
20 rugged] heavy
22 black fir-groves] dark firtrees
23 rooted congregation] sad impassive audience
24 full] slow
26 battling] battlers
30 joy] life
32 quail] fail

NOTES

36 solace] comfort
46 because] most/more } that
55-60 missing in MS. and *N.R.*
64 If toads are nauseous and obscene . . .
65 tigers] leopards
67 living substance struggles . . .
78 us] you
81 What matter some few years . . .
Bear with a few short . . .
XV [Not in *B.M.*]
1-14 were printed in the *Secularist* under the title of 'Universal Interaction'
10 warm] sane/good
16 exiles] wretches
17 evil] baneful
21 incurable] implacable [twice]/ineffable/immutable/immovable
XVI [Not in *B.M.*]
7 sooth] truth
50 There is no comfort in this life . . .
54 thoughts] things/truths
XVII [Not in *B.M.* This is XIII in MS., though corrected in brackets]
2 throb] shine
3 thick] slow; supernal] immortal (*N.R.* also)
5 men regard] sad men watch
10 quivering moonbridge] moonbridge lustrous
14 silver/mystic } lakes gleam level lawns of . . .
19 Fond] Poor
28 is a void] an inane
XVIII
29 Lust of the eyes and pride of life . . .
30 traced] pierced
69 the germ] again
72 -evolving] -evoking/-composing
XIX
16-17 . . any who behold try not to save
But each one thinks . . .
But rather thinks . . .
21 eventual] to follow
29-35 added four months after the rest
35 best] good
XX
4 T. wrote *shore*, then *bank*, then *shore* again
14 The angel's hands beneath his throat . . .
29 looked] gazed
35-36 . . . which kept always
Its unregarding and impassive gaze
46 *sworded* underlined
47 cold] calm (*N.R.* also)
XXI [Not in *B.M.*]
2 bleak] stern
4 sinks] falls

5 stupendous] Titanic
14 beholds] regards
16 see p. 263, note on Dürer's *Melencolia*
21 With the prone (poor *canc.*) creature for dissection brought

On the subject of this line T. wrote to William Rossetti,[1] 30.1.74: 'Though knowing about nothing of art, I have long been profoundly impressed by the "Melancholy" of Dürer, and my sole engraving is a copy of that work signed Johan Wiricx, 1602, which, I am glad to find, Scott describes as admirable. Wishing to bring this great figure into a poem, and rapidly enumerating the accessories which help to identify it, I find myself bothered by the animal prone at her feet. Ruskin in one place terms this a wolf, and in another a sleeping wolf-hound. Scott does not characterize it, I think.

'For myself, I have been used to consider it probably a sheep, and as dead, not sleeping; in fact, a creature awaiting dissection, and suggesting anatomy as among the pursuits of the labouring and studious Titaness.

'Can you, who are an art-adept, resolve the question, and tranquilize my agitated mind?' [T. then quotes his stanza, and ends] 'Must I, as Ruskin dictates, change this last into

With the keen wolf-hound sleeping undistraught—
(a villainous makeshift)?'

Both lines are in our MS., with the 'makeshift' written first.

23 The infant on the millstone perched beside
29 that light] with the
31 baleful] tragic/baffled/gloomy
35 weakness] fancy
36 comet] low sun
37 curved] arched
38 village] hamlet
39 snaky] wriggling
40 batlike leathern] trs.
48 Struggling though hopeless in the conflagration
51 Weary] Baffled/Heavy
55 piercing] cleaving
63 Dawns] Grows;
tenebrous] gloomy/sombre } fixed
65 Fate] life
68 black] dark
71 Titanic] Gigantic
73 sublimity] austerity

[1] *Salt* 77-78.

74 dark metropolis of threne
75 The river with its islands and its bridges
76 stern] bleak
78 *moving* [moon] underlined
81 *often* underlined; up to] upon
82 iron endurance] stern defiance
83-84 . . . terror sapping self-reliance
And all new confirmation of Despair

LINES, 1878
(p. 205)

MS. Don e.36; Unpublished. Dobell paraphrased the poem in his Memoir, and quoted some stanzas, but did not print it in full because Thomson had not wished it to be published, thinking it imperfect in form (see his comments below). To a modern ear its faults are not those of 'hardness and harshness', and it is worthy of a place in this selection, apart from its biographical interest. To our ears, also, it has curious echoes of later poets (see Introduction, p. xliv).

The MS. has several alternatives in the margin: I have made my own choice from these, as Dobell did, and print the variants below. The punctuation follows the MS. except for the omission of one semi-colon, which seems to have intruded by mistake.

The first line of the poem is written with other fragments at the end of the *C.D.N.* pencil draft in *B.M.*

5 tender] young and
10 ways] days
18 sojourn] travel
21 sources] fountains
30 hanging] poising
41 food] feast
56 ancient] very
69 you] ?thou *throughout*
79 must] but
91 that all our little] our little human
94 lasting] during
123 Save as] Except/Beyond
144 brought to life] made to live
149 conscious] human

A star at the end of the poem refers to 'One of the mottoes to the City of Dreadful Night, Poi di tanto adoprar . . . etc.' The MS. continues: 'Above merely copy rough pencil draft; too hard and harsh in both conception and execution for attempt at polishing—Far more truth than poetry in it. Thursday evg. 19.9.78.

'Writing the foregoing lines I have felt like a man making his Will at the gates of Death, summing up Life's scores and settling accounts when about to leave its inn. Yet I do not truly feel very near to Death, for with a seeming partial revival of the creative energies, in thought and imagination, it is impossible to realise death, even when absorbed by its sombre fascination. It may be merely the throes of some new birth that give the lethal illusion; for birth is so like death.

I do not hate a single man alive,
Some few I must disdain; ?contemn
I have loved heartily some four or five,
And of these there remain   ?and
                there remain of them
Just two, I think, for whom I would outface
Death gladly; for the one, death and disgrace.'

A VOICE FROM THE NILE
(p. 208)

MS. Don d.108; *Fortnightly Review*, 1.7.82; *1884*.

MS. dated November 1881; the *Fortnightly* version notes that T. corrected the proof shortly before his death. MS. Don c.73 contains notes for the poem, evidently made some years earlier, chiefly from the Encyclopaedia Britannica. The first line of the poem is written with other fragments at the end of the *C.D.N.* pencil draft in *B.M.* Don d.104 has two fragments of a draft, undated. After four lines, similar to those printed, is a piece of prose:

If I withdrew or swung aside my waters the whole would be drowned in a Red Sea of sand
The corn
The palaces
The doves that swing upon the tender palms
The ibis
The flamingo
The crocodile
The lotus
The human race

Other fragmentary lines follow, and the draft ends with lines 191-6, almost as printed. On the same sheet is the first stanza of 'A Song of Sighing', which was written in 1868.

I have printed the *Fortnightly* punctuation, though the version has one misprint —*lovers* for *loves* in l.153.

TO H.A.B.
(p. 213)

MS. Don d.104; *1895*.
H.A.B.: Harriette Annie Barrs—see Introduction p. xxvii. The manuscript was not available when Dobell published the 1884 collection. Salt writes to him on 7.8.88: 'Mrs. Pelluet writes to say she is going to send me various papers, but they don't come. One is a set of verses addressed to her by Thomson on his birthday in '81'; and shortly afterwards writes that he has received the papers. The version in *d.104* is in pencil, and has corrections or variants added by T. in pen, most of which are used in the 1895 text. It is dated 23 and 24.11.81.

3 onward] forward; for] to
6 looks back to] lingers on *alt.*
7 silver] lead and
14 sightless] sombre
15 darkening] glooming *alt.*
T. has underlined (as a fault) the word *joy* occurring twice in the fourth stanza
28 *Sands*, printed by Dobell, is a good guess at an almost illegible word, which replaces a totally illegible word crossed out.
30 calmly] richly
36 found] deemed
40 the happiest] itself a

THE SLEEPER
(p. 214)

Cornhill, March 1882; *1884*.
Punctuation as *Cornhill* version, date January 1882. In Don d.104 is a fragment, dated 27.12.81, as follows:

The fire is in a { ruddy / steadfast } glow,
The curtains drawn against the gloom.
The house all silent save the flow
Of murmurs from the dining-room.

This stanza is deleted, and its first line written again, followed by:

Yuletide midday blithe as a feast,
By pleasant airs caressed,
With the young moon high in the blue South-east
As the sun in the white south-west.

H. Hood Barrs refers to the poem as 'B.V.'s poem on Dick' (i.e. Miss Barrs): see Introduction p. xxviii. The *Cornhill* paid four guineas for it, which Barrs fears will only be the excuse for 'another sad, sad spree'. (Bodleian MSS.)

AT BELVOIR
(p. 216)

MS. Don d.108 (not in T.'s handwriting, nor Dobell's, except that he has written the last two lines of st. 1); *1884*.
MS. dated January 1882. Epigraph from *A Midsummer Night's Dream*, II.i.163
The poem recalls a visit to Belvoir Castle with the Barrs, made during T.'s summer stay at Forest Edge, 1881 (see Introduction p. xxvii).

MODERN PENELOPE
(p. 219)

No manuscript; *1884*, where it is dated 1882.

PROEM: 'O ANTIQUE FABLES'
(p. 221)

MSS. Don d.104, B.M.; *Fortnightly Review*, 1.2.92; *1892*.
MS. Don d.108 contains an earlier draft of the poem, in four eight-lined stanzas. After the third of these is the date 12.8.71. Both versions recall Leopardi's 'Alla Primavera, o delle favole antiche', from which T. took the epigraph for his 'Naked Goddess'. The first stanza in Don d.108 is similar to the later version, though it has two extra lines in the middle, and ends at l.6. The second stanza runs thus:

Your Heaven was not divided from our earth
Your living held communion with the dead;
Your loftiest Gods were of terrestrial birth,
And wandered here by love and fancy led;
Your men of wisdom and heroic worth
Became true deities when life was sped
And in the marble pure or rhythmic line
Your Gods and mortals were alike divine.

T. had written an early poem (1854) with this title, headed by a quotation from Browning's *Saul*: 'Carouse in the Past'.
Punctuation from MSS., which are dated 5 Jan. 1882. Don d.104 contains some alternative readings, as below:

6 bathe] wash
7 dawn entrancing] dawning upon
21 this death which cometh soon
39 Consumed or frozen] And burn or freeze

THE POET AND HIS MUSE
(p. 222)

MS. Don d.108; *1884*.
Punctuation as in MS., which is dated February 1882. Dobell records that T. has written on the MS.: 'Not true now, but true of seven songless years'; this is not in Don d.108, however.

INSOMNIA
(p. 225)

MS. Don d.108; *1884*.
Punctuation from MS. (which is in pencil) except for one or two commas. There are a number of alternative words, from which Dobell made a good choice: I give most of the other readings below, but not the cancellations.
T. has dated the stanzas as he wrote them, even to the day of the week. I give the dates in abbreviated form:
After l.40, 23.2.82, and a note: 'Little Sister aftn. to Lorna Dance. Mr. Ptaček to tea and supper.'
After l.80, 24.2.82; the same date repeated after l.90.
After l.120, 25.2.82, repeated after l.140.
After l.150, 27.2.82.
After l.180, 28.2.82.
After l.200, 4.3.82.
After l.230, 6.3.82.
After l.250, 7.3.82 (Tues. morning); the same date after l.270 (Tues. evening).
After final line, 8.3.82.

  62 win] lure
  66 awful] nameless, *and a note added*: Quy for the Shadow behind 5th Hour

110 blessings equal] can compare with
170 into] unto *Dob*.
171 paint] hint
189 Inexorable] Immitigable
203 mangled] senseless
204 whirled] swirled
210 storms] storm *Dob*. [The *s* seems to me to be needed here to divide the sounds]
214 fixed] set
253 Pondering] Brooding
264 enormous] immense cloud-
268 workmen] workman *Dob*.
274 charged] black
295 climb] come
299 nightly] common
300 petty] little

DESPOTISM TEMPERED BY DYNAMITE
(p. 232)

MS. Don d.104; *Weekly Dispatch* 4.6.82; *1884*.
The MS. of this, the last poem that T. wrote, is dated 1 May 1882. The *Dispatch* version appeared the day after his death, and is reproduced in *1895*. I give the MS. variants, some of which are deleted and some left as alternatives. Title: 'Divine Despotism' etc.

13 Full] My
14 monarch] King, their
23 lost in its Immense] cannot glut its vast
26 men and women poisoned] evil men corrupted
31-36 added at end of MS.
39 sure it will not stir] that may not stir up

INDEX TO FIRST LINES

A man of genial heart and liberal mind	75
As we rush, as we rush in the Train	85
Come to me, oh come to me	1
Day after day of this azure May	85
Dear Mother Earth, tell us, tell us, tell us	118
Each doth by his birth belong	118
Eastwards through busy streets I lingered on	4
Eight of us promised to meet here	80
Fixed to a tall stem like a mast	122
From out the house I crept	12
From the midst of the fire I fling	89
He cried out through the night	133
His eyes found nothing beautiful and bright	134
How your eyes dazzle down into my soul	79
I come from mountains under other stars	208
I had a Love; it was so long ago	205
I heard the sounding of the midnight hour	225
I looked out into the morning	125
I sighed unto my Muse, 'O gentle Muse'	222
Indeed you set me in a happy place	76
In the early morning-shine	131
In the endless nights, from my bed, where sleepless in anguish I lie	65
Is this the second childhood's feeble sadness	3
Last evening's huge lax clouds of turbid white	54
Let no mortals dare to be	121
Like a soaking blanket overhead	61
Lo, thus, as prostrate, 'In the dust I write	177
Love on the earth alit	76
Mr. MacCall at Cleveland Hall	129
My dear, dear Friends, my heart yearns forth to you	74
My poor friends, I come to you kindly	86
My thoughts go back to last July	216
Nor did we lack our own right royal king	58
O antique fables! beautiful and bright	221
O mellow moonlight warm	86
Of all these women fair and wise and good	75
Oh, what are you waiting for here, young man	125
Once in a saintly passion	122
She sits, a Woman like a Titaness	66
Still thine eyes haunt me; in the darkness now	1
Striving to sing glad songs, I but attain	73
Ten thousand years ago, ('*No more than that?*')	82
That jolly old gentleman, bless his white hat	119
That one long dirge-moan sad and deep	5
The Church stands there beyond the orchard-blooms	58
The fire is in a steadfast glow	214
The fire that filled my heart of old	88
The old man moans, saints' eyes with tears are wet	118
The sun was down, and twilight grey	146
Their eyes met; flashed an instant like swift swords	142
There is no other title in the world	232
This field of stones, he said	176
This is the Heath of Hampstead	78
This is the story	89
Through foulest fogs of my own sluggish soul	67
Through the country to the town	135

Waking one morning	133
Was it hundreds of years ago, my Love	80
Weary of erring in this desert Life	68
Weddah and Om-El-Bonain, scarcely grown	152
Weep not Dearest, weep not so	2
What are these leaves dark-spotted and acerb	74
What did she mean by that crotchet work	219
What precious thing are you making fast	126
What would you have? said I	128
When I trace back from this my death-in-life	75
When one is forty years and seven	213
When the sixties are outrun	175
When too, too conscious of its solitude	74
Wherever on this round earth	118
While the trees grow	54
Who was Lilah? I am sure	176
Why are your songs all wild and bitter-sad	73
Would some little joy to-day	151